Prison

PETER LANG
New York • Washington, D.C./Baltimore • Bern
Frankfurt am Main • Berlin • Brussels • Vienna • Oxford

Jacqueline Z. Wilson

Prison

Cultural Memory and
Dark Tourism

PETER LANG
New York • Washington, D.C./Baltimore • Bern
Frankfurt am Main • Berlin • Brussels • Vienna • Oxford

Library of Congress Cataloging-in-Publication Data

Wilson, Jacqueline Z.
Prison: cultural memory and dark tourism / Jacqueline Z. Wilson.
p. cm.
Includes bibliographical references and index.
1. Prisons—Australia—History. 2. Prisoners—Australia—History.
3. Prisons and race relations—Australia. I. Title.
HV9872.W55   365'.994—dc22   2008015050
ISBN 978-1-4331-0279-0

Bibliographic information published by **Die Deutsche Bibliothek**.
Die Deutsche Bibliothek lists this publication in the "Deutsche
Nationalbibliografie"; detailed bibliographic data is available
on the Internet at http://dnb.ddb.de/.

The paper in this book meets the guidelines for permanence and durability
of the Committee on Production Guidelines for Book Longevity
of the Council of Library Resources.

For Ian, Lachlan, Zara, and Paul.

CONTENTS

PREFACE

This book is the final stage of a journey that began for me as a student at La Trobe University, where I had the good fortune to be taught the principles of ethnography by Rhyss Isaac and Alberto Gomes. The courses they ran combined history, anthropology and sociology, and left me happily unable, ever since, to confine myself to one discipline.

La Trobe University was the home of what had become known internationally (courtesy of Clifford Geertz) as the "Melbourne school" of history, founded informally in the university's early years by Greg Dening, Rhyss Isaac and Inga Clendinnen. This group had developed an ethnographic approach to history, and it was this methodology that I inherited. By the time I started there Greg Dening had long ago moved on to other institutions, but he retained his links with La Trobe and would often drop by, as ready to talk to undergraduates as to catch up with colleagues. During one of those visits he spoke to me of his ethnographic approach to the writing of history, of how we legitimately can and should locate ourselves in the histories we attempt to discover and record. He understood, deeply, how history is at least as much a personal journey as it is a gathering of data, and he helped clarify and give me confidence in my own instinctive sense of this process.

There came a point where the journey was no longer metaphorical. Much of my research for this book involved travelling long distances around and across Australia, sometimes by air, alone, at least once by boat (which produced a bout of seasickness beyond imagining), but more often in the family car with my husband, Ian, and our children, Lachlan and Zara. We travelled mostly during school holidays when Ian was free of his teaching duties, he and I sharing the driving for hundreds of miles at a time. Wherever we stopped he would spend the days with the kids sightseeing, and/or (to their delight) sampling local eateries, cinemas, parks, regional zoos and so on, whilst I spent my days doing fieldwork at various prison sites. This took its toll. At the end of one such trip we arrived home at one a.m., and after three weeks on the road and a dozen or so motel rooms in three different states I could not remember where the cutlery drawer was in my own kitchen.

The "tyranny of distance" made it impossible for me to visit every historical prison site in Australia. And apart from that, there are simply too many. Wherever Europeans have been, they have left behind sites of captivity. The continent seems littered with them. They are some of the earliest and most durable public buildings remaining from the nineteenth and twentieth centuries, and there are few places that do not have some kind of jail embedded into the environment. If one counts all the deserted police cells, "lock-ups," courthouses with adjoining cells, small prisons and the larger Pentonville-style prisons in various stages of decay and restoration, there are literally hundreds scattered about the landscape. Many are now in ruins, such as the convict site on Sarah Island on Tasmania's west coast (my first boat trip), whilst others remain intact, standing high and proud and dominating their neighbourhoods. Some are known only to local residents, whilst others are well known but are so isolated that few visitors are able to access them. Many now function as other historical sites do, serving the tourist trade, selling everything from historical books to brochures to tea towels to ball-and-chain key rings.

Whether tourist or researcher, one does not visit a succession of former prisons as a random, serendipitous exercise; the sites mean something. But their meaning varies with each visitor, myself included. Part of my project was to discern and characterize as much as I could of those diverse meanings. To some extent, then, this book is an account of my own discovery and exploration of the nexus between the personal and the historical, between individual identity and social memory. If the result has any resonance at all for others similarly engaged, the journey will have been worthwhile.

JZW
Mount Helen, April 2008

ACKNOWLEDGMENTS

This book began as a PhD thesis in the School of Historical Studies at Monash University, supervised by Professor Marian Quartly, with Christina Twomey as associate supervisor. To Marian and Christina, my sincere thanks. Marian I first met through our mutual association with the Australian Federation of University Women, and to that organization go also my thanks, both for the invaluable collegiality its members have extended me and for material support in the form of scholarships.

One of Marian's most valuable attributes as a supervisor, for me, was that she was not fazed by my inability (and unwillingness to try) to bed down and locate myself within one discipline; she in fact welcomed and encouraged this in me, giving me great freedom, and hence the confidence, to follow my nose regarding methodology, topic and interpretation. Without such licence my project would have been very different, certainly not as personally rewarding, and perhaps unfinished.

My PhD was itself an outgrowth of my Honours thesis, which I completed at La Trobe University. I wish to thank those mentors and teachers at La Trobe in the Sociology, History and Archaeology departments who provided me as an undergraduate with the scholarly framework and intellectual tools to carry the project through. Among them, my special thanks to Rhyss Isaac, Alberto Gomes, Katy Richmond, Alex Tyrrell, and Estelle Farrar.

I am also grateful to the many people who generously took the time to read my work as it developed and provide valuable commentary and encouragement: Susan Aykut; Joanna Bourke; Marc Brodie; Barbara Caine; David Cannadine; David Carment; Graeme Davison; David Dunstan; John Fitzgerald; Andrew Marcus; Robert Manne; Hamish Maxwell-Stewart; Maria Nugent; Seamus O'Hanlon; Mark Peel; Scott Poynting; Marcus Rediker; Jennifer Rogers; Graham Seal; and David Wilson.

I am indebted to the many people associated with the prisons I studied who consented to participate in my research, especially those tour guides, former prison officers, curatorial staff and other stakeholders who not only gave me access to their workplaces but allowed me to observe and question them as they went about their day. A number of them (listed in Appendix One) also consented to be interviewed, in some cases granting me considerable time and making themselves available for follow-up enquiries. Their contribution was nothing less than vital.

Sections of this book have previously been published elsewhere; for permission to reprint that material here I am grateful to the following journals: *Ethnography*; *Australian Historical Studies*; *Journal of Australian Studies*; *History Australia*; and the *Howard Journal of Criminal Justice*. I would also like to thank the various editors and anonymous reviewers of those publications for their advice and constructive criticism.

I would like to thank my colleagues in the School of Education at the University of Ballarat for providing a supportive and collegial working environment, and in particular my thanks go to Laurie Angus and John and Sol Smythe for their invaluable help in the latter stages of the project.

On a personal note: a very pleasant aspect of life at Monash was the friendship, intellectual stimulation and collegiality of the postgraduate community there, in particular Jamie Agland, Amanda McLeod, Kathy Lothian, Helen Doyle and Rachel Buchanan. To all of them, my thanks.

My friends Latif, Damaris, Merryn, Lee and Kerry have earned my gratitude many times over for their support, ad hoc childcare, meals, and in general just being there. Special thanks also to Mr Campbell Penfold and his colleagues, without whom it would all have turned out very differently.

Finally, and most especially of all, go my thanks and my love to Ian, Lachlan and Zara, who took much of the journey with me.

INTRODUCTION

The eternal questions that concern historians...are the ones with which we grapple endlessly. Whose history is being told? Whose history is left out? Whose collective memory should be celebrated? Whose is forgotten? Which past should be preserved? Which re-created?
        — Jan Penney, "What is History in the Marketplace?"

*

This book is a study of decommissioned prisons in Australia that are deemed to be of historical significance, and which operate, or are expected to operate, as tourist sites. The study focuses centrally on narratives associated with the sites, and on the social and historical processes that bear on their interpretation, representation or exclusion. Due to those processes, a range of the narratives are obscured, neglected or outright hidden, and as these sites are in many cases significant venues of social memory, this loss of narratives has implications for their historiographical integrity.

The lost or neglected narratives in question are in the main those of inmates, who are "othered" by society—not only during their incarceration, by virtue of their having transgressed the community's legal norms, but also, and more significantly for public historians and others with a stake in the remembrance of the sites, as historical entities. This othering occurs, in the first instance, as a seemingly unavoidable consequence of their criminal status, but is perpetuated by the mode of interpretation of many sites, due to the continuing influence of persons and/or groups identified with and representing the prison "Establishment"—that is to say, the custodial staff and their supportive social and professional associates such as prison administrators, community groups and corrections policy-makers. (The class-system connotations of the term, in the context of the prison system, are neither accidental nor trivial.) This Establishment network also receives key support from the mass media, and in certain circumstances from politicians intent on garnering popularity via harshly punitive law-enforcement policies.

The historicity or otherwise of Australian prison museums is of particular moment. The loss of narratives I describe constitutes a diminishment, and hence a distortion, of a collective sensibility which I identify as an aspect of an Australian national character. This contention arises in part from this country's unusual relationship with its sites of incarceration, past and present. The nation-state of Australia has the unique distinction of having been founded as a jail, with convict transportees comprising the bulk of its first colonial population and the initial *raison d'être* of the society-building enterprise.* I suggest that these historical beginnings contribute to a perennial ambivalence on the part of some Australians toward their history, especially where it involves the convicts. Accepted wisdom has it that the "convict stain," which from the early nineteenth century blighted Australians' sense of their historical origins, has largely disappeared from public sensibility;[1] I will be questioning that assumption.

The convict question as such is, however, something of an adjunct to the main thrust of the study. Not all, nor even most, of the sites discussed here held convicts; the majority were prisons to post-settlement persons convicted of crimes committed on Australian soil. And even the jails with a convict history, such as Fremantle Prison, spent far fewer years housing transportees than they did the subsequent generations of "home-grown" prisoners.

Among those with a stake in the representation of prisons decommissioned within living memory, perhaps the most obvious are former inmates. Their stories are essential to any study of such sites. However, none of the active participants in my study was, to my knowledge, a former inmate; for various reasons, I made no attempt to interview or even contact such persons. In the first place, I am primarily concerned with the sites as they present today, as current or potential public history or tourist sites. Although inmates' stories are central to the sites' histories and to my purport overall, the main question I have addressed here is whether those stories, and the inmates' voices, are discernable on-site, or among adjunct narratives. To have sought out a collection of oral testimonies would have amounted to a digression from my chief purpose. A further, important factor was the issue of re-

---

*   *Convict* is used throughout this book in the specifically Australian sense, to refer to penal transportees of the early colonial era.

searcher intrusiveness; I wished to avoid being, or even merely *seeming* to be, yet another researcher compiling dossiers on a group of people who have spent significant portions of their lives under the scrutiny and control of those who hold the dossiers.[2]

This is not to say that past inmates' narratives have been ignored or subordinated; rather they are gleaned, glimpsed or inferred from a variety of other sources. These include published personal memoirs, the many fragmentary accounts quoted in secondary sources and documentaries, and, crucially, examination of the built fabric of the institutions in which they were incarcerated. In the jail's physical structures, which of course constituted the inmates' physical living environment, one encounters history as static display, in the form of architecture, artefacts and décor. Within that purely physical context the stories of those who inhabited or otherwise interacted with the structures are implied—at times with unexpected potency—in those objects of display.

Notwithstanding my interest in the prisons as physical entities, the study is not confined in its analytical scope to the sites themselves; nor is it in any taxonomic sense a report on the content or modes of presentation at the sites, although there is of course some reportage of that kind. Intrinsic to my overall argument is an examination of certain broad historical and cultural aspects of the popular narratives that inform sites' interpretation, and which in turn influence tourist and general public perceptions of prison populations in general, contemporary and historical. In keeping with this breadth of purview, the book addresses questions of self and identity on a personal, community and national level, utilising two disparate, but compatible, theories of the self: the "narrative" model of social psychologist Jerome Bruner; and Erving Goffman's "dramaturgical" model.

Bruner posits the construction of the self as a narrative process; a formulation we present to ourselves as a kind of inner autobiography, ongoing and continually updated, as the basis for our sense of personal identity. This "autobiography" takes the form of a coherent, approximately linear narrative that contextualizes our present self within a succession of life events, and places us within the hierarchy of progressively broader narratives of kinship, community, society, nation, gender, social stratum and so on.[3] The implication of such a concept of identity is that without such narratives to draw upon, neither the individual, nor the broader community in which that individual is "embedded," can experience their existence as meaningful; in social philosopher Alasdaire MacIntyre's view, the life that lacks such "stories" is no longer "intelligible."[4]

Goffman's dramaturgical model of the self is concerned not so much with narratives as with "performance."[5] He pictures the self as a social construction comprising "front and back regions," that is, in effect, "public" and "private." This model is used in my comparative analysis of the public persona of an archetypal "celebrity prisoner," as well as the public presentation of the prison from which he emerges and which he effectively represents.

Goffman also provides the fundamental model used here, of the prison *qua* prison: in 1961, in a ground-breaking sociological analysis of asylums, military establishments, prisons and the like, he identified a special category of institution,

> a place of residence and work where a large number of like-situated individuals, cut off from the wider society for an appreciable period of time, together lead an enclosed, formally administered round of life.[6]

This type of establishment he defined as the "total institution":

> Their encompassing or total character is symbolized by the barrier to social intercourse with the outside and to departure that is often built right into the physical plant, such as locked doors, high walls, barbed wire, [and so on].[7]

*

Principal research for this book chiefly took the form of ethnographic observation at rural and urban prison museums across Australia.[8] Ethnography, as practiced by the social historian, is essentially the study of relatively small groups of people for historiographic purposes, using the methodologies of the anthropologist. This approach translated into my doing the standard tour at each site (often more than once), taking hundreds of photographs, and interacting, both informally and in structured interview settings, with tourists, tour-guides, curators, managers, former prison staff, and various other people having a personal, professional or financial stake in the sites' remembrance. My purpose was to discern and examine the *cultures* I encountered at each site, with the intention of producing what ethnographers call "thick description"—a body of richly contextualized descriptive analysis based on the researcher's watchful immersion in the cultural environment. The method is a continuing search for the meaning of minutiae. Thus ethnographer Clifford Geertz:

The concept of culture I espouse...is essentially a semiotic one. Believing, with Max Weber, that man is an animal suspended in webs of significance he himself has spun, I take culture to be those webs, and the analysis of it to be therefore not an experimental science in search of law but an interpretive one in search of meaning.[9]

Australian ethnographers of recent decades have, as Alice Kasakoff says, "written mainly about clashing or changing worldviews."[10] As we shall see, this is as good a description as any of the world inside Australian prisons during the last three decades of the twentieth century.

Melbourne historian Greg Dening stresses that the ethnographer must be unafraid to acknowledge her own presence in the research environment, and to disclose, as it were, her own agenda. Nor should she fear the explanatory limitations innate to the method. As literary critic Peter Craven puts it, in a review of Dening's writings:

Dening believes that the historian should indicate where he or she is coming from in order to redress any false presumption of objectivity, the better to understand the "otherness" of the past and its participants, who are best represented through a kind of recapitulative historical dramaturgy which is full of partial points of view as well as lacunae, but which tease the reader out of thought so that he or she is left to complete the conceptual jigsaw or to see that it cannot be completed.[11]

Geertz, likewise, speaks of eschewing the pretence of "laboratory" studies, and acknowledging, rather, that

I really did live among these people; I did talk to them. They did react to me; I did react to them. This is...Renato [Rosaldo]'s notion of the positioned scholar. You are somebody: you come out of a certain class; you come out of a certain place.[12]

That said, it is appropriate at this point that I declare my own situation, as both a "positioned scholar," and also as a stakeholder. I have a multi-layered interest in prisons. My current scholarly concern, as a social historian, is mainly with the interpretative questions noted above; but that concern is rooted in a number of more personal aspects. I have a generic interest in institutions of incarceration and detention, having spent some years as a ward of the State of Victoria, and can claim a degree of insight into such institutions' social roles, day-to-day workings, and relationship with their inhabitants. It will be apparent that I am centrally concerned here with the mass of relatively innocuous inmates who by and large were not incarcerated for crimes of violence (but who may well have learnt violence while inside, such being the nature of these places). It is not my intention to beatify or otherwise sentimentalize transgressors, nor do I believe society is always to blame. But it sometimes is. And even when it is not, there is, I believe, a self-evident incongruity in the wholesale mixing of, say, remand prisoners—that is, those still legally innocent—with convicted armed robbers and worse, or young offenders with general-population adults, or petty thieves with professional stand-over men, and so on.

Aside from my own institutional history, I have the further connections of having lived as a child in Melbourne's northern suburbs in the 1970s, in the immediate neighbourhood of the maximum-security prison Pentridge (in a rented house that had an unusually heavy, reinforced back door with multiple locks and bolts, as a safeguard against escapees), and, most importantly, of having had a brother imprisoned there in the late 1980s. I visited him regularly throughout his stay in, variously, "D," "B" and "G" Divisions. By way of more fully explicating this latter association, and to provide some context for subsequent conceptual discussion, I will in due course recount some aspects of those visits.

What do we value? A society is identified, or rather identifies itself, at least as much by what it reviles as by what it embraces. Such is the cultural nature of transgression and social othering. Paula Hamilton speaks of the duality inherent in national identity, a function of both remembering and forgetting—what she terms "socially organized amnesia."[13] Considerations of this kind, of course, weigh on any project of social memory at any scale, not just at "national" level, and remind us that however inclusive is the intent, "real world" choices will continue to be made; some narratives will, inevitably, be excluded. What, then, of the contention central to this book, that inclusive remembrance is essential to the historical integrity of the community? The question at this point becomes not so much *whose* narratives, but rather on what basis, by what standards, is the choice made? A genuinely inclusive ethos, I argue, can only be based on a sense of fairness, on the sort of commitment to social justice that drove E.P. Thompson on his lifelong mission to write "history from below"—to, as he famously put it, "rescue" the anonymous masses from "the enormous condescension of posterity."[14] In the belief that the kind of "rescue" of which he speaks can be effected by listening for the voices of those masses, such a commitment forms the core of this book.

NOTES

1   Marian Quartly, "Convict History," in *The Oxford Companion to Australian History* (rev. ed.), ed. G. Davison, J. Hirst & S. Macintyre (Melbourne: OUP, 2001).

2   Problems of this and related kind were addressed in some depth at a round-table discussion at the Australian Historical Association conference in 2004. Stephen Garton, Anthea Hyslop, Naiomi Parry and Bruce Scales, "Privacy or Politics? Researching Personal Material in the Age of Privacy," discussion convened at Australian Historical Association Conference "Visions," Newcastle, 9 July 2004.

3   Jerome Bruner, "The Narrative Construction of Reality," *Critical Inquiry* Autumn 1991, pp. 1–21; and "Life as Narrative," in *Consumption and Everyday Life*, ed. Hugh MacKay (London: Sage, 1997), p. 105.

4   Alasdaire MacIntyre, *After Virtue: A Study in Moral Theory* (Notre Dame Indiana: University of Notre Dame Press, 1981), pp. 191–203.

5   Erving Goffman, *The Presentation of Self in Everyday Life* (New York: Anchor Books, 1959).

6   Erving Goffman, *Asylums: Essays on the Social Situation of Mental Patients and Other Inmates* (Garden City NY: Anchor Books, 1961), p. xiii.

7   Ibid., p. 4.

8   For a full list of sites visited see Appendix 2.

9   Clifford Geertz, *The Interpretation of Cultures* (New York: Basic Books, 1973), p. 5.

10 Alice Bee Kasakoff, "Is There a Place for Anthropology in Social Science History?" *Social Science History* 23 no. 4, 1999.

11 Peter Craven, Review: Greg Dening, *Readings/Writings*, in *Australian Review of Books* no. 209, April 1999.

12 Clifford Geertz, in "Clifford Geertz on Ethnography and Social Construction," interview by Gary Olson, *JAC* 11 no. 2, 1991, http://jac.gsu.edu/jac/11.2/Articles/Geertz.htm (accessed 29 July 2005).

13 Paula Hamilton, "The Knife Edge: Debates about Memory and History," in *Memory and History in Twentieth-Century Australia*, ed. Kate Darian-Smith and Paula Hamilton (Melbourne: Oxford University Press, 1994), p. 23.

14 E.P. Thompson, *The Making of the English Working Class* (London: Victor Gollancz, 1980); see also *idem*, "The Moral Economy of the English Crowd in the Eighteenth Century," *Past & Present* no. 50, 1971.

PART ONE

Prison Tourism

All over the world, tourists visit the sites of former prisons. London's Bloody Tower, Alcatraz, Auschwitz, Solovki Gulag, the POW Museum at Changi and many others receive thousands of visitors a year. They are part of a growing trend in organized sightseeing, at locales of "death, disaster and atrocity," known as "Dark Tourism."[1]

Apart from former prisons, Dark Tourism sites most commonly include battlefields, assassination and terrorist attack sites, Holocaust memorials, even natural disaster remnants. The phenomenon has been characterized as essentially a "commodification of death"; but the Dark Tourism paradigm is not simple. Far from being "merely" sites of suffering, with connotations of human beings *in extremis* as their main draw card, sites recognizably fitting the Dark Tourism model are usually multi-layered historically and sociologically, and from those layers disparate groups and identities derive subtly nuanced, diverse ranges of meanings.[2] Thus, for instance, Alcatraz Island, which to those who identify with the men imprisoned there was a site of infamously brutal twentieth-century incarceration, admits also of a contested interpretation, as an exemplar of *pre*-twentieth-century *indigenous* dispossession. This counter-narrative was forcefully made clear, after the prison's closure, by the Native American activists who occupied the island from 1969 to 1972 and whose actions, and causes, have since been incorporated into a highly textured, multi-faceted site interpretation.[3]

The Australian variety of Dark Tourism is unusual. In most countries of the world where the paradigm has a significant place in the public history arena, a wide variety of sites qualify for the Dark Tourism label aside from prisons. This is not nearly so true in Australia. With the relatively small exceptions of the 1804 convict revolt at Castle Hill and the miners' rebellion at Eureka fifty years later, no historical battles have taken place on Australian

soil other than those between European settlers—or their armed representatives—and Aboriginal people, and almost none of the relevant sites of those
inter-racial wars of conquest are today exploited or commemorated as tourist
sites. (As recently as the year 2000, American travel writer Bill Bryson made
his way to the site of the 1838 Myall Creek massacre, for which seven whites
were eventually hanged, and found nothing there to identify nor commemo-
rate the event, little tangible interest among local residents, and no sign of
tourist interest.)[4]

No civil wars or internal conflicts remotely on a par with those fought
on other continents have sundered the Australian commonalty, nor has our
history been significantly shaped by assassinations of public figures. There is
no site in this country equivalent in the public consciousness to Gettysburg;
Little Big Horn; the Dallas Book Depository; the D-Day invasion beaches of
Normandy; Hiroshima; the fields of Flanders; nor Pompeii. Australia is replete with war museums and memorials, but with very few exceptions their
meaning for Australians is irrevocably tied to sites of events elsewhere. The
Australian War Memorial in Canberra lists, among the various exhibitions
and services it provides, tours of battlefields; but the battlefields that attract
large-scale tourism by Australians are situated on other shores altogether, in
France and Belgium, on the coast of Turkey at Gallipoli, and most recently
along the Kokoda Trail in Papua-New Guinea. Dark Tourism within Australia is a narrow ground, thus far confined almost entirely to former prisons.

The prisons discussed here were almost all built in the nineteenth century, and remained in operation into recent decades. (Many were decommissioned within the last fifteen years.) In most cases, their architectural design
incorporates the neo-Gothic outward appearance which was more or less
standard for prisons through much of the nineteenth century. This design, as
we will see, is itself a significant aspect of both the sociology of the operational prison, and the social psychology inherent in the post-operational public history site. It accounts for much of the interest in historical prison sites
that draws tourists in the first place.

Exactly why former prisons are so fascinating to so many people is itself
a subject meriting much discussion. The reasons are diverse and complex.
They have to do centrally with our innate need to formulate the stories about
ourselves that locate us in the world, and the stories about the world that locate us within ourselves. In order, then, to make sense of the prison museum—in order to incorporate it into our own personal story, or the story of

the community—we must consider the stories of those who experienced the prison before it shut down.

NOTES

1   John Lennon & Malcolm Foley, *Dark Tourism* (London: Continuum, 2000).
2   Carolyn Strange & Michael Kempa, "Shades of Dark Tourism: Alcatraz and Robben Island", *Annals of Tourism Research* 30 no. 2, April 2003.
3   Ibid; also Tina Loo & Carolyn Strange, "'Rock Prison of Liberation': Alcatraz Island and the American Imagination," *Radical History Review* no. 78, 2000.
4   Bill Bryson, *Down Under* (London: Black Swan, 2001), pp. 253–8; only since his account was published has a commemorative plaque been installed at the site, and it now receives non-Aboriginal visitors.

CHAPTER ONE

Personal:
Visiting Prisons

In the normal course of an operational prison's daily business, large numbers of people pass through its gates specifically to have contact with prisoners. These visitors include a variety of professionals and charitable workers, and, most abundantly, inmates' relatives and friends. The latter category—those undertaking the ordinary "non-professional" prisoner visit—comprise by far the bulk of outsider access to almost any jail.

For the civilian visiting a prisoner, the experience is characterized by two things: the emotions associated with the fleeting encounter; and, intertwined with these emotions and conditioned by them, the glimpse one has of life and circumstances within the jail. Some years ago I drafted an account of a typical visit to my brother Paul, when he was on remand in Melbourne's main maximum-security prison, Pentridge:

> It begins with a queue in the street outside the south door into the Remand section. Once admitted, we file into an ante room, where we endure some minutes of paperwork designed to ensure that the prisoner we are visiting hasn't used up his quota of contact visits for the fortnight. If he has, the visit will consist of a futile, half-shouted conversation through a glass screen (no phone intercoms like you see in the movies). More minutes in a waiting-room, then a guard-box where they wave a metal detector over you before allowing you through the main gate into the prison grounds.
>
> The familiar internal road, which leads to the prison's administration centre, is pleasantly tree-lined and unprison-like, almost suburban-looking. Anyone with less personal reasons for being here could think it quite a congenial introductory vista, never knowing how strange and threatening this road is. If you have an emotional stake in what happens in this place, your xenophobia surfaces here.

The trek to the Contact Visit area takes you off that leafy avenue almost immediately, to wend along a steel-roofed, hurricane-wire-enclosed breezeway, and here, as you glance around at the no-man's land bordering the walkway, the defining reality of Pentridge begins to announce itself. From the outside, the prison's physical personality seems to be summed up in its perennial nickname, "Bluestone College"; but once inside—still in the open air, but *inside*—you realize that it is not only (perhaps not even mainly) basalt walls that symbolize and make tangible the ethos of the place. It is the wire. Everywhere you go in Pentridge, if there is sky above you, then somewhere near you there is wire. Mostly, at eye level, you are looking at, and through, heavy-duty hurricane wire; occasionally you get a glimpse of obsolete barbed-wire. Raise your eyes slightly, anywhere, and there is razor wire.

It's the razor wire that stays most starkly in the mind afterwards. There must be miles of the stuff, obscene, stainlessly shining coils running atop every massive wall, perched above the ubiquitous hurricane-wire fences, draped and strung here and there like the Devil's own foliation, "just to make sure."

Wherever you look in Pentridge, there are fences and walls, demarcating areas segregated and enclosed for no reason apparent to an outsider. The general impression is one of boxes inside cages inside a series of corrals inside an enormous, barren, walled compound.

We reach the Contact Visits area—a longish, cheaply carpeted, tacky pre-fab room with a dozen or so widely spaced cafeteria-style tables. Here, Paul is ushered in through a plain door that leads back to...prison. That door is where freedom ends and inside, *real* inside, begins. Only the prisoner you are visiting knows what is behind that door, what it is like to be inside. Here at a table we spend a tense hour talking.

He hates being locked up, of course—who wants to live in a box?—but confinement isn't the real torture of Pentridge for Paul. It is fear. He is so scared. All the time. He points out various people around us during my visits—"That guy's a real case"; "Watch out for that screw, he's a psycho"; and so on, warning me about them, as if *I* might have to fear them, as though he can no more imagine me walking out and away to freedom than I can imagine what he walks back into.

At the end of the hour, I leave to retrace my steps along the breezeway, and he is escorted back through the door.[1]

Pentridge Prison was shut down in 1997, several years after Paul's release. When running to capacity it had held upwards of 1,000 inmates, and received tens of thousands of "non-professional" visitors a year. Presumably, not every prison visitor was as wide-eyed with anxiety as I (indeed, many I observed were clearly old hands at the process); nor was every prisoner quite as traumatized as Paul. But there are any number of reasons to think that his condition was not untypical, and that the above narrative is emblematic of many—in some respects perhaps the majority—of experiences concerning inmates and those on the outside with a personal stake in inmates' welfare.

Paul spent two years in Pentridge. While still awaiting trial, he was, for banal administrative reasons (overcrowding in the Remand section), transferred to B Division, a maximum-security section housing long-term prisoners with behavioural problems. He had his twenty-first birthday there. He was repeatedly assaulted, and after twice attempting suicide was further transferred to G Division, the psychiatric unit, where he served out his time.

Less than two years after his release, Paul was dead of a drug overdose. In this regard he was all too typical, both in the trajectory of his life and the timing of his death. He had previously spent time in youth detention centres, and research has shown that "young offenders" with a history of youth detention have the highest death rate in the community of their peers; they are generally dead, by a variety of causes, within three years of leaving incarceration.[2]

*

This book is centrally concerned with the diverse personal narratives associated with Australia's historical prisons. The fragment of Paul's story I have presented here, intertwined as it is with my own experience of the prison as an outsider, is included as a sample, as it were, of the manifold narratives notionally available to those involved in the sites' historical interpretation. The book is not, however, simply a collection of such narratives; rather it is an attempt to identify the historical, psychological and social processes that determine to what extent those narratives may be discerned by tourist visitors to former prisons, and to identify in turn the factors that tend to lead to the exclusion of some narratives in favour of others.

In the April 2002 edition of *Australian Historical Studies*, public historians David Carment and Mickey Dewar disagreed over the extent and nature of the pressures brought to bear by government and community groups on the curatorial processes of the Museum and Art Gallery of the Northern Territory.[3] The particulars of their debate are of less concern to us here than the general problem from which they issue, which is that the compilation and presentation of public history—whether in the form of museum collections, re-enactments, or the restoration and display of heritage sites—are inherently vulnerable to the competing demands of the various groups, organizations and individuals who for one reason or another regard themselves as stakeholders in the interpretation. It is, however, neither the multiplicity nor the disparity of such narratives that causes the problem. The chief danger to which popular historical interpretation is prone arises from the tendency for one, or a small number, of the stakeholder groups to exercise significant exclusionary dominance over the others when it comes to the choices and nuances of interpretation, and in the process to influence, whether directly or indirectly, the ultimate decision-makers in the matter of representation. In the final analysis, it is these groups that the present chapter and, ultimately, this book are about.

The daily task of running a prison museum can induce a somewhat beleaguered mentality. Site personnel are routinely beset by funding concerns and the practical problems associated with the upkeep of large, aged and often severely rundown buildings, combined with the abiding imperative to attract and entertain paying visitors. Such necessary pragmatism tends to produce a measure of cynicism—or at least scepticism—toward any research that does not have readily discernable potential benefits for the sites themselves, and the arrival of an independent researcher can introduce tensions. On my arrival at Fremantle Prison, for instance, the site manager made it clear that in principle he supported research, and that this was part of the site's role, but he also left me in no doubt that in relation to his day-to-day concerns, most of the research done there had little relevance for him. He gestured to a large collection of volumes lining his office and said, "Look at that—there's a bookcase full of reports here, and I can't get enough funds to fix the place. These sites suffer from analysis paralysis. There's been too much analysis and not enough action."[4] In similar vein, almost the first thing said to me onsite at Brisbane's Boggo Road Gaol by a former prison officer was, "Are you going to help us fix the place? We're desperate for help here. Look at the place."[5] When I explained that I was simply a social historian with no influence over heritage funding, his disappointment was palpable.

Concomitant with concerns of this kind was a suspicion, occasionally voiced, that I might be somehow associated with the National Trust or a similar "official" heritage guardian body. Across all categories of site personnel there was, I found, a widespread mistrust of such organizations for their supposed authority over aspects such as the preservation of the physical structures and features—what archaeologists term the "built fabric." At one rural Victorian jail, which I toured without prior notice as I happened to be in the town on a family day-trip, I was greeted with outright alarm; the police had visited the site the previous week in response to a complaint that the proprietors appeared to be improperly in possession of artefacts from Pentridge. The items held were legitimate, having been openly purchased at auction, but the proprietors had been unnerved by the experience. When I, knowing nothing of what had been going on, began asking questions about the provenance of what I recognized as Pentridge items, the coincidence was too much for them to believe. They allowed me to tour the jail, but I am not sure I ever fully convinced them that I was not somehow connected with the National Trust (whom they blamed for the original complaint) or the police themselves. (The original complaint to police, although mistaken, was not necessarily as mean-spirited or pedantic as might be thought: the misappropriation of artefacts from historical sites, especially by stakeholders in the latter phases of their involvement with the sites, is a perennial problem for heritage workers. I have been shown extensive collections of prison items, large and small, in the hands of former staff members who either felt they were entitled to souvenirs of their careers, or believed they were "protecting" the items from a notional philistine element they expected to succeed them.)

A study of the social history of a former prison necessarily takes in the interwoven complex of personal experiences that comprise the collective memory of the institution. This network of individual memories is in large part a function of the relations between all the various stakeholders of the site—those, that is, with some interest in shaping the stories told by, about and within the historical prison. Apart from professional curators, these groups comprise former inmates; curatorial personnel such as tour guides; volunteer personnel, who may include members of local history societies and the like; former staff of the operational prison such as prison officers, governors, or welfare personnel, in particular those staff members who have retained a connection with the site after its decommissioning; residents of the local neighbourhood; friends, relatives and/or descendants of inmates; and historical researchers.

My own position as both researcher and inmate's friend naturally influenced the focus of my research and interpretive responses to the sites I visited. I was very circumspect about revealing anything of my personal background while on site, and careful also to maintain an overtly neutral tone during interviews. It became apparent, however, that my interest in certain aspects of the sites prompted some of the people with whom I interacted to align me, whether tacitly or explicitly, to some extent with their conception of the Other. Although at times an impediment to aspects of the research, this labelling, I came to realize, was symptomatic of aspects of the othering process itself, and hence afforded precisely the kinds of narrative glimpses I was seeking.

Cherry Grimwade speaks of the extensive difficulties besetting researchers who wish to examine the operation of functioning prisons (that is, prisons containing prisoners) due to the reluctance of the institutional "gatekeepers"—administrative and operational staff—to expose their practices and systemic environments to disinterested scrutiny.[6] "As gatekeepers," she says, "these agencies tend to be protective of their institutions and practices and are often unwilling to approve particular research unless certain conditions are met."[7] In other words, they insist on having the final say on what *stories* can be told about the place, and indeed whether any stories at all will be permitted to emerge.

In the researcher's encounters with the gatekeepers the respective parties' motives are most likely to become visible, and hence an intrinsic part of the subsequent story. A striking example of this is the subterfuge American writer Ted Conover had to resort to in order to research the routine interior workings of a typical prison: faced with a blank refusal from the New York State Department of Corrections, he concealed his profession and signed on as a corrections officer, completing months of aptitude tests, psychological assessment and rigorous, military-style academy training before working for a year in the notorious Sing Sing Prison.[8] A less spectacular but no less typical Australian example is recounted by ethnographer Barbara Denton, who conducted a study of the female illicit drug culture in Victoria, both in and outside prison. She found that hardening official attitudes to her project as it progressed led to access restrictions being imposed where none had previously existed, and a generally increased level of obstruction and censure toward her.[9]

There are many reasons for such gatekeeper activity in the *operational* prison. Some are obvious—security considerations being the main one—and some are more arcane, to do with the nature of the carceral total institution as a workplace. In such an environment the prospective researcher provokes a complex of reactions. As criminologist David Wilson says, "Prison is about maintaining order, about maintaining control."[10] During the institution's operational life, the prime focus of that control is, of course, the inmate population. For many reasons to do with the business of ordering and controlling a captive population, prisons are secretive entities, and, as in any functional environment predicated on the keeping of secrets, power resides in esoteric knowledge. As long as there remain inmates between the walls, the prison must view outsiders as potential allies or accomplices—witting or not—of those inmates or, at least, persons bent on undermining the established power base. Steps are routinely taken, therefore, to ensure that such outsiders achieve minimal access to, or insight into, the prison's hidden realms—what Erving Goffman terms the "back regions"[11]—for it is in that unseen territory that the engine of control ultimately lies.

At the institutional level, the prison's system of operation is designed to give absolute priority to security, and therefore its "default position" is to reject, or exert very stringent control over, approaches from outside. At the level of the individual staff member, aside from routine concordance with the institution's position, a further factor is the reflexive suspiciousness encouraged by his or her daily working conditions. In effect the prison officer, like the inmates, spends each shift locked up.[12] This fundamental condition of the work, plus its highly specialized, dangerous and esoteric nature, sets the prison officer apart from other people, and encourages an inwardly focused social culture among staff that excludes outsiders. Added to this is the fact that the "legitimate" exclusion of outsiders can foster a lack of accountability, which in turn leads to staff having, and wielding, considerable power within the institution.

Grimwade, in her concerns regarding gatekeepers, focuses on operational prisons. With their closure and subsequent translation into historical entities, both the opportunity and motive for staff members to continue to exercise power would seem at first sight to be lost; but in fact the imperatives for retaining control often remain and can at that point become even stronger, as the potential arises for the newly-open institution's history to emerge, in the form of its manifold narratives. ("Stronger" in part because with the demise of the institution and the disbandment of the group whose collective experience was inextricably bound up with it, remaining individuals who identified strongly with that group or had a personal dependence on its cohesiveness can feel peculiarly threatened by a loss of control of the vestigial narratives. Such attachment is a natural enough feeling, given the sort of situations that can arise in a prison.) And at the same time opportunity is

afforded, typically through the gatekeepers' perennial associations with interested community groups such as Rotary, Apex, and local history societies.
There is a general perception within those organizations and the wider community that these individuals, whose professional lives have been so long
immersed in the institution, are naturally the ones with the definitive "inside"
knowledge. Hence arises the incentive to position themselves so the narratives can be chosen and regulated, and in the process consolidate their social
standing—to retain the function of gatekeepers. In the case of an institution
that becomes a tourist venue, this most naturally involves taking on a role
such as tour guide.[13]

*

It should not be inferred that I advocate any exclusion of the prison officers'
stories. On the contrary, they are as complex, interesting and valid as any—
as is affirmed by memoirs such as that of Conover and, closer to home, Pat
Merlo on Pentridge.[14] As insiders, their experiences are highly important;
and as stakeholders in the prison's representation they have every right to
voice those experiences. If the prison officer's conditions of work set him or
her apart from the mainstream, it also provides a unique perspective, and that
can produce both predictable antipathies and some unexpected empathies.

On my arrival at Boggo Road Gaol, I was shown around by a former
prison officer (the same one who had hopes that I would help them "fix the
place"). I was interested in how he felt about the inmates, and in what terms
he remembered them. I was about to ask if he had any pleasant memories
regarding prisoners, but at that moment we arrived at a caged yard, about ten
metres square, in the back of which stood a large concrete trough and a couple of taps. There was a peculiarly sordid atmosphere about the place, a Spar-
tan aridity which the plumbing did nothing to relieve. And it really was a
cage; even the sky was latticed by hurricane-wire. This area my guide identified as "the shit yard." It was here that the inmates' latrine buckets were
brought from the cells (which had no sewerage connections) for cleaning. In
this secure yard, he said, "the sex offenders, child molesters and so on, the
worst prisoners"—he almost spat the words out—spent their working day:
"The sex offenders' job was to sit here and wash out the shit buckets. They
were segregated from the other crims, they wouldn't have survived in with
the general population, and we gave them the shit yard to work in."

So in the world of Others, there were those even further othered. As we moved on, I got my question out: "Were there any prisoners you *liked*?"

He did not hesitate: "No." But then he paused. "There was one prisoner, could have been any bloke off the street. This prisoner was very well behaved, never gave me any trouble. I used to bring him cups of tea, small favours, you know. I felt sorry for him. His wife had been having an affair. He was off fighting for his country, and when he got back, poor bugger, he found her in bed with a fella. It sent him mad. He cut off her head, took it down to his local pub, sat it on the bar and asked for a beer. I mean, that bloke could have been any one of us."

It takes a certain world view to see the Everyman in an axe-murderer—and we may well profit by taking notice of such perceptiveness. But however insightful the prison officers are in recounting their experiences, however entertaining they are as raconteurs, and however some of them may attempt, in good faith, to empathize with those whose lives they confined and controlled with their keys and uniformed authority, they cannot, in the final analysis, tell those inmates' stories, nor the stories of those for whom the inmates' welfare was paramount, in other than the voices of prison officers. A reliance on this one group of stakeholders in compiling the prison's history omits, as primary source, the voices, and hence the narratives, of those persons who after all comprise the institution's *raison d'être*.

The physical prison informs on two levels. On the first and more general level, there is the characteristic architecture of detention, which comprises permanent structural elements such as stone walls and corridors, skyless cells and so on, and more ephemeral—albeit no less characteristic—features such as the coils of razor wire festooned atop and about those same stone walls, or the steel mesh behind which a common-room television receiver was once enclosed. In such minutiae, I believe, we glimpse a microcosm of the human condition in a kind of banal *extremis* that is by nature beyond the imagining of the ordinary citizen. On the second level—and here we are afforded far more particular insights—there is the inmate's knowing and deliberate impact upon the fabric of his or her world, in the form of graphic and/or textual self-expression—graffiti.

By graffiti I mean, by and large, illicit, usually private, works of individual inmates, rather than the officially sanctioned murals often displayed in open-air exercise yards. My research in this area provides the substance of

Part Two of this book. For now it may be generally stated that prison officers in the main dislike inmate graffiti, and where they are influential in the sites' operation and interpretation, they dislike also the idea of its being studied by researchers. Often the tourist public does not even know of its existence. At sites where inmate graffiti has survived, it tends to be in areas sequestered from public view—a practice noted by sociologist Daniel Palmer in his reflections on Fremantle Prison's extant but hidden inmate graffiti.[15] Palmer also comments that the former prison officers (who make up most of the tour guides there) showed a marked antipathy toward the graffiti,[16] and my own experiences at Fremantle and other prisons affirm his observations; requests to view the graffiti provoked responses ranging from indifference, through suspicion, to outright obstruction. Typical was the response of a retired senior prison officer from an eastern-state prison who was active in the local Historical Society. While being shown the Society's collection of prison artefacts, I noticed an iron cell door leaning against a wall of a back room, covered with graffiti. I expressed an interest in who might be the author, but my host dismissed the enquiry with offhand contempt, unequivocally othering the unknown artist as "just some crim." When I returned to the room a few days later, the door had been reversed to present its pristine outside surface to view.

Among a number of former staff who in one way or another made known their regret at the demise of the institution as a centre of incarceration ("It was a damn good prison!"), and who perhaps also were nostalgic for the personal power they had once wielded, there was patent resentment at the presence of a researcher who would not have been allowed access during the prison's operational life. In other words, whatever my motives, I had no business being there. Opposition of this kind was rarely made explicit, but it clearly underlay a number of off-hand comments made during informal conversations; one ex-prison officer (at J Ward) did say outright, "Of course, you'd never have been getting in here in the old days. You know that, don't you?"

Some former prison staff's distrust of me was based on an idea that my enquiries were politically motivated. (Political trends among prison officers are discussed in a later chapter; suffice it to say at this point that members of the profession tend on the whole to be politically conservative.) At one site, the most direct ill feeling emanated from a former sub-governor who made it clear, with some vehemence, that he categorized me among a cohort from what he termed the "Sociology Block" at my university who had been among those agitating for prison reforms in the 1970s, and against whom he held an enduring grudge. (That I was a child during the relevant period fazed him not at all in forming this judgement.) I found when interviewing him that any line of questioning that could remotely be interpreted as sympathetic to "the crims" was met with marked asperity. My last conversation with him, an impromptu exchange in a car park near the jail, ended with him reacting to what he saw as a loaded question by shouting at me, "Get your facts straight, Girlie! Just get your facts straight!."

The rank sexism of "Girlie" exposes a further facet of the problems associated with the study of prisons, especially for the female researcher. The operational prison is a profoundly masculine, and masculinist, environment—a maxim that even applies, paradoxically, to prisons that also house women—and in the cases where the post-operational prison remains under the control or even merely the influence of former operational staff, this masculinity of tone and ethos tends to persist. In some cases it may well be more evident than ever, due to the departure of whatever female staff and/or inmates there might once have been to (theoretically) leaven the male sway. Although some sites employ female tour guides, none among those I met were former prison officers.

The consequent sexism I found unabashedly blatant in its expression. Ex-prison officers at J Ward, Boggo Road, Fremantle, and Pentridge (tour guides, all) told me, in one way or another, that:

(a) As a woman I could not have real insight into these institutions, because there were things that went on in there that "decent" women were not, and should not be, privy to.

(b) Female prison officers had no legitimate place in a male prison. The men I spoke to tended not to spontaneously mention the women they had worked with, but when I raised the subject (I was curious about the lack of female ex-prison officers among tour guides), they were virtually unanimous that having women staff in an operational men's prison "didn't work." They tended to dwell on the women's shortcomings as colleagues, often with anecdotes about female staff members becoming emotionally involved with male prisoners. In recounting these star-crossed relationships they invoked clichéd notions of women as innately over-emotional and hormone-driven.[17]

(c) Women inmates were morally "far worse than male inmates"—incorrigibly devious and manipulative ("tricky" was a favourite descriptor), malicious and mischievous (they wilfully stirred up trouble with the men), highly problematic for male officers to control, and deficient in an essential forthrightness supposedly present in male inmates. "You knew where you stood with the men, but you never knew what was coming with the ladies," was how one ex-Pentridge prison officer put it.[18] Another facet of this putative wickedness was the female inmates' habitual "foul language"—so "filthy," I was told, it was not fit to be repeated to me.

It goes without saying that without misrepresenting herself the researcher must, out of at least ordinary courtesy and to facilitate the work, make some effort not to offend the social norms of those she is working with and/or attempting to make the subject of study. The ethnographic enterprise requires both a suspension of judgement and a measure of complicity in other peoples' behaviour, or at the least, a conscious adoption of an appropriate façade. (Denton speaks of having to conform to the expectations of the prison officials when visiting prisoners, by "wear[ing] some form of jacket and carr[ying] a briefcase: my professional persona.")[19] The unreconstructed sexism demonstrated at various sites made it necessary for me to adopt a relatively unassertive, "traditional" style of femininity that automatically inhibited certain lines of enquiry (for instance, the aspect noted above regarding female language).

This persona became particularly significant when I was researching the graffiti left behind by the last generations of inmates. The routine, in a number of the prisons where I had requested access to areas normally closed to the public, was for me to be escorted to those areas by a tour guide, invariably a former prison officer, who carried a set of keys. As we reached each cell or sequestered area, my guide would open the door in question, step aside and allow me to enter, then stand and wait while I took notes and photographed the visible surfaces and features. As I worked, I was invariably aware of his attitude to what I was doing (usually because he had made it explicit as we walked about the jail), that I should not by rights be there and that the material I was studying was not suitable for *anyone* from outside the prison system to view, much less a woman.

A great deal of the graffiti, it must be said, is highly confronting, especially in male areas—violent, wilfully transgressive, replete with unalloyed malice, and in many cases viciously misogynistic. I discovered, paradoxically, that if I made something of a show of my disquiet when viewing particularly lurid images or texts, this would often result in my gaining access to further areas housing "offensive" material, including, occasionally, areas I had previously been told were off-limits. Precisely why this should be I am not certain; perhaps by complying with my guide's gender expectations I ceased to threaten his sense of control of his environment. Perhaps, too, the apparent capacity of arcane aspects of "his" jail to shock me on the basis of my femininity had appeal to, and to some extent affirmed, his masculinity. Whatever the reason, I found it necessary to adopt this kind of "feminine" demeanour, to some degree at least, in every prison I visited where former prison officers were in charge or ran tours.

A friend commented to me, when I recounted some examples of the sexism I encountered, that the milieu I was describing seemed "stuck in a 1950s time-warp." I off-handedly agreed, as the assumptions expressed and the mode of their expression indeed seemed reminiscent of that era. On later reflection, however, it became apparent to me that they could be seen as a reversion to, or perhaps even an abiding vestige of, a far more distant period. In the stereotypes embodied in the view that women transgressors are exceptionally immoral in comparison to their male counterparts, and in the radically gendered dichotomy that juxtaposes those shameful female transgressors with "respectable," "good" women, there are perceptible similarities to the judgements voiced by successive generations of custodians of convict women, from the earliest moments of Australia's colonial history.[20] Historian Joy Damousi identifies a propensity in women convicts of the early nineteenth century to subvert their male jailers' capacity to maintain order, chiefly by both utilising and transgressing norms of gender and sexual behaviour, and, crucially, by ridiculing. The men in positions of authority in the Colony of New South Wales were, Damousi argues, radically limited in their frames of reference by which to comprehend a female population who refused to conform to the masculine concept of femininity.[21] Two centuries later, the men in positions of authority in the prisons of the late twentieth century, who spoke so feelingly to me of their problems with the female prisoners under their charge, seemed to me equally limited in their frames of reference, and might almost at times have been speaking from within the pages of Damousi's book.

The enduring nature of such stereotyping is not a trivial matter, even though the sites no longer hold inmates. When the stereotypes are sincerely held and expounded by persons who control the narratives and are publicly perceived as having authoritative expertise, the potential result is at least unbalanced public history, and at worst the perpetuation of a longstanding essentialist diabolising of women offenders, and by extension non-"respectable" women generally, in the public consciousness.

*

The reader could easily have the impression by now that everyone I had dealings with was obstructive or difficult to deal with. This was certainly not true. At a number of sites I received generous access, enthusiastic and friendly support, and in general the type of response a visiting researcher would hope to receive. However, in several cases where personnel extended to me the benefit of their welcoming disposition their good works were offset to a greater or lesser degree by the antipathy of others on site. At one jail, for instance, where the curator extended me every assistance, an ex-prison officer who ran the tours, and whom I had to deal with almost daily, was clearly disgruntled at my presence. At another site, the curator was generous and helpful toward me, and fully supportive of my research. She was, however, already at odds with certain other identities—stakeholders—associated with the historical interpretation and presentation of the site. My presence on site, and the fact that I was seen to have her favour, did not please her antagonists.

The conditions and responses that confronted me at times made it difficult to pursue my planned methodology, and more than once seemed like setbacks. But it became apparent that many of the problems I was meeting were in fact symptomatic of issues directly germane to my study. Insofar as my fieldwork may be seen as an interrogation of our historical prisons, the key questions I was asking of each site I visited were, How is this place being interpreted as an entity of public history? and How inclusive is it of all the narratives that could legitimately be associated with it? If my enquiries were met with sexism, obstruction, prejudice and anti-intellectualism, there are many reasons to regard those attitudes and perceptions as systemic to the institutions concerned, whether in their present or former roles. And if those systemic attitudes bear upon our ability to receive or discern certain narratives or certain classes of narrative that emanate from such sites, then they must be counted as factors potentially affecting our interpretation of the sites, and hence affecting the capacity of those public history entities to inform their clientele, the public, with integrity.

*

As at the beginning of this chapter, I once more offer here a glimpse of the alternative narratives available to those committed to inclusive interpretation of our historical prisons. My earlier anecdote expressed the point of view of an outsider with a personal concern for a specific inmate; the account below is that of an insider professionally concerned for *all* inmates.

In the last decade or so of its operational career, the administration of one of the prisons I visited appointed a young man named Jason Smith to the welfare staff. Smith was given to understand that his primary responsibility would be to provide pastoral care for the inmates. Shortly after starting, however, the realities of the job, and of his professional status in the institution, were brought home to him:

> There was a bloke who wasn't travelling too well in the reception section…This bloke who'd come in that day was a bit loopy and was put in the obso' [observation] cell. Two screws opened the door, 'cause he was carrying on, to have a bit of "biffo." He was as mad as a snake. Now, I started wandering up, I can see one screw in the doorway and the other's giving it to him in the cell, telling him to shut up. But you've got to understand that the structure was, you had on the first and second tier what we call "four out" cells, all just grill mesh, so there was four, eight, sixteen and the same prisoners above, looking down at me in the middle of what we call the "circle." I'm standing there having a look into the obso' cell, and here I am right in the middle, and all the crims are looking down at me. They're going, "Oh, the Welfare's gonna sink the boots in as well." I'm sitting there thinking, "Oh shit." The two screws looked at me, I thought, "Shit, we've fucked up now." They were a couple of heavy types of guys, pretty athletic sorts of blokes. I wandered out of the circle, I thought, "Jesus." It was a real dilemma for me. I said to the boss the next day, I said, "Look I've got to talk to you." I said, "This and this went on last night." He said, "Well, you can go two ways, Jason, you can approach the Governor on paper and go through all that business, or you can just keep quiet about it and just see it as part of the business in this game." He said, "This will happen down the tracks again and again. This guy didn't deserve what he copped, but there'll be others who will deserve what they cop, and on that basis you really have to make a distinction about where you stand."
>
> It's a black-and-white world in there, there are no grey areas.[22]

Faced with a stark choice regarding his professional future and facility in the job, Smith found himself adopting a *modus vivendi* which, for a committed

worker in the welfare field, involved a radical compromise of practice and
values:

> I approached the two blokes and said, "Listen,...don't do it in front of me again. If
> it's going to be on, give me some kind of non-verbal so I can get out of there."
>   It would have made my job impossible...There's a lot of stuff that goes on in
> prison that has nothing to do with discourse. It's just about knowing and looking at
> the right time...I'd often walk down and I'd look around and you could see there
> was going to be some "counselling," or "therapy" going on, as we used to call it,
> and I'd quickly look around, pack up my bags and leave.[23]

Such a choice, it is reasonable to judge, signifies little more than the comparative superficiality of the role of welfare within the institution—and the
concomitant powerlessness of the welfare officer[24]—and implies worlds
about the routine plight of the average prisoner. In characterising the various
forms of his "total institutions," Erving Goffman makes the critical point that
an intrinsic aspect of the prison, and a core facet of its operation, is that it "is
organized to protect the community against what are felt to be intentional
dangers to it, with the welfare of the persons thus sequestered not the immediate issue."[25] This radical diminishment of the inmate's entitlement to protection and general care for his/her welfare, and the cast-iron assumption that
security considerations override all else, means that the relatively benign disposition of individual members of staff will almost certainly count for nothing in crises and/or situations where individual compassion is at odds with
institutional imperatives.[26]

As Smith recounts, the inmates themselves in fact had few illusions
about the nature and efficacy of "the Welfare":

> The true nature of the job never really surfaced; the idea was to ... [help] guys who
> weren't coping with incarceration...You'd say, "I'm from Welfare, what's the
> story?," and a lot of it was just superficial, basic-kind of band-aid stuff, "Ring up
> my mum and tell her to bring in more socks," or "Ring my lawyer and tell him I
> gotta see him," or I was a contact point, "Ring my girlfriend and see how she's go-
> ing and Bubs," and all this sort of stuff. There wasn't a lot of finesse about the way
> we worked.[27]

Stories such as that of the apparently routine "obso"-cell atrocity are, of
course, precisely the kind that under normal circumstances do not reach the
ears of the general public, whether at large or while sightseeing at the site of
the events. But it is just such anecdotes that allow one to make sense of, for

instance, my brother Paul's incessant fear during his incarceration, which seemed at the time like paranoia but very likely had a sound basis in the corporeal reality of his environment. It is, in fact, only through such redolent glimpses, however gleaned, that anything intelligible can be gleaned about Paul's story, for he never recounted in any detail his prison experiences, then or after his release. His story stands as one of the multitude that must be inferred, as best we can, if we are to hope even for a glimpse of the ordinary terrors of life in prison.

NOTES

1   Jacqueline Wilson, unpub. MS, n.d.
2   Julio Szego, "Young Offenders Face Greater Risk of Death," *Age* 19 May 2003, citing a study by the Murdoch Children's Research Institute's Centre for Adolescent Health.
3   See David Carment, "Making Museum History in Australia's Northern Territory," *Australian Historical Studies* 33, no. 119, 2002; cf., in the same edition, Mickey Dewar, "If I was Writing my Own History I'd be a Hero…A Response to Professor David Carment on Making Museum History at the Museum and Art Gallery of the Northern Territory"; and Margaret Anderson, "Oh What a Tangled Web…Politics, History and Museums."
4   Graeme Gammie (Fremantle Prison site manager), interviewed 24 April 2003.
5   Boggo Road Gaol tour guide to author, informal conversation, 20 Jan. 2003.
6   Cherry Grimwade, "Diminishing Opportunities: Researching Women's Imprisonment," in Sandy Cook and Susanne Davies, *Harsh Punishment: International Experiences of Women's Imprisonment* (Boston: Northeastern University Press, 1999), pp. 292–8.
7   Ibid., p. 293.
8   Ted Conover, *Newjack: Guarding Sing Sing* (New York: Random House, 2000).
9   Barbara Denton, *Dealing: Women in the Drug Economy* (Sydney: University of New South Wales Press, 2001), pp. 15, 22–3.
10 David Wilson, "Millbank, the Panopticon and their Victorian Audiences," *Howard Journal* 41 no. 4, Sept. 2002, p. 374.
11 Erving Goffman, *The Presentation of Self in Everyday Life* (New York: Anchor Books, 1959), pp. 106–13.
12 Erving Goffman, *Asylums: Essays on the Social Situation of Mental Patients and Other Inmates* (Garden City NY: Anchor Books, 1961).
13 See Bob McKercher and Hilary du Cros, *Cultural Tourism: The Partnership Between Tourism and Cultural Heritage Management* (New York: Haworth Hospitality Press, 2002), pp. 162–5. Boggo Road Gaol, Brisbane, for instance, had only former prison officers (volunteers) conducting tours when I visited there. A broadly similar situation obtains at Fremantle Prison, and former custodial staff are the chief sources of information and/or training for tour guides at Old Geelong Gaol and "J Ward."

14   Pat Merlo, *Screw: Observations and Revelations of a Prison Officer* (Hawthorn Vic: Hudson, 1996).

15   Daniel Palmer, "In the Anonymity of a Murmur: Graffiti and the Construction of the Past at the Fremantle Prison", in *Historical Traces*, ed. Jenny Gregory (Perth: Centre for Western Australian History, 1997).

16   Ibid., pp. 111–12.

17   For an insight into the female prison officer's viewpoint on these and other issues, see Merlo, *Screw*.

18   Timothy Knapp (ex-Pentridge prison officer), interviewed 7 March 2001.

19   Denton, *Dealing*, p. 15.

20   See Joy Damousi, *Depraved and Disorderly: Female Convicts, Sexuality and Gender in Colonial Australia* (Cambridge: Cambridge University Press, 1997); Anne Summers, *Damned Whores and God's Police: The Colonization of Women in Australia* (Harmondsworth: Penguin, 1975).

21   Damousi, *Depraved and Disorderly*, Ch. 3.

22   Jason Smith (former prison welfare officer), interviewed 30 April 2003.

23   Ibid.

24   This judgement is consistent with much else that Smith had to say to me. See also Barry Ellem, *Doing Time: The Prison Experience* (Sydney, Fontana Collins, 1984), p. 86.

25   Goffman, *Asylums*, p. 5. It should be noted that although Goffman's model was formulated over forty years ago and many reforms have occurred since then that supposedly address the issues of prisoners' rights and welfare, his premise remains relevant and essentially applicable to prisons today. Alison Leibling, *Suicides in Prison* (London: Routledge, 1992), pp. 220–2.

26   Merlo, *Screw*, pp. 43–4.

27   J. Smith interview.

CHAPTER TWO

Gothic:
The Medieval Legacy
in Australian Dark Tourism

We shape our buildings, and afterwards our buildings shape us.
— Winston Churchill

*

Fortifications, by their nature, are built to last. Any traveller to the British Isles with a modicum of interest in historical architecture can hardly fail to notice the remnants of the great fortresses erected in their hundreds during the Middle Ages, and called by their Norman builders *castels*—castles. These structures—always the dwelling-place of the nobility and therefore emblematic of that group— stand, alongside the Gothic church, as perhaps the defining architectural entity of the period.

The first castles were built of timber, but the preference quickly shifted, almost a thousand years ago, to stone; in this material the design was perfected. The masonry castle was a highly utilitarian structure expected to serve as a place of refuge for the local villeins in times of threat, to withstand the worst physical rigours of siege warfare, and to provide a platform from which its armed occupants could defend their ground. In all of these functions it proved eminently successful. The castle's high, crenellated battlements, jutting vantage-points and strategically placed loopholes gave defending archers ample scope to shoot at and otherwise assault invaders from relative safety; the metres-thick ashlar walls, the circular towers and keeps, and the heavily reinforced gates were sufficient to resist practically all means by which besieging armies could directly assault them, until the advent of gunpowder-propelled missiles.

In the centuries following the invention of firearms and the abandon-
ment of feudalism, the castle was gradually transformed, in both purpose and
public sensibility, from its military role to one that emphasized its residential
function, and also from a place of public refuge and concourse to the private
dwelling solely of the lord of the manor and his household. Of those castles
that remained occupied, some were incorporated, through major renovation
and additions, into the extended residential edifices that would come eventually to be termed "stately homes." Many others, of course, fell sooner or later
into ruin, the dynasties they once housed having withered or fallen, or simply
having moved into more comfortable—that is to say, less martial—
accommodation, purpose-built elsewhere in the park.

In the pre-modern social era of rank, the castle, and its successor the
stately home, held a unique place in the landscape as the epitome of exalted
worldly dominion. To the commoners occupying the surrounding lands, the
"big house in the park" commanded not only the physical terrain but the social, economic and legal landscape also,[1] inspiring in the "low-born" individual an acute consciousness of impregnable authority and literally
awesome power.

Although they may not have realized it at first, it was just such an architectural combination of commanding power and physical impenetrability that a
group of prominent Philadelphians, intent on reforming the treatment of
Pennsylvania's incarcerated criminals, were seeking when they first met, in
1787, to develop proposals for a new, humane type of prison.[2] The group,
who counted among their number Benjamin Franklin, styled themselves the
Philadelphia Society for Alleviating the Miseries of Public Prisons. Influenced in varying measure by Quaker spiritual ideals, Enlightenment social
philosophy, and the writings of English penal reformer John Howard, the Society began a dogged lobbying campaign, over three decades, to persuade the
legislature to build a revolutionary style of reformatory prison. Their efforts
finally bore fruit in 1829, when America's first large-scale "penitentiary"
was commissioned and received its first inmate.[3]

One of the largest and most expensive buildings in the world at the time,
Philadelphia's Eastern State Penitentiary was intended, in its physical layout,
amenities, and operational ethos, to give every inmate a forced opportunity to
reflect on his or her crime and life in general, to repent, and ultimately to be
rehabilitated. This was to be achieved by housing each one in seclusion and

isolation, from each other and from the outside world, with minimal diversionary activity and only a Bible as reading-matter.

The "separate system," as it was to be known, required a prison design that was innovative in almost every way: a number of long, narrow, multi-tiered cell-blocks were laid out radially, like wheel spokes, from a central "hub" which afforded the guards a clear view down each corridor (but no direct view into the cells). The prisoner spent twenty-three hours a day in the cell, and one hour in a one-person exercise yard directly attached to the rear of the cell. No voice other than the guards' was allowed to be heard; no contact with, nor even a glimpse of, one inmate by another was permitted; when being led from one part of the building to another, the prisoner was blindfolded by a canvas hood completely covering the head. Each cell had a high, vaulted, skylit ceiling, the better to achieve spiritual communion with God and conscience; also, both for the sake of providing a humane degree of comfort to the confined individual and to ensure the viability of the cell as a living environment sufficient unto itself, each one had running water, central heating and a flush toilet. As the now decommissioned prison's promotional website proudly points out, such facilities were far more advanced than those the president of the United States enjoyed in the White House at that time.[4] (The system's innovative design notwithstanding, however, there were many problems with its function, and neither the running water nor the sewers were reliable.)[5]

It is important to keep in mind that Eastern State's extraordinarily severe regime arose out of a genuine compassionate regard for the soul and character of society's every miscreant, and an unshakeable faith that the innate goodness in each one could be reawakened. Every detail of the prison's internal design was aimed at reform, at returning to the fold the lambs that had strayed. The regulations and disciplinary measures required for the absolute segregation of individuals were never intended, in their conception at least, as displays of cruelty or gratuitous exercise of power per se. Externally, however, the institution's purport was rather different: here, in its physical, visual presentation to the outside observer, the intended keynote was deterrence—a warning to the free citizens beyond the walls of what was in store for them if they did stray from the path of righteousness.

The architect appointed to design the penitentiary was an Englishman, John Haviland, nephew of a friend of John Howard. Haviland was both familiar with contemporary prison design and disposed to pioneer a radically innovative institution. The building, which was situated on high ground in pasture land just beyond the city's then outskirts, was always going to be physically imposing. But sheer size was not deemed sufficient to convey the founders' dire message; the American public was becoming accustomed to grand dimensions in its public buildings, and to the monumental, Jeffersonian-Athenian style routinely employed to emphasize those dimensions. An architectural look was chosen which the designers judged would express, in the most confrontational possible manner, a sense of dreadful consequences, and of the righteous might that wreaked those consequences. Haviland designed the façade, therefore, in the "Gothic revival" style which had been gaining popularity in Britain for some time, and so to the outsider, Eastern State Penitentiary came to resemble nothing other than a castle.[6]

The prison was decommissioned in 1971. The city limits overtook it long ago, and it stands now, huge and profoundly incongruous, in suburban Philadelphia, its ten-metre-high stone walls and massive crenellated towers a radical discontinuity in the streetscape. It was opened for tours in 1994 after two decades of public debate (during which the building survived a number of redevelopment proposals), and is today one of the city's major tourist attractions.

Yet the modern tourist is in a sense re-enacting a long tradition at Eastern State: from the moment of its completion, it attracted visitors from all over the world. By the mid-nineteenth century, while fully operational, the institution was hosting up to 10,000 curious outsiders per year—general sightseers, politicians, diplomats and other worthies.[7] It is, then, arguably one of the earliest examples of large-scale Dark Tourism. This suggestion is admittedly debatable, given that many, and quite possibly most, of the tourists involved were drawn not by the dire connotations of the system which our late-modern perspective dictates, but by the prospect of an uplifting manifestation of Enlightenment optimism and progress. But it equally may be that a significant number were motivated by a morbid or voyeuristic urge to observe, at close hand, human beings in abject captivity. The concept of touring operational prisons, it is worth noting, is not confined to early modernity; in our era, inmates at a number of prisons had to regularly endure the candid scrutiny of guided tour groups from community service organizations such as Apex and Rotary being shown through the fully operational facility by staff in the 1980s and 1990s.[8] At that point—where the perception and treatment of people begins seriously to resemble the perception and treatment of zoo animals—we glimpse, as a core aspect of their social condition within the prison, the othering of the inmates. (An academic colleague has recounted to me his inaugural experience as an "official visitor" to Pentridge in the 1980s, when to his embarrassment his guide, a senior staff member, ushered him without the slightest ceremony into a cell housing two prisoners who simply had to sit where they were, ignored, while the staff member expounded on the features and amenities of their living space.)

Numbered among the visitors to Eastern State from the furthest corners of the world in its early years of operation were designers and policy-makers in the area of penal reform.[9] Penal architects in dozens of countries, including Britain and much of the British Empire, strove in their designs to emulate Eastern State Penitentiary's synthesis of Enlightenment egalitarianism, humane compassion, and God-fearing authoritarianism. As a result of this imitation, which in most cases included both interior and exterior features, over the remainder of the century approximately three hundred prisons were built world-wide on the Pennsylvania model, incorporating, with various local permutations, the radial-spoke "separate system" and the quasi-medieval fortress façade.[10]

These imitators were in their turn influential. Perhaps the most significant, especially in regard to British Empire prison design, was the "model" prison Pentonville, in north London, which received its first inmates in 1842.[11] "Pentonville became one of the most copied prisons in the world," with imitations being built in many of the countries of Europe.[12] It was also the prototype of a wave of prison-building in Britain: "within six years after the new model prison was erected, fifty-four others with a total of eleven thousand cells were constructed [in Britain] after its general design."[13] In the colonies, too, Pentonville served as the exemplar of the separate system, and was duly copied, battlements and all, in the construction of a number of prisons in Australia. These included, among others, Pentridge, Adelaide Gaol, Fremantle Prison, Long Bay, Darlinghurst, Grafton, Bendigo, Geelong, Bathurst, Beechworth, and a major addition to the established Port Arthur complex.

The significance of Pentonville regarding penal policy-making in Britain and its colonies, combined perhaps with the fact of John Howard and his reform movement being English, has led to something of a gap in the social memory—and hence in the historical understanding—of the separate system's development; Pentonville's debt to Pennsylvania has been largely forgotten. In many minds (and not a few supposedly well-informed historical accounts), the "model" British prison was invented in England, under the direct influence of Howard's writings and the activism of certain of his fellow-reformers.

The best known of those adjunct reformers is the social philosopher Jeremy Bentham, who in 1791 published his own concept of the ideal reformatory prison, a radical design he dubbed the "panopticon."[14] His theory was based on surveillance: the panopticon was to be circular, with its cells facing inward to a central hub, giving the jailers a view of every prisoner, while allowing the prisoners no view of either their guards nor each other.

Modern forgetfulness of the separate system's true origins has given rise to a widespread misconception, which has acquired the persistence and ubiquity of a myth, that Pentonville and the many prisons for which it served as the model were built according to, or under the influence of, Bentham's panopticon design. But in fact his design was never put into practice in Britain on any significant scale (the government initially approved construction, then withdrew funding),[15] nor anywhere in the Empire, for that matter, and certainly played no significant part in prison design in Australia.[16] (A conceptual reliance upon Bentham's model is in fact peculiarly inapt in the Australian context, not least because the convicts' location and role in the colonial social and economic structure made surveillance especially problematic, and given Bentham's active opposition to the concept of transportation and hence his prominent role as one of the philosophical "enemies" of Australian convict society.)

One may find, here and there, minor Australian jails put forward by some as panopticons. A typical example is the so-called "Round House" in Fremantle, which was opened in 1831 with eight cells accessed from a central courtyard. But although the Round House's general form superficially resembles Bentham's model, its surveillance capability—the core of Bentham's idea—remains questionable, and in this it typifies the mode of propagation of the myth, in that almost any detention centre taking an even partially circular form is likely to attract the label "panopticon." I have encountered the myth as part of tour guides' patter at Port Arthur, where the separate (Pentonville-style) prison was described as a "panopticon," with a detailed and quite misleading account provided of Bentham's concept; similar misinformation may be found on university websites; in scholarly books and learned journals; and even on the website of the Howard League for Prison Reform, a British group which carries on the reformist ideals of John Howard.[17]

Part of the confusion between the Pennsylvania-Pentonville and panopticon models presumably stems from the radial format; but there the similarities end, for the separate system was not designed to facilitate surveillance of individual prisoners (guards had to walk from their central control point along the radial corridors and look through each cell door's peep-hole to see what the prisoners were doing), and it is in fact arguable that this relative invisibility constituted one of the greatest dangers to inmates' wellbeing, in that suicide attempts and other mishaps went undetected until too late (a drawback to the system unresolved into modern times, and contributing to an enormous number of deaths and serious injuries in custody).

The myth has in recent years acquired further legitimation in scholarly circles through the influence of Michel Foucault's "surveillance" theory of the prison as an instrument of social control.[18] Foucault, whose sociology of the prison may have some validity in today's paradigm of ubiquitous video-surveillance, makes extensive metaphorical use of Bentham's model. This was perhaps apposite in the Frenchman's geographical milieu (some panopticons were tried on the Continent),[19] but in his theory's translation to English, and its consequent implied applicability to the British correctional paradigm, it tends to be historically misleading.[20]

*

As noted above, the genuine castle of yore was, by virtue of its socio-economic status, strategic location and unparalleled robustness, set apart from the community it oversaw and protected. (There were always some castles located within towns, especially where the Norman rulers feared potential local rebellion. Such examples were relatively few, however, and have little bearing on this discussion.) That separation was both literal and symbolic, and for ordinary people, inured from birth, as they were, to "know their place," the castle itself stood as the embodiment of the absolutely unattainable. This of course is no longer the case. The rise of modernity, and with it the age of aspiration, has diminished the castle socially, while also bringing the modern viewer closer to it physically: in the countryside, public access to the parks and buildings themselves is commonplace; in many towns and cities, the local "big house" now stands not in its park, but in the midst of urban life. In those parts of the world where castles may be found by the roadside, as it were, the buildings themselves, whether in ruins or relatively pristine, may well still inspire a kind of awe in the viewer, in appreciation of their architectural grandeur; but they no longer symbolize with any immediacy the might of arms in which their proprietors' power once ultimately resided. In other words, the modern sensibility is unlikely to apprehend the medieval castle as threatening in any substantive sense.

By contrast, the prison built in quasi-castle style can, when operational, provoke considerable unease in the modern onlooker. In the first place, the institution exists, and is perceived by those outside its walls as existing, on something of a "war footing"—that is, although not strictly a *military* fortress, it is, nevertheless, functionally a fortress, and as such is a tangible manifestation of implied or latent violence, of the armed power of the Establishment. Thus if real castles have largely lost their power to intimidate, the quasi-castle-prison may still have that power, may still be able to evoke in the neighbour or observer a sense of dread in some degree equivalent to that intended by the Pennsylvania Quakers who invented the idea. This is not to say that only prisons built in the style of castles are capable of engendering a sense of threat in onlookers; in fact, any centre of incarceration may present itself to public view as highly disturbing visually. But the visual aesthetic of the castle-style prison is peculiarly potent in this regard. And this style of architecture has a particular fascination for tour visitors to historical prisons.

The implied violence of the prison, however, relates directly to the containment and coercive control of the inhabitants; that is, it is directed inward, and thus runs counter to the true castle's purpose of repelling attack from without. This has two effects. Firstly, the implicit reminder of the inmates' existence fosters a social attitude which has its roots in the origin of the castle-style prison itself: the separate system removed the criminal from even notional concourse with the general community, by virtue of both the high walls and the radical segregation policy; as a corollary to this, and in keeping with the astringent moralism underpinning the new penal ethos, the inmate—or more precisely, the *imagined* inmate—became radically othered, in the eyes of "respectable" society.

Secondly, the building's apparently gratuitous outward-facing defensive features—in particular the loopholes and crenellations—in fact carry a subtle implication of potential violence directed, incongruously, at the outsider. This hint of menace of course has no rational basis—there is no reason for the passing civilian to come under attack from the prison—yet it remains an aspect of the building's external persona, and, crucially, is concordant with another, far more realistic concern felt all too acutely by many neighbours of prisons: fear of escapes.

A case in point is the relationship between Pentridge Prison—the epitome of Gothic design—and the suburban community which it dominated for 150 years. Many of those who lived in the prison's close environs (which, in the nervous imagination of some, extended to a whole suburb away) speak of their constant unease at the thought of escapes; but some also speak, usually in vague and general terms—yet heartfelt, for all that—of the awful experiences they believed the inmates were undergoing. Many associated the monolithic grimness of the jail's façade with the inferred violence within, with one lifelong neighbourhood resident summing it up as "a rotten place. Like a medieval torture chamber. Everyone knew what was going on in there. You'd walk past it to get to the lake, and it always gave me the creeps."[21]

Not everyone sees the urban prison in such a negative light, however. My study of Pentridge Prison's neighbours revealed a clear distinction between those who disliked and feared the prison when it was operational, and a significant minority who felt positive about it as a presence in the community. The psychological roots of such division, it turned out, were clear and relatively uncomplicated: almost all of the latter group acknowledged some form of personal link with the prison or the penal system, having been employed there or having had family members or acquaintances who worked there. Others recounted childhood memories of prison-sponsored events such as Christmas festivities mounted within the jail by inmates. In other words, those disposed to feel positive about the institution in their midst tended to be those who for one reason or another identified (whether consciously or otherwise) with the prison Establishment.

Of all Australian historical prisons, the façade of Pentridge is among the most explicitly "medieval" in appearance, and this aspect of the design has always attracted attention. But it was not merely the crenellations, loopholes and castellated gate-towers for which the jail became famous; during its operational career, it was facetiously known throughout Melbourne as "Bluestone College," after the basalt ashlars of which the complex was constructed. This nickname does not appear to have arisen merely out of a general awareness of the institution's built fabric; for many it expressed—

and continues to express—something essential about the prison. In my study of neighbouring residents' perceptions, almost all participants interviewed at some point mentioned the bluestone in terms of its visual aesthetic, historical significance, perceived authenticity, and/or its "unique" connection to the area (local quarries supplied the stone). [22] Among the respondents to a questionnaire survey, 75 per cent cited the bluestone as central to what they regarded as "important about Pentridge." And it should be noted that these statistics included those who responded negatively about the prison *qua* prison.

A wave of prison construction in the early-to-mid nineteenth century was mirrored in the latter decades of the twentieth century by a rash of closures across Australia. The maintenance and upkeep of a densely inhabited complex of huge, antiquated stone buildings presents special problems; retaining them as prisons became increasingly expensive and, ultimately, impractical. Combined with the difficulties associated with simply keeping the inmates' environment liveable and the working conditions of those who guarded them adequate, from the 1970s onwards a new wave of penal reformism began to bring to the public's—and inmates'—attention the notion that prisoners had a right to living conditions which did not in themselves constitute punishment. Newly under scrutiny, also, was the manner in which they were treated by staff.

Notwithstanding the potential improvement in their own workplace conditions, many prison officers were at odds with the proposed reforms, not least because they did not share the belief that the prisons were unsatisfactory as places of containment and punishment, however rundown and unremissive they might be. This stance was in large part a natural consequence of their moral perception of the "crims" they guarded—an aspect of the othering noted earlier. It led to the development of a kind of siege mentality among staff, and hence something of a reactionary backlash, which in turn translated, for a time, into worsened conditions for inmates in some jails. [23] A series of official inquiries ensued regarding alleged abuse of prisoners (most of these inquiries concluded that many staff—in some jails a majority—and the prison system generally had much to answer for), [24] and there was sustained lobbying by various groups for the closure or, at least, massive refurbishment of the nation's Victorian-era prisons. However, the intransigence of prison officers in a number of jails (with, crucially, substantial support from their unions) significantly obstructed many institutional reforms,[25] and de-layed for years closures which were widely seen as both inevitable and ur-gent. This situation was maintained until the advent of the free-market economic paradigm in the 1980s and 1990s, which fostered a new perception of the prisons as intolerably cost-ineffective.

Where argument along humanitarian lines had largely failed to motivate the policy-makers, the financial imperative succeeded, and over little more than a decade most of the nineteenth-century prisons in Australia were de-commissioned. Inmate populations were relocated to new, and in many cases privately operated, prisons on the outskirts of or outside the metropolitan ar-eas, leaving behind not only empty buildings, but also most of the personnel who had staffed them. The "shedding" of many of the long-term staff, espe-cially in cases where the prison system was also undergoing a degree of pri-vatization, amounted in some prisons to a "union-busting" exercise. The numbers retained varied from prison to prison; at Pentridge, for instance, al-most no prison officers were employed in the new facilities; more recently at Beechworth, in rural Victoria—decommissioned in 2005—a significant number made the transition to the replacement prison.

Many prison officers emerged from this period harbouring a degree of bitterness. This arose from the circumstances in which they found them-selves out of work, combined with their existing opposition to the reforms they had been compelled to introduce in the years leading up to the closures ("mollycoddling the crims"), and their opinion that there was no good reason to close the prisons anyway. Such bitterness was clearly evident, and mark-edly consistent in its particulars, in almost all the interviews I conducted with former custodial staff—even, it is worth noting, among staff who had retired before the closures and therefore had nothing material to lose; the parentheti-cal "mollycoddling" comment above was one among a number of strongly expressed summations I heard. Their dissatisfaction tended to intensify the conservatism with which they had long approached the job, and with it, I suggest, served further to consolidate their views regarding inmate popula-tions as massed collections of the Other. These factors, along with certain former officers' manifest sense of vestigial proprietorship over their "cas-tles," have significant implications for public historians, with regard to re-search, interpretation and presentation of the sites. This in turn impacts upon public perceptions and understanding of the sites and, more widely, of the generic institutions and their inhabitants.

*

Just as there is a tourist market in the case of real castles—whether in ruins or whole—so, too, it has been found that people will travel some distance, and pay an admission fee, to look over former prisons that resemble castles. A significant proportion of them in fact come primarily for the visual aspect of the "medieval" edifice. Survey responses from tourists show a predominance of interest in the architecture, over and above consideration of the imprisoned human element; in most of the individual interviews I did with sightseers, the visual aspect was the first factor mentioned in response to the question, What made you interested in touring the site? The notional conflation of architecture and history was made explicit and invested with a markedly personal element in a number of cases, with respondents commonly identifying the physical structure as "our history."

The public preoccupation with "history," and the implicit equation between that ideated history and certain modes or materials of construction, are of a piece with the fascination for the typical Gothic façade. This points up another aspect of the castle design to which the modern individual is sensitive, and which undoubtedly plays an important part in some people's perceptions of the historical prison—especially, I would argue, those who felt comfortable with the operational prison. The true medieval castle was not only a fortress, and the home of the nobility; from the late Middle Ages, it also began to acquire a unique status in the public consciousness as the archetypal setting and symbol of *romance*—of the knight errant, of courtly love, and chivalry.

During the prison's operational career, any romantic symbolism inherent in the Gothic façade is, for the majority of observers, only distantly an aesthetic factor, outweighed as it is by the far grimmer associations noted above. With the prison's decommissioning, however, and its consequent transition from venue of proximate suffering and menace to site of social memory, visual perceptions also begin to undergo a transition. The "romantic" potential of the structure, so long latent, begins to influence the ordering of aesthetic priorities. This element is rarely explicit in any literal, knights-in-armour sense; it remains at the level of cultural subtext, serving to nuance perceptions of the site overall. It leads, in turn, to a tendency among promoters of the site as a tourist attraction to exploit any elements of the physical structure that have a Gothic quality, by featuring appropriately representative images on posters and letterheads, posting them on websites, and so on. The Eastern

State Penitentiary logo, for instance, depicts a stylized rendering of the prison's iconic castellated main entrance and gate towers.[26]

Websites are in fact an important aspect of prison museum promotion, and are employed specifically to display names, events and representations of the physical institution that denote for the prospective visitor some supposed essence of the site. In the process there are generated a variety of what tourism sociologist Dean MacCannell terms "markers"—signifying informational attributes, accessed beforehand, that contribute to the sightseer's "recognition" (as opposed to *perception*) of sites visited.[27] It may be that such markers are peculiarly significant as a component of the sightseer's experience of an historical prison—especially the sightseer who has not previously visited any other prisons—given the relative lack of information normally available about the interior workings of operational prisons, and the consequent difficulty in forming coherent expectations.

Even the first-time sightseer to an historical prison has *some* expectations, of course, aside from the connotations of the architecture. Promotional material routinely utilizes a variety of images and concepts associated with the institution's history, including narrative texts, representative interior photographs, reproductions of historical documents, and, often, "mug shots" of former (usually deceased) prisoners. These, too, constitute "markers," within MacCannell's definition, and as such may be seen as further informing the "recognition" that is the sightseer's unwitting quest. Yet there are subtle lacks and biases inherent in such material which the modern sightseer is culturally and psychologically unlikely to be in a position to discern. Australian historical prisons are almost invariably promoted with a signal emphasis on the period beyond living memory, most often the nineteenth century, and the stuff of these markers, especially pictures of inmates, is generally drawn from those "historical" times. (The main exception to this, to be discussed in due course, is the promotion of particularly notorious prisoners or spectacular events of more recent times—what I term the "celebrity prisoner" phenomenon.) This preoccupation with the *distant* past has a number of effects in regard to the sightseer's perceptions and general sense of the *personal* dimension of the site.

By a combination of promotional markers and the mode of presentation of the site itself, the sightseer is tacitly encouraged to identify with the "historical" characters, that is, the nineteenth-century inmates whose pictures and stories appear on the posters. They are routinely presented as sympathetic characters by virtue of the terrible and disproportionate punishments they received—floggings, solitary confinement, and so on, premised on the classic "transported for stealing a loaf of bread" notion which Australian children have been absorbing as rote for generations. The implication is that "they"— the archaic and hence brutally unenlightened juridical Establishment—"did things differently back then."

The counterpoint to this, and a central aspect of my argument, is that in various ways the tourist is discouraged from discerning or inferring, any more than vaguely, the prison's *recent* inmates. Their representation— insofar as they are coherently represented at all—tends to depict, interpret and/or present them much in accord with the *modern* Establishment point of view of the contemporary prison inmate—the "crim." They are conceptualized, in other words, as the definitive Other. This othering takes a variety of forms and embraces a wide spectrum of tones; it can and often does involve rendering them, in anecdote, media depiction and penal museum representation, gratuitously comical. But it also can, and equally often does, take markedly callous and at times overtly rancorous form.

Othering interpretations often inhere as subtext when, for instance, former prison officers provide the narrative accompaniment to sightseers' tours. Also, static displays of illicit inmate artefacts such as weapons, which are often presented simply as collections mounted under glass with minimal interpretation—the items are assumed to "speak for themselves"—naturally serve to other the original wielders of such instruments. Yet, crucially, this occurs without necessarily eliciting significant sympathy for, much less empathy with, whoever among the "crims" may have fallen victims to those instruments.

*

In defining "markers" for the purposes of his model, MacCannell elaborates on an existing, but far narrower, concept in tourism sociology that defines as markers such signifiers as, for instance, the plaque identifying an otherwise unremarkable meadow as the site of a long-ago battle, or the signs frequently seen in locations about the eastern United States testifying that "George Washington slept here."[28] The typical American sightseer, it may reasonably be assumed, will recognize the connotations of national heritage embodied in such a message, and may well experience a frisson of personal affirmation through their identification with that heritage.

Shortly after Pentridge Prison was decommissioned in 1997, Jesuit Social Services, who had a long association with the jail, were permitted to run public tours of the complex for several weeks prior to its transfer into private hands for development. Among the modest interpretative material they displayed was a small sign on a wall in "D" Division, headed "THE SUM OF HUMAN MISERY." Under this heading was an astronomically large number representing the total number of "prisoner-years" spent by all the inmates kept within the division throughout its history. In an institution whose inmate population had departed mere weeks before and were therefore still a living presence in sightseers' consciousness, the statistic, and its mode of interpretation, stood as one of very few expressions I have seen, in Australian historical prisons, of a curatorial disregard for the customary distinction between archaic and modern inmates, as objects of sympathy. In the mode of its presentation, as a physical plaque on a wall, which identified and located the personal within the viewed space, it was analogous to the "George Washington" sign. And yet, given the general attitudes noted above, it is unlikely to have elicited a corresponding degree of sympathetic identification; for many sightseers to Pentridge, the Jesuits' well-meant "marker" said, in effect, "The Other slept here"—and that Other did so in large (and hence dangerous) numbers. It is possible, in fact, that aside from *who* occupied the space, the statistic itself militated against empathy because of its sheer size.

This points up a significant peculiarity of Australian historical prisons as venues of Dark Tourism. As I have said, Dark Tourism is, broadly, about visiting historical sites of suffering and mayhem such as battlefields, concentration camps, and so on; insofar as the visitor to such sites is in any meaningful degree sensitive to the experience, those places tend by their nature to elicit empathy, a sense of identification with the victim/participants. At most sites this reaction in the tourist is taken for granted, and for curatorial personnel there is usually little at stake anyway. (At one site, the US Holocaust Museum in Washington DC, the visitor is specifically "required" by the format of the tour experience to identify with Holocaust victims.)[29] In the case of most modern Australian prison museums, however, the victims of suffering are the Other. They therefore do not evoke the empathy of any but the relative few who for one reason or another harbour some personal concern for that Other. In this regard, Australian historical prisons are unusual sites within the general model of Dark Tourism, in that they are possibly the only ones where the mainstream visitors' attitudes by and large *endorse* the suffering of the victims. (It must be stressed that this tendency applies almost exclusively toward modern-era inmates; at sites such as Hyde Park Barracks in New South Wales and Port Arthur in Tasmania, for instance, which only ever held colonial-era convict transportees and ceased operations in the mid-nineteenth century, compassion for the inmates is the norm, and governs both representation and visitor response. On the other hand, at sites such as Fremantle Prison, whose history of operations began with colonial transportation but continued unbroken into the 1990s, there is strong sympathy evinced toward the transportees, as represented on-site, while attitudes to the prison's latter-day inmates is markedly harsh.) This inimical view is amply confirmed by the number of tourists one may encounter at jails throughout Australia who speak nostalgically about capital punishment, who decry the "luxury" of modern "motel-style" prisons, and who echo the prison officers' sentiment that the old jails were good jails and should never have closed. The consistency of their animosity toward the former inhabitants does much, I believe, to render explicable the otherwise paradoxical confluence of the romantic aesthetic and Dark Tourism.

A favourable aesthetic disposition toward the "romantic" edifice itself may in fact promote a tendency in the visitor to underestimate the deleterious effect it had as a living environment for its inmates, and hence to contribute to the exclusion of their narratives. I came to suspect, on conversing with some tourists, that a subtle aspect of this psychological process involved a tendency for site visitors in effect to identify with the Establishment, both through their favourable attitude to the building's visual "beauty," and a concomitant impulse to identify with the power element implied in the historical form of the castle.

The converse, of course, also applies: a viewer who has reason to identify not with the Establishment but with the building's unwilling residents may be markedly unmoved by such aesthetic considerations. Thus cultural sociologist Toby Miller (who is himself unlikely to identify with the Establishment), recounts a friend's perception of Fremantle Prison:

> Walking nearby with a friend, I said how beautiful the prison's stonework looked. She averted her eyes and moved away, soon angry and tearful. Her brother had just been released. She had been a regular visitor during his prison term. The stonework did *not* look beautiful to her.[30]

*

Not all of Australia's historical prisons strictly resemble castles. Yet even if they do not literally sport crenellations and cylindrical keeps, virtually all but the most modest rural lockup have in common a markedly wilful architecture that towers and imposes itself upon its surroundings, that gives an impression not merely of size and robustness—the prudent minimum in buildings that must keep hard and determined people confined—but of baleful admonition. It is an architecture that *glowers* at its neighbours. In this quality, even *sans* battlements, they remain faithful to the visual tradition conceived by those long-ago Philadelphian proponents of "muscular Christian punishment."[31]

The institutional history of Australia is relatively short. Because of this, and the imperatives that pressed upon the administrators of our founding population and their immediate descendants, our historical prisons are among the nation's oldest buildings. In the opening lines of this chapter, I suggested that the Norman castle may be viewed as "the defining architectural entity" of feudalism. Given Australia's penal origins and the subsequent influence those beginnings have had on the growth of our society, it is arguable on similar grounds—that is, the edifices in question were intrinsic to and symbolic of the fundamental social order—that the Gothic prison stands in an equivalent defining position in relation to early Australia. If this is so, then it may have particular significance for the twenty-first-century individual who is in any way engaged in a search for an Australian national identity.

NOTES

1   Harold Perkin, *Origins of Modern English Society* (London: Ark, 1986), pp. 42–43.

2   Norman Johnston, *Forms of Constraint: A History of Prison Architecture* (Urbana Ill.: University of Illinois Press, 2000), pp. 67–70; Eastern State Penitentiary (hereafter ESP) website, "History of Eastern State Penitentiary, Philadelphia," http://www.easternstate .org/history/sixpage.html (accessed 10 Mar 2005); Mike Walsh, "Black Hoods and Iron Gags: The Quaker Experiment at Eastern State Penitentiary in Philadelphia," http://www .missioncreep.com/mw/estate.html (accessed 10 Mar 2005);

3   *Penitentiary* in the sense of a reformatory prison had long been used in reformist writings, on both sides of the Atlantic, but it would become, and remains today, chiefly an American usage. The word was used to denote the "experimental" English prison at

48   *Prison: Cultural Memory and Dark Tourism*

Millbank, the opening of which preceded Eastern State by a year, but which was deemed a failure. See David Wilson, "Millbank, the Panopticon and Their Victorian Audiences," *The Howard Journal* 41, no. 4; also Johnston, *Forms of Constraint*, pp. 62–3.

4   ESP website, "History".

5   Johnston, *Forms of Constraint*, p. 73.

6   Ibid., pp. 70–73.

7   Ibid.; Walsh, "Black Hoods and Iron Gags."

8   Craig W.J. Minogue, "Human Rights and Life as an Attraction in a Correctional Theme Park," *Journal of Prisoners on Prisons* 12, 2002. Minogue was an inmate of Pentridge; former staff at various other Australian jails told me that the practice went on there, too.

9   Johnston, *Forms of Constraint*, pp. 68, 80, 90; Walsh, "Black Hoods and Iron Gags."

10   Johnston, *Forms of Constraint*, pp. 91, 99, 110, Ch 7 *passim*; Walsh, "Black Hoods and Iron Gags"; ESP website, "History"; Peter Scharff Smith, "The History of Solitary Confinement: Rehabilitation, Insanity and Cultures of Control," Danish Institute for Human Rights, http://www.humanrights.dk/departments/Research/resProj03/psseng01/ (accessed 20 Feb 2005).

11   On the process by which Pentonville came to be modelled on Eastern State, and the ways in which it varied from the original, see Michael Ignatieff, *A Just Measure of Pain: The Penitentiary in the Industrial Revolution* (London: MacMillan, 1978), pp. 194–7; also Johnston, *Forms of Constraint*, pp. 90–91.

12   Johnston, *Forms of Constraint*, p. 93.

13   Ibid.; see also Amy Edwards and Richard Hurley, "Prisons Over Two Centuries", extract from *Home Office 1782–1982*, United Kingdom Home Office, http://www.homeoffice.gov.uk/docs/prishist.html (accessed 10 March 2005).

14   Jeremy Bentham, *"Panopticon": or, the Inspection-House; containing the Idea of a New Principal of Construction Applicable to Any Sort of Establishment, in Which Persons of Any Description are to be Kept Under Inspection* (London: T. Payne, 1791).

15   On the tortuous circumstances of this episode see L.J. Hume, "Bentham's Panopticon: An Administrative History" parts I and II, *Historical Studies* 15 and 16, nos. 61 and 62, Oct 1973, April 1974; also David Wilson, "Millbank."

16   Conservation architect Roger Beeston provides a useful comparative summary of the two designs in his "Sandridge (Bendigo) Gaol, Victoria," *Historic Environment* 14 no. 2, 1999, pp.17–24; see also Wilson, "Millbank,"; James Semple Kerr, *Design for Convicts: An Account of Design for Convict Establishments in the Australian Colonies During the Transportation Era* (Sydney: Library of Australian History, 1984); *idem, Out of Sight, Out of Mind: Australia's Places of Confinement, 1788–1988* (Sydney: S.H. Ervin Gallery, National Trust of Australia (NSW), 1988); John Hirst, *Convict Society and its Enemies: A History of Early New South Wales* (Sydney: Allen and Unwin, 1983), pp. 10–14.

17   Examples of the myth may be found in, e.g., Helen Marshall, Kathy Douglas and Desmond McDonnell, *Deviance and Social Control: Who Rules?* (Melbourne: Oxford University Press, 2007), pp. 110–12; Pat Cooke, "Kilmainham Gaol: Interpreting Irish Nationalism and Republicanism," *Open Museum Journal* 2, August 2000, http://amol.org.au/omj/volume2/volume2_index.asp (accessed 23 Mar 2004); Howard

League for Penal Reform, "A Short History of Prison," http://www.howardleague.org/studycentre/historyofprison.htm (accessed 25 February 2005).

18 Michel Foucault, *Discipline and Punish* (Harmondsworth: Penguin, 1986).

19 See Johnston, *Forms of Constraint*, pp. 108–9.

20 Ibid., pp. 1–2; Beeston, "Sandridge Gaol."

21 Sally Collins, interviewed 10 February 2001.

22 On the Coburg quarries see Richard Broome, *Coburg: Between Two Creeks* (Melbourne: Lothian, 1997), pp. 130–4, 174–5.

23 This "siege mentality" was graphically evinced for me in a number of the interviews I conducted among former prison officers.

24 See, e.g., Kenneth Jenkinson, *Report of the Board of Inquiry into Allegations of Brutality and Ill Treatment at H.M. Prison Pentridge* (Melbourne: Victorian Government, 1973); idem, *Report of the Board of Inquiry into Several Matters Concerning H.M. Prison Pentridge and the Maintenance of Discipline in Prisons* (Melbourne: Victorian Government, 1973); J.F. Nagle J, *Report of the Royal Commission into New South Wales Prisons* (Sydney: New South Wales Government, 1978); James Kennedy, *Final Report of the Commission of Review into Corrective Services in Queensland* (Brisbane: Queensland Government, 1988); Peter Lynn, *Inquiry into the Victorian Prison System: Instituted to Inquire into a Report on Allegations of Maladministration, Corruption and Drug Trafficking within the Victorian Prison System* (Melbourne, Victorian Government, 1993); on aspects of corruptly "authorized" prison violence generally, see Peter Grabosky, *Wayward Governance: Illegality and its Control in the Public Sector* (Canberra: Australian Institute of Criminology, 1989), Ch. 2.

25 David Brown, interview, *Four Corners*, ABC Television, broadcast 7 November 2005; Ombudsman WA, *Report on an Investigation into Deaths in Prisons* (Perth: Western Australian Government, 2000); Grabosky, *Wayward Governance*.

26 See ESP website, homepage: http://www.easternstate.org/; also, among Australian historical prisons, Fremantle Prison, http://www.fremantleprison.com.au/tours/tours8.cfn; Adelaide Gaol, http://www.adelaidegaol.org.au/.

27 Dean MacCannell, *The Tourist: A New Theory of the Leisure Class* (Berkeley CA: University of California Press, 1999), Ch. 6.

28 MacCannell, *The Tourist*, p. 110.

29 Lennon and Foley, *Dark Tourism*, p. 146. Unusually for an Australian site, the interpretative gallery in the Port Arthur Visitors' Centre invites similar (albeit optional) commitment on the part of the tourist—although this could be regarded as consistent with the abovementioned tendency for prison tourists to be encouraged to identify with 19th-century inmates. This aspect of the Port Arthur site is briefly discussed in Chapter 11. See also Carolyn Strange, "From 'Place of Misery' to 'Lottery of Life': Interpreting Port Arthur's Past," *Online Museum Journal* 2, 2000, http://amol.org.au/omj/volume2/strange.pdf (accessed 12 March 2005).

30 Toby Miller, *Visible Evidence Volume 2: Technologies of Truth: Cultural Citizenship and the Popular Media* (Minneapolis: University of Minnesota Press, 1998), p. 232 (italics *sic*).

31 Jonathon Glancey, "Within these Walls," *The Guardian* 1 February 2001.

CHAPTER THREE

Public History, Dark Tourism, and Real Estate:
The Case of Pentridge

Until recent years it was axiomatic that the operation of prisons in Australia was the exclusive province of government. But the advent of increasingly comprehensive laissez-faire economic policies during the latter decades of the twentieth century brought a shift toward an embracement of the concept of "privatization" of prisons, and this has resulted in a number of privately operated prisons and "detention centres" being commissioned in various locations around Australia.[1] An attendant and more general trend in the state of Victoria, arising from the same laissez-faire policies and reaching a peak during the 1990s under the Kennett government, saw a large-scale "rationalization" of publicly owned institutions (including many schools, local government centres, and so on) with resultant windfall exploitation of those sites' potential, once closed, as simple real-estate. "Under Kennett, Victoria embarked on the biggest privatization program of any regions in the world, selling public assets for more than $30 billion, and redirecting services valued at a further $10 billion into private hands."[2] Uniquely among the former prisons discussed in this book, H.M. Prison Pentridge, in north-suburban Melbourne, falls into this category.

In many ways Pentridge may be seen as an archetype of the Australian prison of the post-convict era. It was established in 1850, in answer to overcrowding at the Melbourne Gaol, as a mainly timber "stockade" built by the inmates it was destined to house.[3] The site chosen was eight kilometres north of Melbourne, closely adjacent to a growing village which would come to surround it, and which would change its name in 1867 from Pentridge to Coburg, in an effort to dissociate itself from the prison.[4] In the decades following the prison's founding, the original (inadequate) structure was replaced by an increasingly extensive complex, still in large part the product of inmate labour, and utilising in its construction the locally quarried bluestone. At its peak it would hold over 1,000 prisoners and cover 140 acres.[5] The iconic medieval gatehouse was in place by 1870, and with it was consolidated the prison's visual impact upon the surrounding suburb: "a massive shape, without adjacent trees to soften its high walls…Its bluestone construction was dark and alien…and the gothic allusions of its main gate and towers made it all the more forbidding."[6] Pentridge served as Victoria's main high-security prison for almost 150 years, and as such was acknowledged as an intrinsic and highly significant feature of Coburg's and greater Melbourne's social history.

In the mid-1990s a State government resolution saw Pentridge decommissioned and its population transferred to alternative centres. Although the prison's closure was not universally welcomed (most of Pentridge's prison officers, for instance, were not re-employed by the new prisons),[7] it was regarded by many as long overdue. The jail's harsh and antiquated amenities and generally rundown condition had attracted much criticism as a living environment (and attempts to interpolate into the complex modern, "state-of-the-art" facilities, such as the infamously unremissive "high-tech" super-maximum-security division known as "Jika Jika," had tended further to degrade rather than improve the prison's reputation).[8] Far more controversial was the government's decision to sell the entire site, as found, to private-sector land developers committed to replacing the prison with a prestige housing estate, dubbed a "walled village," and a "piazza."[9]

It is by virtue of this relatively sudden transformation, from functioning public institution to private land-development site, that Pentridge merits particular examination. The former prison is discussed here as a dual case study, regarding both the problematic interface between public history and radically commercial imperatives, and the role of the gatekeepers and other stakeholders in the process of creating and/or affecting that interface.

The ongoing public unease provoked by the sale and redevelopment of Pentridge rested on a trivet of concerns. In the first place, the deal was done under a cloak of "commercial" confidentiality which among other things permanently concealed the precise terms of the sale and the price paid by the developers. These secrecy provisions survived the 1999 change of State government, with even the local council remaining largely "not privy" to the terms of the contract.[10] (A contemporary report at the time of the sale stated that the price was "understood to be about $20 million.")[11]

Secondly, there was a widespread perception of inadequate local community consultation, both before and subsequent to the sale. The government publicly acknowledged the historical significance of the site and the concomitant need for community involvement in its development;[12] but the announcement of the sale proposal attracted immediate criticism from National Trust Australia (Victoria) on the grounds that the government was "go[ing] against its own recommendations and [its] building protection agency [Heritage Victoria]."[13] The "recommendations" referred to were those of an architectural consultants' report commissioned before the jail closed.[14]

Once the sale took effect, a number of the Trust's fears regarding the possible destruction or misuse of classified Pentridge structures apparently proved justified, with various of those structures being demolished in short order, notably some sections of the perimeter wall and the whole of the ultra-high-security division, Jika Jika. Relations between the developers and local council (City of Moreland) were strained from the first, and in 2001 a "demarcation" dispute over who should pay for the upkeep of the site's original buildings led to a hearing before the State Department of Infrastructure Planning Advisory Panel, which ruled that the owners were exempt from heritage site upkeep costs.[15] (This and related disputes between Council and the developers continued to simmer for some time, with heritage upkeep costs once again becoming a focus of public contention in 2003.[16] The two bodies eventually came to an accommodation.) Long after redevelopment began, local residents were bemoaning the developers' "habit" of short-circuiting community participation, through the expedient of too-short notice of meetings and vagueness of proposals upon which residents were invited to comment.[17]

Thirdly, and consequent upon these first two factors, there was (and remains) concern in many quarters regarding the potential assault on historicity inherent in the appropriation of a major element of social memory by (profit-driven) entities of the private sector. A notable aspect of the tender process was that it occurred without any agreed-upon "master plan for heritage interpretation." [18]

Aside from the highly confronting visual quality of the external boundary walls, the physical features for which Pentridge has always been best known are the Gothic elements comprising its westward-facing front-entrance façade. These, along with the original internal buildings clustered behind the façade along the western side, have been preserved, with the intention of exploiting their historical significance. The form and method of that exploitation was the subject of several years of speculation and at times rancorous debate between Moreland Council, the developers, the National Trust, Jesuit Social Services and local community groups such as the Coburg Historical Society (CHS) and Citizens Advocating Responsible Development (CARD). These organizations pursued a diversity of goals: the National Trust was primarily concerned that the site's heritage-designated built fabric should remain pristine;[19] the Jesuits expressed unease about the unmarked graves of over forty executed prisoners buried beneath a lawn near D Division (including the partial remains of Ned Kelly, and Ronald Ryan, the last person executed in Australia);[20] the Council, aside from its above-noted contention that the developers should take more responsibility for heritage-related funding, reacted forcefully to reported breaches of the planning permit in the form of unauthorized demolition of wall sections;[21] the CHS proposed, among other things, a "sound-and-light" show;[22] and CARD lamented the lack of community consultation regarding the development overall, and was instrumental in forestalling a developers' plan to extend the site's residential construction zone outside the western boundary walls, that is, in front of the prison's iconic facade.[23]

The site's corporate owners, Pentridge Piazza Pty Ltd, finally revealed their full intentions in mid-2002, when they announced their architectural "master plan" for the development.[24] Alongside various new constructions, including a controversial sixteen-storey apartment tower, the refurbishment of existing buildings was to see the surviving divisions become, variously, a "boutique" hotel, a backpacker hostel, and an aged-care facility.[25] The project, expected to cost $300 million, aimed "to turn the former jail into a commercial and residential hub."[26] Little trace of the various interest groups' historical proposals was visible in the master plan, nor in subsequent elaborations and extensions to that plan.

Not that Pentridge Piazza's directors intended to eschew entirely the incorporation of some sort of formal historical presentation into their project; but their avowed concept of the site's history, and the consequent form of that presentation, were such as to cause the social historian considerable misgiving. According to press statements by the company's "community liaison officer," Reg Macey, the motivation for compiling and displaying an "historical record" of Pentridge rested primarily on an analogy drawn with the classical history of the northern-Italian "walled town" of Treviso—the family home-town of one of the directors, and the model on which the piazza-centred redevelopment plan is based.[27] "In 1969," according to Macey, "in Treviso, [archaeologists] discovered part of the old Roman forum and some of the tessellated pavement was revealed. It's there with a board explaining what it was all about."[28] In other words, once having conceived the idea of transforming the jail into an entirely different type of architectural and cultural entity, the developers responded not to the original site's inherent and specific historical narratives, but to the generic, inferred narrative of its proposed replacement. That this is an unconvincing basis for historical interpretation is evidenced by the following elaboration by Pentridge Piazza director Luciano Crema, whose markedly ambiguous explication implies a desire simultaneously to deny *and* celebrate the prison's existence:

> If you can remove the fact that it was a prison and just think of it as a new beginning, and activate it with a lot of people, you can see something that's been done in Europe in many towns, yet we don't have anything like it here in Australia. The history of this place is what makes it different and I think people will want to live there once they understand the concept.[29]

The immediate question, of course, is just how one is to "remove the fact that it was a prison," as it is precisely this fact that constitutes the site's "history" and is therefore what "makes it different." Clearly, from the developers' point of view, there were strong reasons for wishing somehow to achieve this feat: people had to be persuaded to "want to live there," or at the least to visit the place as tourists, if the redevelopment was to turn a profit. Such commercial and populist imperatives—the epitome of what has been termed "marketplace history"[30]—must inevitably result in attempts to render the site palatable to the envisioned audience (with the commercial need to ensure, of course, that that audience is as numerous as possible).[31]

Like almost any nineteenth-century prison (almost any prison, in fact), Pentridge is well qualified to be numbered among those "places with difficult histories"[32] that present a special challenge to the public historian—and to entrepreneurs such as Luciano Crema. Decisions become necessary as to what type of history audiences will tolerate. Here, then, arises the incentive to "remove the fact that it was a prison." Of course, even the directors of Pentridge Piazza knew that such "removal" was not literally possible nor even desirable—the site's history as a prison, after all, constitutes its chief tourist potential—so the project was in fact to render the prison emotionally innocuous to the mainstream visitor, while preserving the impression of "authenticity" that is so vital to the sightseer.[33]

I have noted the perennial concern of public historians over the tendency for key decisions regarding interpretation and representation of sites to be overly influenced by relatively small numbers of stakeholders, or narrowly motivated groups. In the case of Pentridge, it seems clear, the central decisions have been made by just such a narrow spectrum of interests, and with, at best, only distant involvement of professional historians. This is not to say that the involvement of such "professionals" at a key level would ensure the site's historical integrity; as public historian Margaret Anderson has observed, even major museum curators can find themselves susceptible to such "compromises," most especially when the key determinant is "community pride."[34] A straightforward inference from this is that the push toward compromise is all the more potent when profits are at stake.

Such concerns in the field of public history are not new. In outlining the pitfalls inherent in presenting history in the popular "marketplace," Jan Penney speaks of the rise, in recent decades, of historical venues that were

> all concerned with presenting the sort of past their visitors liked to see. A sanitized, neat and clean sort of history that did not threaten, that presented a good story, an unreal sort of reality.[35]

To this she adds, tellingly, "Most often these museums presented the history of the dominant class."[36] Insofar as the concept of class has meaning within institutions such as Pentridge Prison (and I would argue that it does indeed have much meaning),[37] Penney's observation has a singular resonance.

In July 2002, concurrently with the release of the "master plan," Pentridge Piazza Pty Ltd made it known that future tourist visitors to the piazza would be able to take in an "audio-visual" exposition given on film by a retired Pentridge prison officer, Colin Nash, and several of his colleagues, all of whom had volunteered their time.[38] Mr Nash was among those who presided over the 1997 decommissioning, and this virtual walking tour of his former workplace, filmed by Pentridge Piazza's Reg Macey, spans the twenty-two years of his employment there and takes the form of a succession of anecdotes retailed in the various "authentic" locations of their origins about the prison.[39] The video presentations, intended to be viewed from an "observation platform" described as "a central part of the [piazza] development,"[40] recount episodes such as escapes and escape attempts, sabotage conspiracies, celebrity concert visits, and at least one suicide.[41]

Given the stakeholder-gatekeeper imperatives discussed earlier, it is apparent that even a "virtual" tour guide is motivated to facilitate the fullest possible public acceptance of the site. As Bob McKercher and Hilary du Cros point out,

> A number of tactics are available to transform a cultural asset into a consumerable tourism product:
> - Mythologize the asset
> - Build a story around the asset
> - Emphasize its otherness …
> - Make it fun, light, and entertaining.[42]

Clearly, McKercher and du Cros's criteria could have been formulated with Pentridge in mind. The "mythologising" of "the asset" began long ago with the emblematising of the structural fabric—the bluestone itself—in the epithet "Bluestone College." This characteristic has always been consonant with the inherent mystery embodied in the boundary walls, and the prison's quasi-medieval façade—all elements that featured prominently in the site's promotional publicity. On a personal level, the narrated mythology tends to rest in large part on such notorious historical figures as Ronald Ryan and (to a lesser extent) Ned Kelly, along with contemporary inmates of the "celebrity" type such as the assiduously self-publicising Mark "Chopper" Read, whose autobiographical works have done much to augment that mythology.[43]

As we have seen, "building a story"—by way of a formalized accumulation of anecdotes permanently committed to the record in the form of the Piazza video—is the avowed project of the gatekeepers, and as is made further clear below, an integral aspect of their intent is to make it "fun, light and entertaining" through an abundance of "jokes," apparently authentic recounting of intrinsically "exciting"—hence "entertaining"—episodes such as escapes, and general euphemization or tacit rejection of the site's more "difficult" aspects. It is axiomatic, for instance, that they initiate no discussion regarding sexual violence.

Of particular significance in relation to the role and influence of the gatekeepers is the emphasis of otherness. In keeping with the factors noted earlier, an abiding component of the popular historical interpretation of the sites is the routine affirmation of that otherness by those who conduct tours (or at least provide the informational basis of the tourist experience). This stance, in its apparently straightforward distinction between good guys and bad guys, embodies an intrinsic drama of the sort that may be expected to resonate with the majority of the visitors to the site. Visitors are relatively unlikely to question, in any substantive way, either the veracity of the stories they hear, or, more importantly, the process by which those stories have been chosen above other candidate stories.

Also complicit in the othering process is the mass media. An instance of this is the manner of treatment the prison officers' involvement in the Pentridge project received in the newspapers. The occasion of Colin Nash's initial video session was reported both in the local newspapers and the *Age*, with the latter adopting a notably flippant tone reliant on heavy-handed word-play, and angled on the discovery that "Mr Nash does a nice line in prison jokes."[44] Even the local paper, whose proximity to the issue prompted a generally more sober tone, could not resist the odd pun.[45] It is to a certain extent *de rigueur* in reporting what might be termed "safe" prison stories— that is, those not involving scandals, such as bashings or deaths in custody, nor the direct social threat of escapes—that they be treated with a levity appropriate to the more innocuous sort of "human interest" story. In such an approach the media unwittingly fall in with the gatekeepers' agenda of euphemising the unpalatable—"making it fun, light and entertaining," "mythologising the asset," and generally furthering the prison's transformation into "a consumable tourism product."[46]

*

Port Arthur curator Julia Clark speaks of the need, in the interpretive representation of historic sites, for a turning away from the incessant curatorial quest for an illusory "authenticity," in favour of an inclusive "integrity"—a readiness to present and acknowledge the manifold strands of narrative from both sides of the Us–Other divide, and from the fuzzily demarcated no-man's land in between that gives the lie to that divide. As Clark says, "It is [in] these social and emotional intersections that meaning lies."[47]

If we are, at least notionally, to make a beginning in the formulation of an inclusive interpretation / representation of former sites of imprisonment, we must address the obvious questions: What *are* the other candidate narratives; and how, in practice, can a fairly selected sample be presented? The second of these questions can be no more than briefly touched upon here; in addressing the first, however, certain guidelines suggest themselves through the nature of the materials that become available.

In the first place, it should be noted that the Pentridge developers might well defend themselves against the above criticisms on the grounds that they *have* included other voices and accounts: shortly after acquiring the site they commissioned documentary film-maker Catherine Birmingham to shoot an hour-long video about the prison *qua* prison, and with their blessing she interviewed not only former prison officers but also a small number of former prisoners.[48] However, her approach, although resulting in an undeniably fascinating and at times sobering glimpse within the jail, falls short of being substantially inclusive (and in the process confirms, albeit in a subtly different way, the media tendencies described above), in that the ex-prisoners interviewed were of the "celebrity" type already noted—in particular playwright Ray Mooney and "Chopper" Read, who in their respective ways were among the "elites" of the prison population, and who have gone on to turn their prison experiences into highly public non-criminal careers. Mooney, the first Australian prisoner to gain a university degree while in jail, was also an outstanding athlete, twice granted day-leave to compete in top-level decathlons.[49] The case of Read is examined in some detail in later chapters. Birmingham herself lamented the exclusionary aspect of her documentary, telling me that she had found it impossible, within the available time, to recruit a wider range of ex-prisoners.[50] To what extent the likes of Mooney and Read can be said to represent the far less spectacular, anonymous and unremarkable mass of ordinary prisoners is very much open to question.

In the effective absence of an oral history project, the built fabric comes into its own for its inferential narrative potential, as also do the views and experiences of non-prisoners who, for their various reasons, had a professional or personal stake primarily in the inmates' well-being, rather than their confinement. The narratives that emerge from both of these types of sources are anathema to many of the gatekeepers.

To consider first the physical. It will be recalled that during my visit to my brother in the operational prison I found the most ubiquitous and visually oppressive outdoor element of the place as a living environment to be the various types of wire—heavy hurricane-wire, wire mesh, and especially dominating, the razor wire, a frieze of imminent violence imposed upon every inmate's day-to-day existence.

There is no razor wire to be found in what is left of Pentridge today. The vestige that crowned a few of the remaining walls for some years after redevelopment began has been removed. It is, one must concede, hardly surprising that redevelopers intent on promoting a site as both liveable and worth touring should have removed such a visually disturbing feature during the initial excavation and subsequent refurbishment; but in the process they did away with a defining feature of the operational prison, and hence emasculated a key signifier of the banal brutality of the inmate experience. Such euphemization in a supposed public history site is of a piece with the routine "sprucing up" such sites undergo before their presentation to the public, and stands, along with jocular dioramas, display-cases full of de-contextualized weapons, souvenir artefacts for sale in the tea-rooms and so on, as active yet unrecognized impediments to the imagination needed to empathize with the multitudes of ordinary prisoners who spent their days and years endeavouring simply to get by.

There are, of course, physical elements of the jail that are intrinsically affecting; as in almost any former jail, it can be edifying for the sightseer to stand inside a cell and contemplate the idea of making it a home for several years; yet even here, within the proverbial "box," the sensation for the tourist can easily be more of an emotional "blank" than anything else. This sense of "anti-climax," as one sightseer put it, was reported to me by visitors at a number of sites. One could argue that this is, indeed, what an inmate might very well feel (or, rather, *fail* to feel) in such an environment; but this overlooks the natural impulse, responded to by inmates everywhere, to provide for themselves some emotional stimulus and affirmation of personal identity in the face of the radically dehumanising influence of blank walls and iron doors—that is, to decorate, and/or otherwise personalize, the walls.

In the case of Pentridge, as in many other prisons, there is little likelihood that any graffiti has survived in areas destined for public viewing. The responses of former Pentridge staff to my expressed interest in graffiti on the site were fully consistent with the attitudes recounted in Chapter One. Yet it would be well within the capacities of a skilled conservator to remove overlayers of paint at selected locations, such as certain cell interiors, and actively present the restored "textualized" surfaces, with accompanying (nonjudgemental) interpretation, as an edifying feature of a tour rather than shutting it away as shameful evidence of refractory inmate behaviour. The restoration process itself could conceivably become part of the tour, with visitors permitted to watch conservators at work. (But there can be little doubt that such a proposal would meet strong resistance from the gatekeepers.)[51]

There *is* an example of Pentridge graffiti that is just visible to this day (especially after rain), as "unofficial" historical text. It was certainly not the work of a serving inmate, however, for it is on the *outside* of the jail. In the 1970s there appeared on the external walls, stark white against the bluestone in letters two feet high, an exhortation for prison authorities to "Ban the Bash." This redolent message referred to a wave of media revelations of violence regularly committed against prisoners by prison officers, with the apparent acquiescence of their superiors.[52] A major inquiry,[53] spurred in part by protest movements within and outside the system, led to significant reforms, and comforted many with the idea that such brutality had been relegated to Pentridge's past. But habits die harder than that—especially when they are perceived as effective. Thus former prison officer Timothy Knapp:

> Anyone who stuffed up in Pentridge went to H Division—could have spat on a prison officer, could have killed his mate next door, violent, raping the boys, stealing, so they took 'em up there and used to give 'em a clip 'round the earhole in the seventies and eighties, and it worked.
>
> Say a prisoner down in D Division [remand] comes in and he's a cheeky little bugger, he's probably been the school bully, Mum's a de facto, can't handle him, righto, he's been warned by the courts thirty times,... he's been into boys' homes and he comes into jail: "I'm not making my bed"; "I don't want a haircut"; "I'm not working"; "You can go and get nicked." All of a sudden he flicks a prison officer or spits on him, so it's down to H Division, they beat the Christ out of him, within thirty days he's as good as gold.[54]

Knapp, who retired some years before the prison's closure, states today that he is on good terms with ex-prisoners because of his basically non-violent management style; yet in matters of passive complicity, such as those that faced welfare officer Jason Smith, for instance, Knapp's position was uncomplicated and, we may infer, typical:

> We [prison officers] stick together; ... we don't work as a fragmented group, dobbing each other in, we get together. If a prison officer gives a prisoner a clip over the earhole we support him, we didn't see a thing, we get up in court and say so....In H Division in my day they used to bash them down there, give 'em a thumping. I stood there and watched it, but you couldn't say it in court.[55]

Such an ethos of unaccountability is both a product of and contributor to the closed and secret nature of the total institution; and there is much anecdotal evidence that it survived the decades of inquiries and systemic reforms. The result, in the case of some Pentridge staff, was feelings of moral and legal invulnerability, combined with increasingly flagrant attempts to alleviate the stresses of what has been termed "working the game." One former administrative staff member had the following to say on the prison in its last decade of operation:

> Crims would always cop a biffing if they thought they deserved it; they'd say, "Oh well, I mouthed off, I spat, they hit me, I threw one back, they hit me with ten, big deal, it's all over, tomorrow's another day." But when crims cop biffings for no reason, even they won't cop that. You don't biff someone for no reason. I think what was going on was that officers were going over to the pub at lunch time, which was "Drum's" across the road, coming back half-tanked. They were fighting amongst themselves in the car parks, a bit of a macho ritual. It's well known, you know [laughs]. One of 'em became a governor in the end.[56]

That revelations of this kind should be acknowledged among the prison's public historical narratives is, I would argue, axiomatic; but once again we may be sure that in the normal course of business nothing of the sort will be included among the stories received by tourist visitors to the site. Such inclusion would be of value not merely for the sake of exposing scandalous behaviour, but rather because of the implications such stories hold for our understanding of the inmates' daily experience of prison.

*

There is a sense, of course, in which all citizens are stakeholders in the public history of our historical prisons—not least by virtue simply of our right to be truthfully informed, and for the historical interpretations we receive to be formulated from reliable evidence. In this regard, too, it should be noted that the influence of the gatekeepers can extend well beyond the bounds of the site and its environs. The development of the Pentridge site, one of Victoria's oldest architectural structures and by rights a major entity of Melbourne's social history, resulted in the appropriation of significant strands of the component narratives of social memory associated with the jail, through a combination of relatively untrammelled commercial imperatives and the concomitant rise in the influence of the gatekeepers—in this case, chiefly the former prison officers, who may be judged to share with the developers a vested interest in a packaged, "authentic" and "palatable" representation of the "historical" prison and their own role in it.

Although it would be expecting much to hope for a change of heart and mind in the boardroom of Pentridge Piazza Pty Ltd, for what it is worth I have presented glimpses of some alternative narratives, of the sort that have been or are likely to be excluded from the prison's public history as determined by those criteria of popular acceptability, but which I argue are nevertheless deserving of inclusion in an honest examination of the history of Pentridge. Here we confront the distinction so tellingly made by Julia Clark between historical "authenticity" and integrity, at the interface between packaged populist "history" and a history inclusive of all stakeholders.

NOTES

1   There have been signs in recent years of this trend being "wound back" somewhat, in response to reports of unsatisfactory operational practices at certain prisons; however, this development and others relating to the merits or otherwise of private-sector involvement in the prison system are beyond the scope of this book, as is the overall issue of prison privatization. See: Amanda George and Sabra Lazarus, "Private Prison: The Punished, the Profiteers, and the Grand Prix of State Approval," *Australian Feminist Law Journal* 4, March 1995, pp. 153–73; David Biles and Vicki Dalton, "Deaths in Private Prisons 1990–99: A Comparative Study," *Trends and Issues in Criminal Justice* no. 120, Australian Institute of Criminology, June 1999; John van Gronigen (former Director, Dept of Corrections Victoria), interviewed on *The National Interest*, ABC Radio National 8 October 2000.

2   Richard Webb, "The Long Goodbye," *Age*, 14 March 2004; see also Michelle Gratten, "Doing Business with Jeff Kennett," *Australian Financial Review Magazine*, March 1997; Peter Ellingsen, "Deconstructing Jeff," *Age*, 4 September 1999; Russell Wright, "Accounting for Our Souls," *Overland*, No. 158, Autumn 2000, pp. 5–13; Cindy Davids and Linda Hancock, "Policing, Accountability and Citizenship in the Market State," *Australian and New Zealand Journal of Criminology*, Vol. 31, No. 1, April 1998, pp. 38–68.

3   The best historical account to date of the founding and development of Pentridge is Richard Broome, *Coburg: Between Two Creeks*, Melbourne: Coburg Historical Society (CHS) 2002, Chs 5 and 10.

4   Ibid., p. 97.

5   Ibid., p. 118.

6   Ibid., p. 7.

7   Knapp interview; George Armstrong (ex-Pentridge Governor of Security), interviewed

31 January 2001; Mark Forbes, "Prison Officers Offered $10,000 as 'Incentive'," *The Age* 19 December 1993.

8   Jika Jika, a largely automated division designed to minimize contact between prison officers and inmates, was closed in 1987 after a fire started by inmates as a protest against conditions got out of control and killed five of them. The subsequent Coroner's report placed substantial blame on the division's design and operation. Coroner, State of Victoria, file 4771–75/87, PRO No. 24P7, Box 79.

9   Goya Bennett, "Walled City Hope for Site," *Moreland Community News* (hereafter *MCN*) 18 June 2002.

10   Cr Leigh Snelling (Moreland City Council), interview 4 April 2001.

11   Rachel Hawes, "$250m Hard Cell for Des Res, Mod Cons," *Australian* 30 April 1999. See also *Age* Letters, "Why Can't We Know the Price?" 5 May 1999.

12   State of Victoria Office of the Minister for Finance, "Government to Offer Coburg Prison Site for Redevelopment," News Release, 10 September 1998.

13   See National Trust of Australia (Victoria), "Pentridge Under Threat," Media Release, 10 September 1998.

14   See Allom Lovell and Associates, *HM Metropolitan Prison Pentridge and HM Metropolitan Prison (Coburg Prison Complex): Conservation Management Plan*, Prepared for the Dept of Treasury and Finance, and the City of Moreland, 1996.

15   Julian Kennedy, "Jail Funds Gap," *MCN* 19 February 2002.

16   Royce Millar, "Planning Work at Pentridge Shuts Down," *Age* 4 January 2003.

17   Interview, Laurie Burchell, vice-president, CHS, 30 May 2003; CHS, "Response to Pentridge Piazza Proposal," correspondence to B. Kosky, 5 July 2002; group interview, CARD membership, January 2002.

18   *Moreland Planning Scheme Heritage Interpretation Issue: Pentridge Prison Complex* (Report, Ministry for Planning Panel 2002), p. 18.

19   National Trust, "Pentridge Under Threat."

20   Cheryl Critchley, "Recognition at Last for Ryan," *Herald Sun* 4 Feb 1998; Vanessa Williams, "Pentridge at Risk," *Herald Sun* 11 Sept. 1998; Nerida Hodgkins, "Save Grave: Chaplain," *Moreland Courier* 28 April 1997;

21   Annabel Woodward, "Bluestone Blue," *MCN* 17 April 2001.

22   CHS, "Coburg Historical Society: Interpretation Concept" (paper prepared for CHS by The Shirley Spectra, 1999); CHS, "Interpreting Pentridge: Sound and Light and Other Options" (prepared for CHS by Carol Atwell and The Shirley Spectra, n.d.); CHS, correspondence to Moreland City Council, 5 July 2002.

23   Moreland City Council, correspondence to CARD, 27 August 2001; author's observation of CARD meetings, December 2001 and January 2002; Farrah Tomazin, "Lockout for Pentridge Townhouse Plan," *Age*, 8 May 2002; "Unit Plans on Hold," *MCN*, 14 May 2002.

24   See Farrah Tomazin, "From Prison to Piazza, Pentridge gets a Makeover," *Age* 1 August 2002; Julian Kennedy, "Going Green: 'Environmental Village' Plans for Pentridge," *MCN* 6 August 2002.

25   Tomazin, "Prison to Piazza"; Kennedy, op. cit.; interview, Burchell, op. cit. (Note that some accounts refer to H Division by its original designation of "A" Division.) The con-

troversial nature of the "mini-tower" plan prompted a local newspaper to canvas Coburg residents' views on its advisability, but reportage of the results was sketchy, indicating some disagreement but providing no statistics. *MCN* 6 July 2002.

26 Tomazin, "Prison to Piazza"; also Pentridge Piazza website: http://www.pentridge-piazza.com.au (accessed 13 May 2005, but now inoperative).

27 Goya Bennett, "Prison Yields its Terrible Past," *MCN* 2 July 2002; Tomazin, "Prison to Piazza."

28 Bennett, "Prison Yields Past."

29 Crema quoted in Tomazin, "Prison to Piazza."

30 Jan Penney, "What is History in the Marketplace?" *La Trobe Forum* No. 17, December–Febuary 2000–1, p. 26; see also Strange, "From 'Place of Misery'."

31 Although the development's official website listed a "History" page, the historical account it presented was very brief and highly selective, concentrating mainly on extant aspects of the prison which featured in the commercial project, and recounting markedly innocuous historical events. http://www.pentridge-piazza.com.au/pages/history.html (accessed 3 June 2005, now inoperative).

32 Julia Clark, "Talking with Empty Rooms," *Historic Environment* 16 No. 3, 2002

33 Ibid., drawing on Donald Horne.

34 Margaret Anderson, "Oh What a Tangled Web…Politics, History and Museums," *Australian Historical Studies* 33 no. 119 (2002), pp. 182–3; see also Penney, "What is History"; Graeme Davison, "Museums and National Identity," paper to Museums Australia National Conference, Adelaide, 20 March 2002.

35 Penney, "What is History," p. 28.

36 Ibid. Penney tells of touring the American South, where she "visited many a museum or historic site that ignores the fact that a complete social and economic life was founded on the use of slaves" (p. 27). Clark makes a similar point regarding significant lacunae in the class structures implied in modes of interior display prevalent in "heritage" houses.

37 See, e.g., David Denborough, "Inside/Outside", http://www.anu.edu.au/~a112465/Y/InOut (accessed 10 September 2002).

38 Bennett, "Prison Yields Past"; Andrew Rule, "The Inside Stories from a Man Who Should Know," *Age* 1 August 2002.

39 Bennett, "Prison Yields Past"; Rule, "Inside Stories."

40 Tomazin, "Prison to Piazza."

41 Bennett, "Prison Yields Past"; Rule, "Inside Stories."

42 Bob McKercher and Hilary du Cros, *Cultural Tourism: The Partnership Between Tourism and Cultural Heritage Management* (New York: Haworth Hospitality Press, 2002), p. 128.

43 See, e.g., Mark Brandon Read, *Chopper: From the Inside: The Confessions of Mark Brandon Read* (Kilmore, Vic.: Floradale Productions 2001) (1991).

44 Rule, "Inside Stories."

45 Bennett, "Prison Yields Past."

46 McKercher and du Cros, *Cultural Tourism*, p. 128.

47 Julia Clark, "Talking with Empty Rooms," *Historic Environment* 16 no. 3, 2002.

48   Catherine Birmingham (dir.), *Pentridge: Some Ghosts and Memories from the Big House*, video recording © Pentridge Village Pty Ltd 2000.

49   Ray Mooney, "Bluestone Shadows," *Sunday Age* "Agenda," 14 September 1997.

50   Catherine Birmingham, interview 5 April 2001.

51   Pentridge Piazza publicity outlets promoted an exhibition of murals painted by inmates of Jika Jika, and preserved, on their concrete wall sections, when the division was demolished. Although the artists clearly put their all into these works, they stand as the "respectable" face of inmate creative self-expression, and as such are of rather less interest, vis-à-vis the considerations addressed by this book, than the illicit, but far more candid, utterances penned secretly on the jail's internal surfaces.

52   See, e.g., *Herald* (Melbourne), "Restrictions on Jail Inquest: Pentridge Will Get 'Bash' Probe," 17 May 1972; "Inquiry Told of Breakdown," 12 October 1972; "'I Could Have Been Killed' says Ex-prisoner," 2 November 1972; *Sun News-Pictorial* (Melbourne), "Prisoner Wins Attack Appeal," 12 February 1972; "Lawyers to Probe Jail Complaints," 20 February 1972; "Two Warders 'Deserve Jail'," 22 September 1972; "I'm Afraid to Leave H Division—Pentridge Guard," 6 October 1972; "Jail Bash Men Needed Aid: Inquiry is Told," 12 October 1972; "2 Warders 'Attacked'," 26 October 1972; "I Wanted to Die After Beating: Prisoner," 12 December 1972; *Truth* (Melbourne), "Grim Story in Prison Papers," 27 May 1972.

53   See Kenneth Jenkinson, *Report of the Board of Inquiry into Allegations of Brutality and Ill Treatment at H.M. Prison Pentridge* (Melbourne: State Government of Victoria, 1973).

54   Knapp interview.

55   Ibid.

56   Confidential communication to author. This account was confirmed for me by a former senior administrator, who stated that there developed among some prison officers "a culture of drinking on the job."

PART TWO

Graffiti

In the field of conservation of historical structures, the unearthing of material traces of the human beings formerly associated with those structures is commonly regarded by conservators as something of an event, a high point in the process. Such traces usually take the form of personal artefacts, documents, or evidence of the individual's direct effect on the built fabric itself, and it is not unusual for work on a site to cease temporarily and for all personnel to gather, in a state of some excitement, at the location of a find. In the case of prison conservation, however, curatorial enthusiasm for such glimpses into the personal tends to be far more partial, especially when it comes to the category of the inmate's effect on his or her physical living environment. Such effect most often takes the form of graffiti.

This inversion of customary values is analogous to my earlier point that in the case of Australian historical prisons the Dark Tourism paradigm is in some ways inverted, in that sightseer sympathy for the victims, the norm at Dark Tourism sites, is often missing or even actively countermanded by mainstream social attitudes toward the prisons' former inhabitants.

It is a fact of prison life that prisoners routinely "vandalize" their cell interiors and other surfaces with graffiti, verbal and pictorial, offensive, satirical or innocuous. It is equally a fact that the practice is forbidden, and that periodic cleaning and repainting are undertaken specifically to obliterate the graffiti that appears. Among former prison sites open to the public, therefore, much graffiti has been lost, most of it falling victim to the routine actions of custodial staff during the prisons' operation. In this regard staff attitudes are broadly equivalent to the views held by municipal authorities toward urban graffiti outside prison. Criminologists Mark Halsey and Alison Young define such outside authorities' official reactions thus:

> [T]he graffiti is seen as something out of place, which must be erased in order to return the social space to its proper condition. Removal is thus a way of *re-appropriating* the space, both taking back the space from the graffiti writer, and returning the space to a condition of propriety.[1]

This idea, of authorities reclaiming physical and moral control of surfaces, has clear parallels in the prison context.

Even in cases where graffiti has survived decommissioning, curators and other authorities in charge of former prisons, by and large wedded to a turnstile agenda, rarely see the value in leaving extant and on public view samples of the candidly violent and sometimes grossly offensive thoughts routinely expressed on prison walls. Surfaces are usually scrubbed and repainted before their public exposure, specifically to hide the graffiti. Tourist visitors are then often told that the resulting white or drab pastel surfaces of the cells and other interior spaces are the "authentic" conditions of incarceration as experienced by the prisoners—"exactly how they were" when occupied.[2] Both Old Geelong Gaol and "J Ward" at Ararat, Victoria (each decommissioned in 1991), are explicitly presented to visitors as being in "original condition," despite having had all graffiti expunged before public tours began (a fact even some tour guides were unaware of when I toured there). At Boggo Road much graffiti survives, but as at Fremantle it is nearly all in locked—that is, non-public—areas. No significant graffiti is visible to the public in Old Melbourne Gaol, but as this was decommissioned in 1929 and has since been put to a variety of uses, custodial and otherwise, it would perhaps be unrealistic to expect rigorous conservation of surfaces.

There are, it must be noted, exceptions to the general disapproval and reflexive concealment described above. Adelaide Gaol makes a feature of some of its graffiti; and the Melbourne City Watch House, which at this writing is not yet open to the public, contains an abundance of possibly unique graffiti (discussed in Chapter 5) that the site management are committed to preserving as far as is practicable. Nor, it needs to be said, is the motivation for removing graffiti always moralistic or venal: at Fannie Bay Gaol in Darwin, for instance, the graffiti was removed by the site's administrative board, after careful consideration, on the basis of inmate privacy concerns.[3] Such instance of curatorial toleration are, however, rare.

Graffiti is recognized by sociologists and social historians as a potential source of insights into culture, society, psyche and times. And prison graffiti is invaluable for the social historian interested in the implied narratives inherent in sites of incarceration. In the spontaneity and purport of graffiti may be found a degree of candour, an unleashing of inhibition, rarely discernable in the more "respectable" modes of artistic expression in prison such as mural painting. Also, of course, the creation of graffiti requires no presumption of artistic skill—literally anyone who is so disposed can express their feelings or beliefs candidly upon a wall, and hence one may find there fragments of literally anyone's story. But prison graffiti's value is far from being merely academic. Daniel Palmer makes a persuasive case for unrestricted inclusion of the graffiti in public tours of prisons, arguing that it stands

> as a resonant textual layer in an already signifying site. Articulating specific moments of past confrontation with power, the graffiti provides evidence that prisons are "about people" and, more specifically, about relations of dominance. If we view the heritage site as a source of "collective memory," the silenced graffiti can be read as a suppressed subtext beneath the "official history" of the site given by the prison guides.[4]

There have been many studies of graffiti, mainly in the fields of sociology and criminology, and the resulting extensive literature discusses the phenomenon in various contexts, including diverse forms of street graffiti, as well as the graffiti found in places such as schools, public toilets and so on; but these studies are almost all concerned with graffiti found in the outside world.[5] There has been relatively little work done on prison graffiti.[6] As indicated in my remarks on authorities' responses, outside graffiti studies can provide analogies in some degree applicable to the graffiti found in prison;[7] also, a number of the analytical categories into which graffiti are divided may be identified within prisons. Halsey and Young propose three categories which have some readily perceived relevance in this regard: "latrinalia"; school classroom graffiti; and "slogans."

> Latrinalia has a specific communicative tone (often involving a conversational format)....Graffiti on school desks is very similar: often conversational...and involving commonly used tools such as ordinary pens....Slogans range from the personal ("Jane loves Ted," or "J. Kaminski is a slut"), through the gamut of political issues...but all share the common feature of being declaratory in nature, expressing a view to an audience.[8]

There are, however, traps in assuming too close an equivalence. Practical environmental differences come into play; for instance, the prison equivalent of latrinalia, which still occurs on the walls of toilet cubicles, is often rendered in conditions of far less privacy, and with far less assurance of anonymity, than its outside counterpart. Integral, too, to the study of graffiti are questions regarding the graffitists' motivation. It is in this area—the possibility of discerning perpetrators' motivational impulses—that the study of prison graffiti in particular is instructive. In their study of the gendered semiotics of (non-prison) graffiti, Bruner and Kelso articulate the apparent truism that: "To write graffiti is to communicate; one never finds graffiti where they cannot be seen by others."[9] This common-sense dictum is echoed, with no less certitude, by criminologists Rob White and Daphne Habibis: "[W]hether written by pen, spray can, or paintbrush, it is always public and displayed on someone else's property."[10] But these statements are of only limited application in the study of prison graffiti, for they do not account for one of the most commonly occurring instances of inmate graffiti, which are those rendered by the occupants *inside* their cells.

Certainly, much prison graffiti, including many of the examples discussed here, is done in communal spaces such as exercise yards, toilets, and holding cells where residence is transitory, with a view to either an immediate or a notional future readership; but in the prison cell one does, indeed, find graffiti written or drawn for no discernable audience other than the writer, a message or sign evidently intended purely as self-affirmation. The cell is effectively a quasi-private sphere, a residential space where under normal circumstances the occupant rarely receives visits from peers, and where the unauthorized text is often located—on the inside surface of the door, for instance, or behind a bed—such that casual inspection by authorities will not discover it. This is not to suggest that all cell graffiti is so exclusive; some, clearly, is intended to convey a message, either to persons in authority or future cell occupants; but there remains a significant portion which, by virtue of its position within the cell and/or the evident duration of the graffitist's residence there, cannot plausibly be judged to have had any intended audience other than the graffitist alone. It is worth noting also that even when clearly visible, the content of much graffiti more resembles brief diary entries than messages to others. These aspects suggest a need to treat prison graffiti as a unique category of text, worthy of far more study than has been the case.

NOTES

1   Mark Halsey and Alison Young, "The Meanings of Graffiti and Municipal Administration," *Australian and New Zealand Journal of Criminology* 35 No. 2, 2002, p. 175 (emphasis *sic*).

2   On-site observation; see also Daniel Palmer, "In the Anonymity of a Murmur: Graffiti and the Construction of the Past at the Fremantle Prison," in *Historical Traces*, ed. Jenny Gregory (Perth: Centre for Western Australian History, 1997).

3   See Mickey Dewar and Clayton Fredericksen, "Prison Heritage, Prison History and Archaeology at Fannie Bay Gaol, Northern Australia," *International Journal of Heritage Studies*, 9 no. 1, 2003, p. 54.

4   Palmer, "Anonymity of a Murmur," p. 105.

5   See, e.g., Nancy Macdonald, *The Graffiti Subculture: Youth, Masculinity and Identity in London and New York* (Houndmills UK: Palgrave Macmillan, 2001); S. Geason and P. Wilson, *Preventing Graffiti and Vandalism* (Canberra: Institute of Criminology, 1990); E. Wales and B. Brewer, "Graffiti in the 1970s," *Journal of Social Psychology* 99, 1976, pp. 115–23; Halsey and Young, "Meanings of Graffiti". On gender aspects of graffiti see Kerry Carrington, "Girls and Graffiti," *Cultural Studies* 3 no. 1, 1989; Edward M. Bruner and Jane Paige Kelso, "Gender Differences in Graffiti: A Semiotic Perspective," *Women's Studies International Quarterly* 3, 1980; J. Green, "The Writing on the Stall: Gender and Graffiti," *Journal of Language and Social Psychology* 22 no. 3, September 2003. There is also a substantial body of work on the aesthetics of graffiti as art, and a further, relatively marginal, activist literature that advocates and in some cases provides practical advice on the "editing," i.e., altering or obscuring via graffiti, of "offensive" advertising (e.g. tobacco); although of undeniable interest to the student of general graffiti, neither of these areas is any more than distantly relevant to the present topic.

6   On prison graffiti see Palmer, "Anonymity of a Murmur"; J. Klofas and C. Cutshall, "Unobtrusive Research Methods in Criminal Justice: Using Graffiti in the Reconstruction of Institutional Cultures," *Journal of Research in Crime and Delinquency* 22 no 4, November 1985, pp. 355–73; Commission for Racial Equality [hereafter CRE], "Racial Equality in Prisons: A Formal Investigation by the Commission for Racial Equality into HM Prison Service of England and Wales, Part 2," 2003, http://www.statewatch.org/news/2003/oct/crePrisons.pdf (accessed 14 Feb. 2004).

7   Certain of Bruner and Kelso's findings, for instance, regarding the gender differences in the semiotics of civilian graffiti, are echoed in the gender comparison of prison graffiti I undertake in Chapter 5.

8   Halsey and Young, "Meanings of Graffiti," p. 169.

9   Bruner and Kelso, "Gender Differences in Graffiti," p. 241.

10 Rob White and Daphne Habibis, *Crime and Society* (Melbourne: Oxford University Press, 2005), p. 86.

CHAPTER FOUR

Power:
The Men

My interest in prison graffiti first arose during the early stages of my study of Pentridge, and the specific graffiti that piqued my interest then was not in-side the prison, but on a developer's promotional billboard located outside the perimeter wall, during the site's initial excavation. The billboard in ques-tion was an architect's rendition of a supposedly typical streetscape in the proposed "Pentridge Village." It had been embellished with a marking-pen, pictorially and verbally, by a person I judged, for various reasons, to have some inside knowledge of life within the prison, possibly as a former inmate.

Firstly, the graffiti included, *inter alia,* two jocular messages naming real persons. The most prominent, written high on a wall of one of the houses of the depicted street, stated, in the stock graffiti manner, that "CHOPPER WAZ HERE" [*sic*]. Of course, such an announcement could have been written by anyone with a modicum of general knowledge and a flair for mischievous irony; however, its significance goes beyond the facetious invocation of a celebrity prisoner, and I will return to it shortly. Below it on a "sidewalk," and less noticeable, another person was named, in similar style, as having also been "here." This person I knew to be a prisoner who, while remaining virtually unknown to the general public, had become notorious within the prison system in the 1980s through his refractory behaviour.[1] The mere cit-ing of that one individual does not of itself prove that the graffitist had spent time "inside"; but it does suggest a relatively esoteric level of knowledge of the prison's resident personnel.

The graffitist had also applied his pen to the only people depicted in the scene, a family group in the foreground consisting of a young couple with a child, and an elderly man. The child appeared to be a boy of primary-school age; he and his mother stood together forming a visual and emotional unit, mother playfully hugging him from behind. The graffitist had spared them his attentions. One cannot say whether this was because of lack of time, or because he could not think of anything to do to them, or because he was sensitive to the child's innocence and the mother's respectable femininity and could not bring himself to despoil those qualities. There are aspects of the condition of incarceration that make the latter possibility the more likely one, but whatever his motive, he had concentrated on the two men, and in so doing revealed a good deal about what was on his mind—subconsciously, at least—and the minds of prison inmates generally.

The young husband/father, who stood with a robust, arms-folded posture, had been given a firearm, in the form of a carbine or automatic rifle with a telescopic sight, tucked into his folded forearms in a semi-vertical position. The weapon was not directly threatening anyone; he simply possessed it—at the ready, as it were. The older man had acquired a grotesquely hyperbolical phallus, which emerged from the region of his crotch and reared upward above his head. In thus disfiguring the two adult males in this way, the graffitist had, wittingly or (more likely) unwittingly, expressed dual, innately entwined preoccupations of the typical inmate: sex and power. A simple and highly plausible interpretation of the firearm is that, given the self-assurance embodied in the man's folded arms and relaxed yet vigorous stance, he had been rendered into an authority figure such as a prison officer.[2] The other man, over-endowed as he was with apparent sexual potency, signified something rather more ambiguous.

Sociologist Katy Richmond speaks of the ubiquity of homosexual talk in prison, arguing that such talk is not merely a signifier of the prevalence of homosexual behaviour but is also, and perhaps more centrally, an expression of the incessant anxiety and fears to which that behaviour gives rise among inmates.[3] She points out that those fears are in fact a product, but also a further source, of the "precarious sense of masculinity" of men in prison,[4] and that this in turn is a chief contributing factor in the extreme violence that routinely accompanies sex acts between inmates.[5] This violence most commonly is a component of rape; but inmates who become compliant when threatened with assault or rape in order to avoid violence are as likely to receive a bashing anyway for "wanting it."[6] It becomes apparent, when such aspects of prison sexuality are taken into account, that the graffitied phallus on the billboard effectively translated the older man into an inmate; yet the appendage that achieved this rendition was only superficially a "sexual" image, in the sense in which the word is usually apprehended. Within the idiom of the total institution, *both* figures had in fact been given *weapons*.[7]

In this crudely rendered and spontaneous (it is tempting, in fact, to use the word *instinctive*) graphic addenda to Pentridge Village's idyllic orderliness, we find an implied comment on the nature of the adversarial relationship between the inmate population and the prison Establishment, and with it a summary of a fundamental power dichotomy of prison life. The rifle, as a device for killing at a distance, is the antithesis of flesh; it is an ultimate physical denial of the corporeal, not simply because it can kill, but because it does so without proximity, without the need to acknowledge the flesh it destroys. The phallus, which in the billboard overtopped all the figures, stands as a reply to that denial, a symbol of the inmate's intensely organic world in which personal agency is achieved through nothing other than proximity, and in which the physical expression of sexuality is synonymous with coercive power.

The theme of power relationships, which lies at the core of almost all substantive social considerations in jail, is further affirmed in the graffitist's choice of prisoners to name: both Chopper Read and the other prisoner were, in their day, "kings" of their respective divisions; by invoking these power-figures, and by doing so via humour, the graffitist implicitly identifies with the prison's "rulers," and notionally places himself on an equal footing with them.[8] Thus apparently simple, facetious irony is revealed to denote something far more serious in the context of the graffitist's presumed former milieu. But the content is not the only signifier. In expressing such intrinsically prison-related matters, the mode of communication itself accords with the idea that the graffitist's background includes some time in the company of those "kings" or their ilk.

In defiance of the most diligent efforts of prison staff to eradicate it and punish the perpetrators, graffiti is ubiquitous in prison. It might well be characterized as the most natural avenue of non-violent self-expression in an environment where illiteracy and partial literacy are pervasive, and where lifelong voicelessness is the norm for many, stemming as it does from economic and cultural poverty combined with lack of education. In this regard, the motivation for prison graffiti does approximately parallel that for much outside graffiti; as Nancy Macdonald found in her study of New York and London graffiti subcultures, at least one of the complex of reasons underlying street graffiti is the artists' subjective sense of voicelessness.[9] Given that, and given, too, the personal and social tensions and pecking-order preoccupations evident in the billboard example, it becomes clear that prison graffiti is not merely natural, but may well be inevitable, as an outgrowth of the typical inmate's day-to-day state of chronic distress.

Nor is illiteracy a necessary prerequisite: the simple fact of incarceration, of spending one's hours in a "box," can result in even well-educated prisoners taking to the walls of their cells with writing implements.[10] The following, for instance, is a twenty-eight-line poem on a cell wall in Fremantle Prison, entitled simply "JAIL," which evinces both above-average literacy for a prison environment and a certain bitter poignancy in its explication of the prison experience:

> WALLS WITHIN WALLS,
> LOCKED AWAY AND FORGOTTEN BY SOCIETY,
> LOVED ONES FULL OF GRIEF AND PAIN,
> ONLY OUR BASIC NEEDS SUPPLIED,
> WITH MONEY YOU JUST SURVIVE,
> WITHOUT IT YOU DO IT HARD,
> THE SAME DAY IN DAY OUT,
> BOREDOM SETS IN WITH NO HOPE IN SIGHT,
> WEEKS INTO MONTHS, MONTHS INTO YEARS,
> NO WAY OUT,
> YOU ARE FREE IN YOUR MIND AND SOUL,
> YOUR BODY IS STILL LOCKED BEHIND BARS,
> DYING FOR FREEDOM,
> AND THE SOFT TOUCH OF A WOMAN,
> PRIVACY IS A FORGOTTEN WORD,
> RULES, RULES, RULES.....
> NEVER MAKING YOUR OWN DECISIONS,
> FRUSTRATION, ANGER, HURT BUILDS UP INSIDE,
> RELEASE IS DIFFERENT FOR US ALL,
> SOME FIGHT, SOME CRY OTHERS JUST DIE,
> THE STRONG SURVIVE AND BECOME HARDENED MEN,
> FREEDOM COMES TO US ALL ONE DAY,
> IS EACH MAN READY FOR THE WORLD AGAIN?
> HOW MUCH HAVE THEY CHANGED FROM WHEN THEY FIRST CAME
>   IN...
> LIVING IN THIS HELL HOLE DOES,
> LEAN, MEAN AND WITH HATE IN THEIR HEARTS,
> SOCIETY DOESN'T GIVE A FUCK!!
> IT JUST STARTS OVER AND OVER AGAIN......

The poem is signed only with a string of anonymous initials and the date, 22 September 1991—two months before the prison was decommissioned.

Inmates have much time on their hands for reflective musings, but it is unusual for them to express their thoughts verbally in the form of graffiti at such length. Most graffiti found on prison walls, although at times startlingly revealing of the inmate's inner world, is far more succinct; much is highly spontaneous, and of course much of it is at least partly pictorial. In Chapter One I referred to graffiti as "the inmate's knowing and deliberate impact upon the fabric of his/her world"; it will become apparent that the use of *deliberate*, implying as it does full consideration and forethought, may be imprecise. Much graffiti arising from the experience of being inside is undoubtedly highly impulsive in both conception and execution; *deliberate*, then, should be regarded here as synonymous with *wilful*, and in many cases little more than that.

The Pentridge Village billboard graffiti's gratuitously rancorous imagery, the manner in which the elderly male is pornographized, the adversarial juxtaposition of archetypes, and, especially, the use of the phallus as an instrument/symbol of aggression, are all entirely consistent with the tone and style of most graffiti found in prisons. But the billboard "artist" was, as street graffitists tend to be, clearly in a hurry. By contrast, the serving prisoner intent upon expressing similar rancour and power-relationship concerns can often rely on many hours in which to work undisturbed, and hence may produce texts on a far more elaborate scale. An exemplar of inmate graffiti that makes the conflation of sexuality and coercion both explicit and signally unambiguous is a very violent drawing done in lead pencil on the wall of a cell in Fremantle Prison and captioned "HOW TO BECOME A PIG."

The scene depicts a grotesquely pornographic fantasy of vengeance, in the form of oral rape, on a presumably especially hated police officer who is not only named but identified by badge number (commentary on police in general is, of course, also implied in the generic "PIG"). The police officer is on hands and knees, the rapist stands naked before him. Handcuffs attached to the dominant figure's wrist identify him as a prisoner; but they hang open, as a sign of his recent liberation. He has acquired a cat-o'-nine-tails with which both to punish and spur on, as he abusively exhorts the officer (via a "talk balloon") to increase his fellating efforts: "SUCK HARDER YOU ROOKIE FAGGOT DICKHEAD." Consonant with the paradoxical nature of prison sexuality noted above, and notwithstanding his current avenue of gratification, the prisoner affirms that he is not really homosexual, by othering his fellator as a "faggot"—an epithet implicitly confirmed by the policeman's abject compliance, also via talk balloon: "ANYTHING YOU SAY DARLING."

The pictured inmate's gratification is total, as is, therefore, his ideated revenge, achieved through the artist's attention to both the physical and the figurative details. The officer (labelled a "CUNT-STABLE") must not only perform the primary sex act, but has also to maximize his subjugator's stimulation by the deployment of multiple sex aids. In identifying the victim as a "rookie," (whether literally true or not) the vengeance inherent in the rape is compounded by the victim's symbolic "virginity."

By imagining a revenge exacted in this way, the inmate overturns the power-dichotomy norms of the prison as defined above, by forcibly bringing the establishment figure into *proximity*, and dealing with him in the organic idiom of the flesh. The policeman's capacity to affect the body at a distance is utterly negated; the only artefact depicted which is in any conventional sense a weapon is the inmate's whip, yet even that is, in the context of the tableau, little more than a prop, a symbol of the theatre of revenge; the physical instrument with which the deed is actually done—the true weapon of the encounter—is the phallus.

Needless to say, not all inmate graffiti is as elaborate, nor as comprehensive in its characterization of the prison's thematic relationships, as the image just examined. Some is simply rancorous and succinct. But even here, there is scope for idiosyncratic nuances. On one cell wall at Boggo Road is a stark command in red marking pen: "FUCK OFF & DIE!". Such straightforward aggression is extremely common in prison graffiti. What strikes the viewer in this case, however, is the juxtaposition of sentiment and calligraphy. The inmate has rendered his message of hostility toward whoever may happen to see his handiwork—or whomever he was thinking of at the time—in meticulously lettered, but markedly incongruous, "Old English" script.

Such ornate, almost oratorical presentation does lend the message a kind of authority; it has connotations of a proclamation. Perhaps this was the intended effect; or perhaps the graffitist simply liked the look of that style of script. We cannot know.

Revenge, which we have encountered above in the rape of the "pig," is a recurring graffiti topic, expressed with varying degrees of succinctness—in some cases notionally against specific persons or groups, such as the "cops," or the "lagger" supposedly responsible for the inmate's incarceration, but equally often as a manifestly heartfelt, yet nevertheless targetless, abstraction. On a cell wall in Fremantle Prison is a typical example of the latter variety. A stylized skull (drawn in black marker pen with considerable care and some skill) grins straight at the viewer, radiating a sense of animate menace despite three bullet-holes in its forehead. It lends to the accompanying declaratory caption distinctly macabre connotations. The first line is banal: "REVENGE IS SWEET"; but the cliché is revitalized and made caustically vivid by the appending, on the second line, of the single confrontational epithet "MOTHERFUCKER."

In contrast to this, at the Melbourne City Watch House carved into the paintwork of a wooden seat, the target of vengeful intentions is made specific, in the form of the person whose supposed infidelity caused the graffitist's incarceration. In the process the graffitist eschews the gratuitous malice of the "skull" graffiti, presenting himself, rather, as one among the many "good men" who have been corrupted by imprisonment itself, and who therefore have an excuse for contemplating violence.

JAIL MAKES GOOD MEN BAD
SO NOW ITS REVENGE TO THE BENT CUNT WHO PUT ME HERE
POETIC JUSTICE

The language used here is of some interest. The main section of the text is, in its way, a small masterpiece of succinctness. Composed almost entirely of Saxon monosyllables (*jail* and *revenge* are the only Latinate words used), and evincing a fine instinctive ear for assonance, it has a plainspoken directness, an emotional integrity, well suited to the assertive declaration of the avowedly wronged individual. And yet, having found perhaps the truest form of words by which to vent his outrage, the inmate inadvertently reveals more of his anguish than he might have wished. The voice that speaks to us so spontaneously from that cell, of the retribution due "the bent cunt" responsible for his current condition, is virtually shouting out precisely the kind of impotent fury, the "chronic distress" of imprisonment defined earlier, which leaves grown men feeling they have no resort but to carve their thoughts into the nearest woodwork.

Like the author of the previous image, this graffitist attempts to encapsulate his meaning in a rhetorical cliché—"POETIC JUSTICE"—although here it is the cliché itself that is appended as a coda. By its inclusion, as a kind of slogan (and in the process reverting to Latin polysyllables), he reasserts a sense of emotional control; the window through which we have glimpsed his inner feelings is closed, and he resumes the hint of swagger needed to maintain personal and social equilibrium within the prison environment.

Despite being in jail for transgressing society's moral paradigm, inmates tend, by their own lights, to be highly moralistic. Just as the desire for revenge can provoke lurid and intense displays of affect, so, too, the inmate can take a signally uncompromising stance when expressing his sense of moral outrage. In a Boggo Road cell I found a very graphic message to paedophiles, a particularly hated category of inmate in most prisons:

> THIS IS A CELL WHERE EVERY KIDFUCKER HANGS THEMSELF. DO IT DOG.
> RUFF: NOW. IT'S THE LEAST YOU CAN DO.

The text is accompanied by a detailed representation of a hangman's noose. Although its author's moral stance is clear, this particular graffito is otherwise puzzling; we cannot know whether the graffitist was targeting a specific individual or sending a general message to any future occupants of the cell with such proclivities. It may be that the cell at that time held more than one inmate—a scenario implying an atmosphere of rancour that could well have proved intolerable in such a confined environment. The graffito may, on the other hand, even be an expression of *self*-loathing. The one certainty is the degree of disapproval evinced.

The violence expressed in the above examples, although shocking, is at least comprehensible in that it is linked to an intelligible affect—the impulse to avenge or respond to perceived wrong. But it is in the nature of prisons that much of the violence there has no apparent connection to any motivation or cause which the ordinary member of a civil society can relate to, and some of the graffiti one encounters reflects this. In another cell at Boggo Road is one of the more disturbing examples of graffiti I viewed. In large block letters is printed:

> WHO WILL BE NEXT TO BE FOUND WITH A BULLET IN THEIR HEAD AND
> DRESSED IN WOMEN'S UNDIES?

The text is a cryptically graphic question that gives away nothing about the writer or his relationship to the event(s) he refers to. One cannot say whether it is a threat, an expression of fear, or an entreaty for protection. It may be a complete fantasy. It has a bizarrely menacing quality arising in equal parts from the mystery, from the juxtaposition of violent death and implied transgressive sexuality, and from the incongruous deliberation with which the message has actually been applied to the wall, in careful block capitals—complete with serifs.

It is a truism that extreme violence, without the "excuse" of being a vengeful response to betrayal or offence, is the natural currency of many people who go to jail—and some, of course, are in jail precisely because of such propensities. One may guess that something of the sort lay in the background of the inmate responsible for the marking-pen image drawn on a cell wall, again at Boggo Road. The life-sized drawing is a detailed, accurate profile view of a type of military shotgun, much used by police forces as a "riot gun," known as a "Franchi SPAS 12." The caption identifies the gun by make and model, and adds that it is "THE BEST IN '89." Notwithstanding its law-enforcement credentials, the Franchi's compact dimensions, pistol-grip and semi-automatic action make it an ideal weapon for criminal activities. To judge by the caption and the drawing's degree of detail, the artist was something of an aficionado.

Not all the preoccupations of prisoners, as depicted in their graffiti, are transgressive, nor are they motivated to write and draw upon their walls solely by anguish or rage. They are also moved by simple enthusiasms, ordinary annoyances and conventional loyalties. A commonly expressed interest on cell walls is motor vehicles. This tends to manifest in the form of quasi-adolescent proselytizing on behalf of specific marques, and in "collections" of models and makes by name. Thus we find such assertions as "GOD DRIVES A HOLDEN V8 HOT" (Boggo Road); HARLEY DAVIDSON RULES (Melbourne City Watch House); and HOLDENS RULE FOR EVER (Boggo Road). In one Boggo Road cell, on the back of the door, the occupant has listed every model of Holden ever manufactured.

In somewhat similar vein, declarative support for favourite rock music artists and bands features very frequently in cells and common areas, with one band in particular a stand-out: in cells everywhere I went, I found expressions of an Australia-wide prison following of the rock band AC/DC. Most simply reproduce the band's logo, including the trademark lightning slash between the letter-pairs, and sometimes with an addendum that they "rule." Occasionally one finds a design commemorating the death of AC/DC's original lead singer, Bon Scott, who died of alcohol poisoning in 1980. The band in its original line-up was especially favoured by inmates for its on-the-record identification with prisoners and the small-time underworld in general, and for the fact that Scott had actually served some time in juvenile prison in the early 1960s for an assault. On one cell wall in Fremantle, pencilled heavily onto the grey paintwork, a fan confusedly misspells the band as "AC/AC." Beneath this an inscription, also in pencil, states, as a sort of passing aside absolutely typical of the setting, "ALL COPPERS ARE CUNTS."

Having noted the low levels of literacy and general education typical among inmates, it is apparent that the authors of some of the graffiti examples discussed here are relatively articulate, at least within the parameters of expression of the kinds of affect and conceptualization associated with such texts. And even among this group, instances such as the extended poem quoted above are exceptional. In the same cell, and almost certainly by the same inmate-poet, is a rather more succinct comment: "FUCK THIS PLACE *FOREVER*." The last word is in fact underscored four times, an eloquent rhetorical touch that sets off the brevity of the composition. Of particular note here, however, is not the wording but the equally pithy graphic element in which the message is framed—a clenched fist with upraised middle finger.

As we have seen, inmate power—that is, the power to coerce—inheres in the corporeal, in the palpable, and the natural, primary mode of expression of such power is the fist. Yet among the graffiti I observed the fist, *qua* fist, was actually rare. It was the basis, however, of the most commonly rendered single image in all the prisons I visited—the "one-fingered salute." As an image, the simple fist has connotations only of force; there is nothing in it to laugh about. But extend the middle finger upward, in the time-honoured gesture of rude defiance, and the fist becomes the basis for an image of far greater complexity and distinctly different tone—a signal of combined belligerence and mischief, of aggression and resistance, with implications of solidarity in its irreverence for establishment norms and values. The insolent finger as graffiti is iconic, an exemplar of the idiom of the prison, and an archetypal signifier of the imprisoned.

As in the example described above, it is sometimes captioned, and hence serves as an illustrative adjunct or visual frame to an explicit message of defiance—which may be as straightforward as a simple "FUCK U," or, as in one Fremantle Prison cell, decidedly more nuanced and cryptic: "EVIL HANDS / ARE NO LONGER / HAPPY HANDS." But it also often occurs *sans* caption or with only minimal comment, as a symbol sufficient unto itself, of generic rebelliousness. Some I observed were clearly intended to amuse, and in this the versatility of the extended finger is most evident, for it readily lends itself to precisely the style of dark or iconoclastic irony which tends to characterize much inmate humour. The most elaborate instance of this I encountered was in Boggo Road, in the cell of one of the "Holden" enthusiasts. In red and black marking pen is a picture of Santa Claus, complete with talk-balloon ("HO HO HO"). In a darkly ironic comment on Christmas as experienced in prison, Santa is giving the viewer "the finger."

It has long been demonstrated that groups of human beings suffering chronic hardship at the hands of other human beings will attempt to derive humour from their circumstances, or create humour despite those circumstances. Two obvious examples are the humour of soldiers on the battlefield, and the very large range of political jokes that served for decades to leaven the plight of citizens of the Soviet Union. This tendency is, I would suggest, more pronounced among groups that have, or at least have reason to hope they will have, a degree of personal or collective agency within the context of their situation. Prison inmates may be classed among groups of this kind, in that they exhibit the capacity for both immediate, mostly personal agency (most often in the form of violence toward each other) and long-term, or aspirational, agency within the limitations of power relations discussed above. The characteristic style of humour which emerges is often dark, at times vicious, and almost always ironical.

Typical intentionally humorous graffiti found in cells in maximum-security prisons varies widely in style and tone. Much of it is very simple—laconic, cartoon irony such as inked-in dots, framed and captioned with labels such as "PANIC BUTTON," or "ROOM SERVICE," and so on; a target with the bullseye offering a "GET OUT OF JAIL FREE" prize; mischievous, pseudo-confrontational skulls (a recurring motif); oddly dressed animals sporting knowing smiles; bizarrely disfigured people confronting giant bugs (what I think of as "facetious hallucinatory"). Some graffiti plays on popular-culture or media references, such as the slogan in a Boggo Road cell, "QLD / SUNNY ONE DAY! / IN JAIL THE NEXT," bemusedly parodying a well-known promotional campaign by the Queensland Tourist Board in the 1980s which characterized the "Sunshine State" as "Beautiful one day / Perfect the next".

Popular-culture allusions are in fact common. In a Fremantle cell there is a large cannabis leaf, drawn in black marking pen, atop a suggestion to "MULL UP." The puckish heading above the leaf, "JOHN AND CRAIG'S EXCELLENT ADVENTURE," is a direct and archly knowing reference to the 1989 motion picture comedy *Bill & Ted's Excellent Adventure*, a fantasy aimed at, and highly popular within, the "pot"-oriented drug culture of the day, about two "inseparable teenage airheads"[11] who go time-travelling to rescue their failing History grades. Also in Fremantle, another cell has been decorated with a "brick wall" motif borrowed from and celebrating the rock band Pink Floyd's 1978 album *The Wall*. This "wall" extends right around the cell, albeit interrupted here and there with cartoon-style animals (smoking a "bong"), a depiction of Ned Kelly in his iconic armour, and the "REVENGE IS SWEET, MOTHERFUCKER" graffito discussed above.

The interest in marijuana evinced by the adventurous "John and Craig" and the author of the "wall" is typical of a preoccupation among prison graffitists almost as pervasive as sex. Drug references abound on prison walls. Most are unremarkable, aesthetically and textually—simple declarative proselytizing such as "BONG ON," "SHOOT SKAG" (inject heroin), and so on; sometimes these are accompanied by depictions of drug paraphernalia such as hookahs and other smoking devices, hypodermic syringes, and so on, or, occasionally, portraits of people in the act of using. Occasionally someone gets inventive with the theme, as in the Boggo Road graffito which, while advising one to "BONG ON," achieves a degree of ironic ambiguity by combining two icons in one in that its illustrative bong doubles as a highly explicit phallus, and in the process cocks a snook at authority on two levels. Some examples signify a degree of competitiveness between aficionados of dissimilar drugs: for instance on a Fremantle exercise yard wall where a bong, characteristic equipment of the marijuana user, has been placed to obscure a previous statement that "SPEED RULES."

In the typical "user portrait" type, the drug is being smoked, and is most likely (judging by other aspects depicted) to be cannabis. In at least one example, in a Fremantle cell, a somewhat hallucinatory visual incoherence in the drawing suggests the graffitist was high while executing it. This is confirmed by the central figure's "thought balloon": "RIPPED OFF MY NUTS ONCE AGAIN IN THIS SHIT HOLE FREO."

The urge to pictorially celebrate the moment of ingesting the drug seems, for some reason, to be peculiar to cannabis users; although the proponents of injectable drugs such as heroin commonly promote their choice in words and/or with drawings of syringes, I saw no example of a person depicted actually using such equipment. I have no explanation for this disparity, beyond a speculative sense that a person intoxicated on cannabis might be more likely to engage in some form of creative endeavour directly inspired by the activity that led to their pleasurable state of mind, than a person who has taken a major central nervous system depressant such as heroin. But such an explanation is, of course, inadequate to account for the absence of depictions of "speed" users.

One of the inmate's most potent enemies is boredom. Playwright Ray Mooney, who served seven years in Pentridge, has stated that he actively enjoyed being locked in his cell, as it gave him the opportunity for reading and reflection.[12] But he is clearly the exception. The average prisoner is in no position to "enjoy" time spent in his or her cell. Illiteracy and educational deficiency deprives the inmate of vital defences against solitude-related boredom: aside from an inability to while away time by reading, under-education often results in an impoverished "inner world"—the individual has no basis upon which to derive any joy from being alone with his or her thoughts, and may well experience it as torture.[13] Even the well-educated can have trouble; a former inmate who had been a science teacher before going to prison recalls: "You live by yourself for fifteen hours a day...you re-live your whole life, things that were horrible, you re-live those."[14] The problem of boredom, of apparently empty hours, Goffman associates with the inmate's peculiar "sense of dead and heavy-hanging time":

> [A]mong inmates in many total institutions there is a strong feeling that time spent in the establishment is time wasted or destroyed or taken from one's life; it is time that must be written off; it is something that must be "done.".…In prisons...a general statement of how well one is adapting to the institution may be phrased in terms of how one is doing time, whether easily or hard.[15]

That the subjective interminability of incarceration can contribute significantly to the inmate's torment is graphically expressed in a large—it occupies almost an entire wall—cell mural in Fremantle, a nightmarish hallucination executed in red and black pencil, ink and possibly crayon, in which a number of the inmate's thematic concerns are juxtaposed in the one chaotic vision. A robed and cowled figure is seated in the foreground, styled after the traditional personification of Death, his head a grinning skull but coloured red and wild-eyed, clawed hands resting on an open book; behind him at his right shoulder a naked woman, markedly androgynous in general appearance, holds before her a burning candle; framing the duo, two fiery hell-demons in red descend with flaming arms outstretched to embrace and devour all before them. Various pertinent details—a string of small skulls, a revolver, bat wings—are scattered in the background. And, in the midst of all this death in various guises, sexual ambiguity, demonic possession and hell-fire, is centrally placed a thematically crucial, symbolic depiction of the cessation of the passing of time, in the form of a handless clock-face containing only the numbers (in Roman numerals) and, in the centre, the words "TIME STOPS?". This clock is a core motif. Suspended behind the foreground death's-head like a rising moon, it fills the space between the cowled skull and the woman, visually uniting them; it draws the eye by virtue of its centrality, its plain geometric regularity—it is perfectly circular—amid lurid turmoil, and by providing the tableau's only verbal element—which thus effectively becomes a caption. The whole terrible image fills the viewer's visual field, inescapable without turning away altogether. It is of interest not only for its pictorial archetypes, but at least as much for the fact that its author chose to render it in his "bedroom" and, given that it then survived whatever remained of his tenure, he presumably felt comfortable about living with it.

Whatever kind of catharsis, personal affirmation or stimulation the artist derived from the completed painting, it seems unlikely that its intended audience was only himself. For the purposes of this study I have generally drawn a distinction between graffiti, which I define as in general transgressive, opportunistic and often very crudely rendered, and the officially sanctioned (mostly outdoor) mural art which the media, and hence the general public, are likely to picture when discussing inmate art. But there are instances where the distinction is problematic. The author of "TIME STOPS?", for example, and the inmate who decorated his cell with Pink Floyd-style "bricks" and various other large figures, were clearly creating a kind of mural art, and, given the works' extensive nature, were presumably working with some degree of co-operation, or at least relative unconcern, of staff. At a number of prisons during the latter years of their operational life, as decommissioning grew to be a realistic prospect it became the practice to allow certain privileged inmates to decorate their cells as they saw fit—a reversal of the usual policy regarding graffiti, and undertaken by staff with a conscious eye to the future historical image of the institution.[16] Hence there are works, such as "TIME STOPS?", which may plausibly be regarded as straddling the divide between the spontaneous, at times unwittingly revealing, style of illicit graffiti rendered in an essentially solipsist mood that admits of little or no broader audience, and the self-consciously "artistic" large works one encounters usually on outdoor surfaces. In some cases at least, I would suggest, these works are aimed at an imagined post-operational audience of outsiders—"civilians"—and have, at least in part, a didactic purport: *This is what it is like.* Such also appears to be the case in the text quoted below, a short rhetorical message composed by the author of the long poem quoted earlier, which it seems likely was written with imminent decommissioning in mind. This concise report unequivocally addresses its closing questions to a non-inmate reader:

> SIXTEEN HOURS A DAY
> WE ARE LOCKED IN HERE,
> WITH THE COCKROACHES AND RATS,
> AND WITH OUR SHIT BUCKET,
> COULD YOU HANDLE IT?
> HOW WOULD IT CHANGE YOU?

In the conventional world outside prison, the serious creative artist routinely works with an eye not only toward an imminent audience, but also toward whatever he or she conceives as "posterity" (irrespective of whether that particular word figures in their thinking). In the prison, however, in the normal run of things the motivation to achieve a place of honour or respect in the wider community's social memory is radically truncated—both by the obvious physical isolation from the public, and by the othering inherent in being labelled a criminal (othering of which the inmate is fully aware). Some prison artists, it is reasonable to assume, content themselves, perforce, with the recognition of future inmates; others (perhaps a majority) may practise a consciously cultivated focusing of thought and sensibility on the present, eschewing the temptation to dwell on a future with which they can feel only minimal natural connection. This sense of timelessness, of the eternal non-arrival of the future, may be felt even by short-term prisoners; by its nature the total institution imposes a regime on the individual immediately upon entry that tends to render each day much like the last, while cutting him/her off from the teleological life narrative to which we routinely refer in order to navigate our way in time. There is evidence, both in the graffiti described above and in further examples to be discussed here and in subsequent chapters, that the news of the prison's closure within the foreseeable future, and with it the further news that inmates upon whom staff looked benignly were to be permitted to express themselves freely on their cell walls, gave those so favoured some reason to hope that their artistic endeavours might one day affect viewers from the outside world.

Just as there are graffitists who are more literate than the prison average, so also there are inmates with more artistic ability than others. Perhaps the most visually spectacular example of all the inmate art I saw indicated such ability, and was, I suggest, done with just such a sense of future audience. But if it was conceived with a conscious desire to convey a "message" about the condition of being in prison, that message was conveyed far more subtly than is the norm in such environments. It is, once again, a cell mural covering much of one wall, and once again in Fremantle, but it could not be more unlike "TIME STOPS?"—thematically, aesthetically or in terms of technical execution. Although consistent with the themes of power and violence discussed above, it is—almost uniquely—painted with a full palette, and translates those themes into a fantastical celebration of colour, form and dynamism.

The motif is east Asian. Two fighting creatures are aloft in the clouds: a long-tailed Oriental rooster, wings spread and talons outthrust, confronts a Chinese-style dragon that spirals down from a fiery, stylized sun in an upper corner. The bird is rendered in blues, turquoise and shades of maroon, the dragon in traditional shades of green and orange. By virtue of their visual relationship the two symbolize the Taoist concept of the universal duality of opposites, yin and yang, with the roughly circular composition representing the traditional depiction of their relationship as intertwined halves of a unified whole. As an original work of art the picture is unremarkable—formulaic, reminiscent of the more elaborate styles of tattooing and body art—but it is executed with striking assurance and technical command of both composition and medium. In the context of the prison cell it is undeniably arresting. The painting is dated 1989—only two years before the prison closed—so there is every chance that the artist was to some extent consciously painting for "posterity"; but equally, it was an image he chose to live with. Precisely what the painting meant to him it is impossible to say, other than to make this observation: whatever symbolism was intended, in both style and subject matter, it is, indisputably, a *masculine* painting.

The meaning and significance of this statement will become apparent in the next chapter, in which I examine prison graffiti created by women.

NOTES

1   I had been told about this particular prisoner during interviews with former prison offi-
    cer Timothy Knapp, and had subsequently read of him in confidential Office of Correc-
    tions internal reports.

2   Staff did not routinely get about the prison carrying rifles, but the image of a prison
    officer so armed would have been familiar to inmates, as that was the standard accessory
    of officers on guard-tower duty. Broome, *Coburg*, p. 281.

3   Katy Richmond, "Fear of Homosexuality and Modes of Rationalisation in Male Pris-
    ons," *Australian and New Zealand Journal of Sociology: Symposium on Deviance,
    Crime and Legal Process* 14, no. 1, February 1978, pp. 51–3.

4   Ibid., p. 55.

5   Ibid.

6   See David M. Heilpern, *Fear or Favour: Sexual assault of Young Prisoners* (Lismore
    NSW: Southern Cross University Press, 1998).

7   I would suggest also that the fact that the mother and child have been left pristine further
    confirms the asexuality of the apparently sexual imagery; had the graffitist really been
    bent on pornographising the group in a manner typical of such defacement, one would
    expect the addition of some sort of sexual features to the female figure, at least.

8   It might even be argued that the relative placement of the two names—Read's up high,
    in a "triumphal" position, the other on the ground below—constitutes a further statement
    about ascendency within the power structure; but I suspect this is reading too much into
    the minutiae of what is, after all, a hurriedly rendered, opportunistic text.

9   Macdonald, *The Graffiti Subculture*, pp. 3–5.

10 It will be recalled that Arthur Koestler's philosophical epiphany, which he experienced
    while languishing in a military prison during the Spanish Civil War, occurred as he was
    whiling away time by scratching mathematical calculations on the wall of his cell. Ar-
    thur Koestler, *The Invisible Writing: The Second Volume of an Autobiography: 1932–40*
    (London: Hutchinson, 1969), pp. 427–30.

11 The phrase is critic Leonard Maltin's, and sums up the protagonists perfectly. Leonard
    Maltin, ed., *Movie & Video Guide*, 1998 edition (New York: Signet, 1997), p. 118.

12   Ray Mooney, "Bluestone Shadows," *Sunday Age* Agenda 14 September 1997.
13   Hoffman interview; Ellem, *Doing Time*, p. 42.
14   Cited in Kevin Childs, "Pentridge: A Prisoner's View," *Age* 20 May 1972.
15   Goffman, *Asylums*, pp. 67–68.
16   John Banks (former prison officer, Boggo Road Gaol), interviewed 20 January 2003.

CHAPTER FIVE

Networking:
The Women

All the inmate graffiti examples discussed thus far have been in male sections of the prisons studied, so whatever we may infer about their underlying motivations, their authors' gender is in no doubt. But the reader may have noted my assumption that the Pentridge Village billboard graffitist was also male, despite the billboard being in a public place accessible to anyone regardless of gender. There are several reasons for this assumption. On its face, to assume that billboard graffiti which is neither ideological nor activist is unlikely to be the work of a female accords with the maxim that, as one researcher puts it, "Very few girls seem to write graffiti."[1] However, this assertion is too simple. Various studies of female graffiti have revealed that "girls" in fact write a lot of graffiti; the chief difference is that it is rarely done on outdoor public surfaces, and even more rarely is it pornographic or aggressively sexual. Most commonly it appears in female-only areas such as public toilets, and it tends to be highly social in content.[2] Both the public nature of the Pentridge Village billboard, and the generally masculinist content of the graffito's pictorial and textual elements, suggest a male author.

In this chapter I will compare women's and men's graffiti in a prison context. As I recounted earlier, gatekeeper attitudes tended to be markedly negative toward graffiti at the sites I visited, and toward the notion of an outsider examining whatever examples had survived. At one site, however, a contrasting view prevailed. The Melbourne City Watch House, a nineteenth-century jail attached to the rear of the former Magistrates Court complex near the Old Melbourne Gaol, was decommissioned in the mid-1990s, and at this writing stands locked and empty.[3] Thus far it retains its interior surfaces in almost exactly the condition they were left in when the last prisoner departed over ten years ago. The single exception to this at the Watch-House is the male exercise yard, which has been repainted. I am told that this occurred shortly after the jail's closure. Surprisingly, a handful of graffiti survive in this space, but the current wisdom at the site is that police officers who had access to the jail after its decommissioning probably wrote them.[4] The reason for the repainting of the exercise yard is unclear.

The present site-owners and custodians, a partnership between Royal Melbourne Institute of Technology (RMIT) and National Trust Australia (Victoria), are currently planning the jail's future as a public history venue and tourist site, and have expressed a commitment to conserve and, as far as practicable, present the site's interior spaces and surfaces as found, for the sake of narrative integrity.[5] Consonant with that intention, they granted me untrammelled access to the entire site and explicitly endorsed my investigation of the graffiti—of which there is an abundance, in the cells, the toilets and washing areas, and the female exercise yard. It is in fact the only site, among those where I was able to view the graffiti, in which the female section of the jail was still accessible with the surfaces intact. (The pattern in the other jails I visited was that the women's sections, where an outsider could gain access at all, either were in sufficiently poor condition as to make inspection unfeasible, or showed signs of having been repainted with consequent obliteration of whatever graffiti was there.)

The Magistrates Courts were always the busiest courts in Melbourne, dealing with the full range of prosecutions either as courts of judgement, in the case of lesser offences, or as the venue for committal hearings in more serious cases. As the Courts' holding facility, the City Watch House at one time or another held almost every person, male and female, indicted in central Melbourne up to 1995, with defendants spending anything from hours to weeks within its walls, and with inmate "turnover" constant and heavy. Thus brand-new offenders, awaiting their first court appearance, were routinely incarcerated in at times overcrowded conditions alongside inmates of long-term prison, transferred for the day for court appearances relating to additional charges, and so on. Unlike normal prisons, the Watch House was staffed by members of the police force.

The fact that the Watch House received both male and female prisoners (housed in separate sections), combined with the current untouched state of the walls and fittings, affords the researcher a unique opportunity. One is able to view and directly compare the graffiti left behind by both groups.

Such a gender comparison reveals that there are both similarities and radical differences between the kinds of graphic sentiments, messages, and self-affirmations bequeathed to us by the men and women who spent their hours there, as they awaited either their day in court or the journey to prison.

It may be said at the outset that what can be found in the City Watch House further contradicts the researcher's maxim quoted above, that "girls" do not in general go in for graffiti-creation. When they are in jail they create a great deal of it. The prevalence of female prison graffiti seems to support my earlier argument that intrinsic aspects of the experience of being imprisoned impel relatively mature adults to become reflexive graffitists.

The Watch House, of course, is only one site—and a site, at that, in which no convicted person actually served out a long-term sentence. It is therefore reasonable to ask whether meaningful generalizations about female inmate graffiti can be made from such a limited sample. Did the inherently transient inmate population of a venue for temporary detention produce graffiti typical of inmate graffiti generally? One approach to this question, and the most obvious, is to consider the graffiti produced by *male* Watch House inmates and compare it directly with the male graffiti at other sites, on the basis that if male graffiti in the Watch House is typical, then it may be inferred that the female graffiti is probably also typical.

A comparison of male graffiti at the Watch House and its equivalent elsewhere does indeed indicate that, by and large, short-term male inmate graffiti tends to follow similar patterns in terms of expressed affect, ideals and values, albeit with certain qualifications. Like his long-term counterpart, the Watch House inmate was preoccupied with power relationships, violence, the impulse to seek revenge, hatred of custodial staff, and the need for self-affirmation. In fact, one of the graffiti discussed in the previous chapter as examples of these categories of affect was from the male section of the Watch House. The short-termers' graffiti is generally more hurried in execution and, with that, less elaborate, less aimed at producing works of art or high-flown calligraphy to live with than at expressing spontaneous sentiment regarding their immediate situation. In the Watch-House there is much declarative graffiti, many vengeful or simply hostile messages directed toward police and other Establishment figures, but relatively few toward other inmates—a reflection, perhaps, of the relative transience of relationships between male inmates compared to the situation in the long-term prison.

Unsurprisingly, there are no examples of elaborate, full-colour mural art of the kind discussed in the last chapter—there are no true paintings at all, nor, it seems, did inmates have access to a range of coloured pencils. Most graffiti in both sections is done in lead pencil or marking pen, or, very commonly, is scratched into the paintwork on metal surfaces or incised into wooden fittings. Presumably because of inmates' short tenure in the jail (weeks at maximum, with only vague foreknowledge of the duration of their stay), large-scale works, even in these media, are rare, although one cell in the male section contains a drawing of significant size and imposing draftsmanship presenting a racial-political slogan. The significance of this work will be considered in the next chapter.

A situational difference between the Watch House and long-term prisons is that it was rare, in the Watch House, for prisoners to be confined one-to-a-cell. Overcrowding at the jail was almost the norm, especially late in its operational career. Given this factor, it is perhaps surprising that so much of the male cell graffiti is so typical of that found in prisons elsewhere, in terms of the preoccupations and concerns the inmates feel compelled to express on the walls. (Some graffiti might have been done during relatively solitary periods, such as when cellmates were preoccupied with their own pastimes, or asleep.) There is one difference in the graffiti content, however, that could well have something to do with the communal nature of conditions, and may also have been influenced by the relative transience of relationships generally: there is very little male homosexual graffiti anywhere in the Watch House. This contrasts directly with the female graffiti, which contains numerous expressions of apparent lesbian relationships (whether formed in the Watch House or previously, outside or in a long-term prison). Expressions of this female homosexuality, however, usually place far more emphasis on the emotional than the physical, and tend to blend seamlessly with the more general expressions of friendship, alliances, and solidarity against adversity. An obvious difference between the male and female graffiti of this kind is that the women evince no aversion to the word "love," which if used in male graffiti tends to be qualified, embellished, and/or caricatured. Also absent in the women's section was sexually aggressive graffiti. There was, for instance, nothing among the females' graffiti remotely equivalent to a male inmate's declaration, atop a heart pierced by an arrow: "WHEN I GET OUT I'M GOING TO FUCK MY GIRL SO HARD SHE BLEEDS."

It is noticeable that there is relatively little graffiti in the women's cells, compared to those of the men. The impulse to draw or write on the walls of the "bedroom," demonstrated so liberally by the men wherever they are imprisoned, seems much reduced in most of the women in the Watch House. By far the majority of women's graffiti is in the exercise yard. This, I believe, reflects a very significant difference between the motivation of male and female graffitists in the Watch House, and also something peculiar about the Watch House itself, vis-à-vis women prisoners.

In the men's communal areas there is a considerable amount of straightforward "tagging"—recording of names, and sometimes dates, without further commentary or message. An example is the men's exercise yard urinal, a doorless facility where scores of men over decades documented their presence by scratching at the enamel on the flusher to expose the metal beneath (in places obliterating the names of predecessors by the same technique). The earliest date visible is 1970. The absence of any messages, comments, boasts, et cetera, suggests that the chief motivation in scratching one's name on the fitting was the simplest kind of abstract assertiveness directed into the future, a statement effectively saying nothing more than "I was here," and taking almost no account of the statement's social context.

Tagging is also present in abundance in the female exercise yard toilet; but in this case the facility had a door. Here and elsewhere in the yard we see a noticeable difference between the male and female graffiti, in terms of what sort of record they wished to leave, and, more importantly, why they wanted to leave it. The women's graffiti shows a two-fold preoccupation almost completely absent in the men's graffiti: the personal relationships already mentioned, and autobiographical "narratives" in the form of "rap sheets"—summarized records of convictions and charges, police station lockups previously held in, time yet to serve, and so on. The women's graffiti is, in other words, both intensely social and, within certain parameters, highly informative.

The aspect peculiar to the women's section of the Watch House, which has to be taken into account if we are to properly understand the nature and significance of the women's graffiti, is this. A male inmate, upon conviction, could be sent to any one of a number of prisons around the state, and once there would be assigned to one of a number of divisions within that prison. But for most of the period under discussion here, all women remanded or convicted in Melbourne, which is to say all the convicted or remanded women in the Melbourne City Watch House, went to only one prison—H.M. Women's Prison Fairlea, in suburban Melbourne. Fairlea opened in 1956 and until its closure in 1996 was the maximum-security reception prison for all women in Victoria.[6]

Despite its "monopoly" on detaining the state's female inmates, Fairlea contained a relatively small community of women, many of whom knew each other—for better or worse—from previous contact outside or, perhaps more commonly, through repeated periods inside. (The percentage of imprisoned women being much less than males, the prison at its busiest held less than a hundred inmates.)[7] In her ethnography of the women's drug culture, Barbara Denton tells of a number of women inmates, of varying degrees of experience of jail time, speaking of the "network" of friends and allies necessary to get by in jail:

> Experienced prisoners…knew the best way to function in prison: "If you want to survive in prison, you find yourself a close friend, and you look after each other," Betsy explained. Her networking had commenced in the police cells. "The first thing I do when I'm arrested is find myself a mate, someone to watch my back."[8]

The period in the Watch House or other police cells could be harrowing, especially if the inmate was "known to police" and hence prone to ill-treatment at their hands,[9] and some women looked forward to Fairlea as a familiar environment where treatment was reasonably fair, and they were likely to meet old friends.[10] For some, however, the prospect was more complicated:

> [I]t was not the power of the prison [Establishment] that was most feared by many of the women. Rather, it was the power of other prisoners….The usual backchat [from prison officers] did not worry Vicky [on her arrival at Fairlea]; she was more concerned about who was in prison. "I was thinking, I wonder who's in here, if I was going to get my head belted in. You might have done something wrong to them."[11]

The key to the process, then, was to establish—or re-establish—one's network *before* arriving in Fairlea, shore up old alliances, negotiate new ones, find a protector if especially vulnerable, and then, crucially, *announce* the fact, via the communal "notice board."

The Watch House exercise yard may therefore be seen as a kind of ante-room of Fairlea, in which the hierarchy within the main prison was modelled, rehearsed, manipulated and discussed, via dialogic "postings"—graffiti—on the toilet door. Thus a graffito proclaiming, for instance, that "MANDY L'S WENDY," which appears on its face merely an affirmation of friendship or romantic attachment, in the Watch House also—quite possibly primarily—means that Mandy enjoyed the protection of Wendy (or vice versa), and as Wendy happened to be well known and respected—or feared—among the Fairlea community, then anyone with a grudge or complaint against Mandy would have more to deal with than her alone. In this and various other "functional" aspects noted below, the women's Watch House graffiti is typical of tagging-style graffiti outside in certain sections of the urban underclass subculture. (On this I can claim some insight, having spent the main part of my youth living in West Heidelberg, a notorious public-housing estate in Melbourne's northern suburbs, where we routinely went about equipped with marking pens for the purpose of tagging. For several years as a teenager, my closest friend was a popular but markedly fearsome girl a year older than I, who was in the habit of tagging bus stops and similar fixtures with her name and mine together. It was understood that the advertised association of our names in this manner virtually guaranteed my own safety from certain aggressors.)[12]

In the same way that taggers outside prison often competitively obliterate previous, rival, taggers' names, so in the Watch House we find certain names scored out, often replaced with obscene epithets or other abusive signals of ill-fame. (This obliterating also occurred in the male section, but generally without the abusive replacement.) It is instructive to note the names that remained pristine because no-one dared cross them out, in some cases appearing repeatedly in company with various other names—thus effectively defining a "crew"—as well as recounting arrest records, plus conveying jovially self-confident messages of good will to the jail population in general. The most visible example of these "top dogs" among the Watch House graffitists is an inmate known by the diminutive "Yonnie." Yonnie features in no less than eight brash proclamations of her presence, associations and story, some of notable length (two comprise more than twenty words each), presented in almost exactly the format outlined above. Her contributions, all but one of which of which she has dated, indicate that she spent an initial three days in the Watch House while attending court, resulting in her remand to Fairlea, then reappeared twelve days later for a further three days, perhaps to answer more charges or due to an adjournment. Despite her having created this record as long ago as 1980, Yonnie's name was never crossed out.

Just as there is more to the affirmation of friendship than meets the eye, so, too, the "rap sheet" signifies more than mere memoir: a list of charges and/or convictions can convey important information to others about who they will be dealing with; thus the inclusion of, say, "LETHAL WEAPON," or "THEFT OF GUN" in effect says to potential rivals, "Don't mess with me, I'm dangerous." But further: a common "admission" among such rap sheets is that the inmate faces, or has previously faced, drug charges. Denton's study reveals that, far from being an acknowledgement of weakness and/or victimhood, as a conventional social viewpoint (and even traditional feminist viewpoints) would assume, this sort of self-declaration in fact may be read as an assertion of agency, in that it places the graffitist within a core locus of power in the prison's social structure and, especially, its illicit economy.[13] (Nor is a "trafficking" charge essential for such status to be inferred; within the closed society of prison, the distinction between dealer and customer tends to blur, as simply using drugs can bring a prisoner into intimate contact with the power network, and anyone merely "holding" becomes a distributor more or less automatically through the routine expectation that drugs will be shared if and when acquired.)[14] Viewed in this light, at least one seemingly bizarre juxtaposition among the graffiti I found becomes suddenly comprehensible: Near the bottom of the female toilet door is incised a "love heart" containing, in large block letters, only the word "SMACK" [heroin]. Immediately below the heart, in the same hand, is the message "JESUS IS COMING TO SAVE YOU." The graffitist's "loving" identification with her drug of choice may be seen as a self-affirmation, a statement of empowerment—and hence her added declaration of spiritual faith may be seen as emanating from a sense of self-confidence, rather than despair.

In the context of the networking imperative, even the very common abusive declarations of enmity against the police may, in any given instance, be more than they seem. A "cleanskin," that is, a newcomer to the prison system,[15] especially one from, say, a rural centre, may begin with no social capital other than to declare her in-principle solidarity with the main group by othering the local police in her area of origin. Thus, for example, the statement that "BENDIGO COPS ARE CUNTS," or "COPS IN SHEPP[arton] ARE DEAD SET CUNTS, DOGS, PIGS," while seeming to fit the previously identified vengeful affect so prevalent among the male graffiti, is also a statement about the graffitist as, at least, a potential ally against the common enemy. (This might also be true to some extent for male prisoners, though in a more generalized way, but I saw very little of this kind of declaration among the men's graffiti.)

This is not to say, of course, that some of these resistant declarations are not more heartfelt and angst-driven than others; the image of imprisoned women with agency through group solidarity and mutual support that emerges from aspects of Denton's analysis should not allow us to forget that their confrontations with law-enforcement, and the concomitant experience of prison, were for many women at least as unremittingly awful emotionally as anything suffered by imprisoned men. Feminist lawyer Amanda George points out that there are times when "the woman [in prison] is completely powerless. There is no real accountability in prisons. It is a closed hypermale military environment demanding a slavish submission to hierarchy and authority."[16] Hence one Watch House graffitist, for instance, presumably arrested in Melbourne's southern suburbs, not only tells her colleagues, in the standard style, that "FRANKSTON COPS ARE CUNTS," but is moved to elaborate about a particular policeman: "...AND SGT MORRISON FROM KEYSBOROUGH CRIME CAR SQUAD YOU FUCKING DOG / HOPE YOU DROP DEAD YOU PIG."[17] It may be inferred that, whatever passed between this inmate and the vilified sergeant, the encounter seems to have left her, figuratively speaking, bloody but unbowed. Such defiance is, however, beyond the capacities of an inmate identifying herself as "LOU A.," who is apparently well into her second week of imprisonment, and tells us, with palpable anguish, "MILDURA CELL'S [*sic*] SUCK / 8 DAYS OF HELL & HEART-ACHE / 3 DAYS OF LONLEY [*sic*] HELL HERE / BALLARAT [illegible]."

Such glimpses remind us that the networking techniques we have seen here and the continual questing for solidarity and support arose from real, urgent need; that if a declaration of friendship and love for another inmate is a signal of an alliance formed, it is very likely also a declaration of friendship and love; that if two young offenders who have been remanded to appear before the Children's Court for arson end their account with the lament "BAIL REFUSED," the appended reply "WHAT A BUMMER" by another (almost certainly adult) inmate is most probably a genuine expression of sympathy;[18] that if an inmate's compendium of arrests and charges is written as a manifesto of potency and status within the system, it may also be written as a result of the simple human impulse to tell one's story, to give voice to the personal history that has led her to this dreadful pass, and thus perhaps render it intelligible, to herself as well as others; and that if an inmate's avowed enmity toward the "Jacks" at a particular police station helps earn her some credentials inside, it may also indicate that she learned the hard way that at least some of the officers of that police station really do merit the abuse she heaps upon them with the point of her nail-file in the paintwork of an exercise-yard toilet door.

It is apparent that in general the women were more socially inclined than the men in their approach to the constant problem of how to cope with being inside. Although the graffiti record attests to the fact that some men do set great store on the friendships and alliances formed in prison and are prepared to express their feelings on the subject, women are less reserved about the process of forming and cementing those relationships. And just as there are examples among the male graffiti that approximate the affect shown in the female section, so, too, female graffiti can simulate male graffiti: hence we find in the female section a fist-and-upraised middle finger in the standard position, but "feminized" with long fingernails, and captioned unequivocally "UP YOURS TO ALL OF YOU." This example of female graffiti giving the "finger," which although less common in the female section than the male, does indicate a shared sense of the coded idioms of the prison across the gender divide.

*

In the centre of the toilet door, in mid-1983, a number of women recorded their collective grief over the death of a colleague, "RHONDA." One of the mourners identifies as Rhonda's cousin. It is possible—likely—that Rhonda was at some time a prisoner; it is also possible that the tag "RHONDA B" elsewhere on the door is a record of the same person's former presence in the Watch House. No further information is available to us, so we cannot say how or where Rhonda died; it is clear, however, that the event was felt deeply by a significant number of people in the prison system (such commemorative graffiti are rare), and that her memory commanded sufficient respect for her name to survive the activities of subsequent taggers.

Rhonda's memorial emblematizes a perennial, half-hidden aspect of the women's prison system: its death toll. As I have mentioned, the chances of a woman meeting an unnatural end in Fairlea were far less than those for a man in, say, Pentridge;[19] but on the edge of the system, in the twilight-world just outside prison, the chances of coming to grief greatly increased. A woman ending a sentence of any length is exceptionally vulnerable on release.[20] Lack of emotional, logistic and/or financial support can leave her bereft, and if her life is complicated by poverty and substance-addiction, as so many prisoners' lives are, the likelihood of her surviving to her next arrest declines even further. There are no figures for the period that saw Rhonda's passing, but between 1990 and 1995, the number of female inmates who died immediately or shortly after being released from prison in Victoria officially stood at sixty-three, or over one a month. (There is reason to think the actual number was considerably higher.) Only a very small percentage of those deaths were from natural causes; although a significant number died violently (including in motor accidents), the majority were, predictably, drug-related. In the last weeks of 1999, women were dying, post-release, at a rate of more than one a week.[21]

If we consider the relatively small number of women in the prison system, it comes to seem very likely—almost a certainty—that virtually everyone in Fairlea (and its successor institutions) at any given time would have known or been related to someone who had died an unnatural death. Yet such a fact is only incidentally a function of the *size* of the prison population; it is centrally contingent upon the socio-economic demographic of that population, and on their cultural, intellectual and educational expectations. More subtly, it is also a function of the degree to which they as a group are othered by the mainstream. In any ordinary peacetime walk of life, a comparable steady attrition of group members by unnatural causes would be regarded as shocking and intolerable; yet in prison populations such statistics can accumulate for decades without being thought remarkable, much less galvanising into action anyone with agency in the realm of policy-making, or with influence over public opinion.

The above death-rate figures were made publicly known in the first instance by the Somebody's Daughter Theatre Company, a group founded by Fairlea women; at a performance marking Fairlea's closure in 1996, the players began with a dedication to the sixty-three. Legal academics Susanne Davies and Sandy Cook, who attended the performance, were moved to take up the issue of post-release deaths among women prisoners, and began research into the causes of death and the implications of those causes for penal and social-welfare policy-makers. They subsequently reported significant resistance to their work from official circles and also the academic funding committees to which they applied for research grants, along with a dismaying

prevalence of inappropriate, stereotypical views on women offenders as expressed in criminological, corrective services and scholarly publications.
Their proposed methodology, which was centred on interviews of women
prisoners specifically "to ensure that their voices are heard," was criticized as
"anecdotal" and therefore "unscientific." The sum effect, in their view,
amounted to a wholesale neglect and hence negation of the subjective experience of women prisoners, which contributed in turn to the continuing
accumulation of mortality statistics:

> [T]he lives of women who have been in prison—their experiences of criminaliza-
> tion and imprisonment and their struggles to re-establish themselves post-release
> [—]...are rarely acknowledged in academic literature or in the popular media. Nor
> are they usually considered in shaping practices and policies. What we might ask is
> the basis for this exclusion? Why is it that the voices of these women and the ex-
> periences they speak of are not being heard? Does the refusal to hear their voices
> mean that more women will die? What can be learned from their experiences that
> will help to ensure a meaningful future for other imprisoned women?[22]

We seem to have moved some distance beyond the Watch House and
Rhonda's *in memoriam*, and given that there is no direct evidence that her
death fits the paradigm of post-release mortality outlined here, the connecting chain of reasoning by which I have arrived at this point may seem tenuous. The common ground is grief. Whatever the actual circumstances of her
death, the event moved women for whom the loss of friends was all-too-
familiar territory to make a permanent record of their sorrow at her passing,
and by implication their pride in having known her. On a larger scale and in
a different setting, but out of similar feelings, the women of Somebody's
Daughters put on record their grief for the sixty-three.

But for grief to be an intelligible, personally supportable affect, the loss
from which it arises must be equally intelligible; its narrative must be comprehensible and congruent with the survivors' understanding of the world.
When grieving must confront, or is confronted by, a *false* narrative of loss,
that is, a narrative that radically misrepresents its protagonists, it is impotent,
giving no comfort and instead fuelling frustration and a sense of injustice. It
is, I believe, this perennial misrepresentation that ultimately created the need
for a group of theatrical players to give public voice to their grief, and to
which Davies and Cook instinctively responded.

The misrepresentation I refer to inheres in the theories, policies and
practices that govern women's incarceration. Davies and Cook take particular

exception to the predominance of "needs" discourse in theoretical and policy-related literature, which focuses on the assumed or deduced special requirements of women in prison, and tends to result in essentialist and in some cases blatantly patronizing policies of treatment.[23] They point out that this discourse, as applied to women in prison, is a misuse, or over-use, of a body of feminist theory which originally identified specifically gendered needs of women.[24] Within a corrections paradigm, this both stems from and in turn further fosters an underlying view of women as inherently problematic—with their "neediness" a symptom of this—and as a result "endlessly draining" on resources, infrastructure, funding, and so on.[25]

Crucially, such demand also saps the professional energy and goodwill of the jailers themselves. With such perceptions of relentless (and hence unfulfillable) demand prevailing at senior policy-making levels, it is hardly surprising that at the other end of the corrections spectrum, among the staff who are in daily charge of the women, "endlessly draining" tends to be tacitly (or even, at times, explicitly) translated into "not worth the trouble." (Although this phrase is mine, it is fully consonant with views and attitudes expressed by almost every former prison officer I interviewed.)

I am not suggesting that all custodial staff share this attitude; many are well-intentioned and properly professional in their approach to the work, and some are certainly motivated by genuine compassion. The two-fold problem in the total institution is the combination of a systemic ethos which tends to reflect attitudes and beliefs of the upper hierarchy and policy-makers, and the disproportionately potent effect of indifferent or actively malign individuals in positions proximate to the inmates—in the total institution, it only takes one person inclined to act with neglect or malice toward inmates to effectively negate all the good works of others. A further exacerbating factor is that if the prevailing official ethos is aligned with such neglect or malice, those officers whose motivation is benign tend to find themselves working against the tide, and over time may become increasingly isolated and feel pressured either to conform or leave.[26]

This reflexive abdication of care and responsibility is driven not only by a perception of women's excessive neediness, but also by a widespread attitude that women inmates are by nature *morally* beyond the pale. Barbara Denton, whose investigation was in part an exploration of the scope and nature of women prisoners' agency, is critical of "superficial researchers who simply accepted the depictions [by] prison staff and criminal justice officials that women prisoners are 'the lowest of the low'."[27] In the sense in which she quotes it, this damning phrase is used to refer to a condition of radical abjectness and pitiable lack of autonomy in their lives generally; but it is of relevance here, for I have heard exactly these words used by tour guides at former prisons when discussing the female inmates during tours, and in those cases the intended connotations of the phrase clearly included the women's moral character.

As I recounted earlier, the former staff I interviewed who had had occasion to come into contact with female prisoners were almost unanimously scathing about what they saw as the women's low morals and deviousness compared with male inmates, their "filthy" language, manipulativeness, and general propensity for causing trouble. (Especially if they had an opportunity to have any contact, however fleeting or distant, with male prisoners; the reason I was familiar with the name of the prisoner graffitied on the "sidewalk" of the Pentridge Village billboard was that a former prison officer had retailed to me at some length the trouble caused by the appearance of that prisoner's girlfriend as an inmate in Pentridge B Division.)[28] At sites where tours are conducted by former staff, or where the historical content of the tour guides' presentation has been informed to a significant extent by former staff, these essentialist and fundamentally misogynist attitudes are clearly evident, in some cases forming the basis of important features of tours.

The most significant example I encountered was in the representation of the gallows at Fremantle Prison. There, visitors received a notably graphic and morally charged verbal account of the notorious Martha Rendell, who was hanged in 1909 for a particularly vicious and sadistic murder, that of her 15-year-old stepson, by incremental poisoning. (She was also widely believed to have similarly poisoned her two younger stepdaughters.) Rendell, we were told, derived pleasure in watching her stepchildren's weeks of suffering, as they sickened progressively under her ministrations. Her method was to apply a topical solution containing hydrochloric acid directly to their "infected" throats, thereby causing intense pain and exacerbating their symptoms (which may have been real sore throats to begin with). The children eventually died, emaciated, in agony, their throats and internal organs having been gradually seared away by the acid.

The tour guides' account of Rendell's crimes and execution presented her very much as she was portrayed in the daily press of 1909: as archetypally evil—unrepentant and devoid of normal emotion, a classically wicked stepmother murderously jealous of her stepchildren's claim on their father's affections. That she calmly protested her innocence all the way to the gallows was taken to show a complete lack of remorse.[29]

Tour visitors responded to the Rendell story with understandable vehemence: emotional groans of distress accompanied each grisly detail in the recounting of the murders, and spontaneous comments I noted included "Bring back hanging"; "Hanging's not enough for the likes of her"; and, to general murmurs of sympathy, "Those poor little kids." Such comments, and the tour guides' telling, were, I discovered, very much in accord with the prevailing view in Perth, where the Martha Rendell story holds a prominent place in the criminal folklore. Whether the visitors to the prison on the days I observed the gallows tour were already familiar with the story I cannot say, but there was no doubt in my mind that by the time they left the prison the majority of them knew with certainty that Martha Rendell thoroughly deserved to be executed, and a significant number undoubtedly knew also that crimes as vile as hers would justify a revival of capital punishment in Western Australia.

What the tourists who visited Fremantle Prison were not told, however, is that there is significant doubt—probably well above the threshold of "reasonable" doubt necessary for an acquittal in a fair trial—that Martha Rendell was guilty of anything, other than transgressing a highly conservative society's customs regarding adultery and living in a de facto relationship.[30] The latter situation she had kept secret from the neighbours, passing herself off as the children's mother, and this deception weighed heavily against her in the media's—and hence the public's—assessment of her. This in turn spurred the government to uphold the death sentence against pressure brought by groups opposing capital punishment. As social historian Anna Haebich has established, Rendell's defence counsel missed many opportunities to cast substantial doubt on the prosecution's evidence; much of the testimony, expert and otherwise, which contributed to the jury's guilty finding was at best questionable and at worst outright unreliable. And virtually all those involved in her trial—jury, judge, expert witnesses, prosecution barrister and perhaps to some extent even her defence barrister—plus the State's political leaders, who after the trial had the power to commute her sentence as an act of mercy, appear to have been influenced in their view of Martha Rendell by the gendered social construction of her as manifestly evil.[31] In other words, there is every chance that the only woman ever hanged at Fremantle Prison—the only one in Western Australia—was not guilty.

No trace of the alternative narrative of Martha Rendell, canvassing any possibility that the State may have put an innocent woman to death, was touched upon by any Fremantle tour guides during the seven or eight tours I observed. This, I suggest, is a significant omission in the public-history exposition of the prison—not merely because credible alternative narratives should be considered when presenting and interpreting an institution's historical events, but because in this case the alternative narrative is readily available to those conducting the tours: a draft typescript of Haebich's article, dated 1997, resides on-site, in the prison museum's archive, and was offered to me by the archivist when I asked for "any information" on Martha Rendell.

The execution of women tends to make tour guides, and the visiting public, uneasy. At sites where women were hanged, guides almost invariably dwell on the enormity of their crimes; it is as though they feel the women must be diabolized in order to justify their execution. Hence it is not in the gatekeepers' interest to explore alternative narratives regarding the likes of Martha Rendell. And in terms of the prison's representation, Rendell is not merely an example of the "wicked stepmother" and generic "evil woman" stereotypes; she is also what might be termed the prison's "featured hanging"—an exceptionally depraved criminal who the public can readily be persuaded transgressed society's moral norms so grossly as to unequivocally forfeit her right to life. In principle, the Featured Hanging can be male or female. But whereas the hanging of, say, Ned Kelly at Old Melbourne Gaol, or even Ronald Ryan at Pentridge, may be represented with at least a nod toward the controversy and lingering doubts as to the moral justice of their executions, the hanged woman must be unambiguously bad.[32]

To return to the women's exercise yard of the Melbourne City Watch House: in an earlier chapter I alluded to certain aspects of the behaviour and, especially, the "foul language" reportedly used by female inmates, which (male) former staff found so offensive they could not bring themselves to recount it to me. On examining the female graffiti, and taking into account the tone of former staff members' sentiments when discussing the issue, I came to suspect that their dismay rested in part, at least, on the women's very free use of the word "cunt."

Cunt is the most confronting word in mainstream Australian English, and perhaps in every major variety of English spoken anywhere.[33] It is used by both male and female prison graffitists as a term of extreme, albeit routine, abuse. This usage, it is reasonable to assume, reflects the spoken-language habits of the prison population in general, which in turn reflect the language of the urban underclass that overwhelmingly supplies the prison population.[34] The word appears most often in graffiti reviling authority figures or groups such as prison staff or the police.

Semiotician Rob Cover discusses a political graffito he installed on a wall in inner-suburban Melbourne in which he directly equated the then (Labor) premier of Victoria, Steve Bracks, with his "overbearing" predecessor, (Liberal) Jeff Kennett, conflating them in a hyperbolical political epithet: "BRACKS = KENNETT: FASCIST CUNT."[35] A subsequent graffitist provided an addendum to Cover's work which read: "CUNT IS A BEAUTIFUL WORD. DON'T USE IT ON BRACKS."[36] Cover observes that, despite various attempts over several hundred years of usage to "resignify" *cunt* to resume its original, feminine-anatomical meaning, the word steadfastly maintains its "'offensiveness' and 'taboo' status...in contemporary Western culture":

> "Cunt" can be understood as a *protected* term: protected from usage such that it be *most* offensive in its deployment—a term of injury which cannot be pinned down to a group identity (such as racial and homophobic terms) but is widely available— if rarely used—as a term of intense injury. The term in its use today can probably be said to offend at least two identifiable groups. Firstly, those opposed to the use of "foul" or "vulgar" language who view the term as fixed in signifying offence always and are possibly—if unconsciously—reinforcing a taste-based demarcation of class. The second...group...are women following a feminist reclamation of the term in order...to further a cultural project of divorcing womanhood from terms of abjection.[37]

Whereas the overall purport of his article leads Cover to focus chiefly on the second group, for our purposes here they have little relevance; there is no evidence of any attempt by female graffitists in the Watch House to engage in "a feminist reclamation of the term" along the consciously directed cultural lines he envisages. More persuasive, however, would be an argument that the female inmates' use of the word constitutes an aspect of a broad (albeit in this case unwitting) "claim of *ownership* of the terminology" by women.[38] Two aspects of the Watch House graffiti give some support to this idea. The first is a single graffito among those we have already discussed.

Yonnie's casually affectionate use of *cunt* in a "letter" to another inmate, Kerry—a message, it is clear, of unalloyed friendship—effectively negates the word's abusive connotation. I found no examples anywhere of male graffiti in which men used the word with the slightest connotation of affection.

The second and rather more substantive aspect is that *cunt*, as an abusive epithet, is used significantly more by the women graffitists than the men. In the Watch House (which I acknowledge is a limited sample) the ratio is approximately two-to-one. Although no directly comparative survey was possible at other prisons due to the absence of female graffiti, the relative scarcity of *cunt* among male Watch House graffiti accords with my findings elsewhere. Where the male graffiti is extant, the word occurs only rarely: among all the graffiti I photographed at Boggo Road and Fremantle, *cunt* is evident only a couple of times at each prison.[39] As we have seen, male inmates' vocabulary of abuse—both verbal and graphic—can be highly colourful and inventive; although the Watch House women's graffiti does show some signs of similar inventiveness, there is visible a tendency among the women to gravitate directly toward the most extreme language, especially when referring to police.

There are two possible reasons for this. Firstly, women may feel the emotional burden of incarceration, and especially the oppression of abusive treatment by (predominantly male) law-enforcement officers in the intensely masculine world of the prison system, significantly more deeply than do men. Numerous personal accounts attest that this is, in fact, the case,[40] and the possibility fits with Amanda George's assessment. As she points out, even routine prison procedures such as strip-searches can amount to arbitrary and gratuitous punishment on a gendered basis.[41] If such affect is a significant factor in the writing of graffiti, it might give rise to a need for a more complete cathartic release, and hence an impulse to use the strongest language available, when expressing their anger.

Secondly, women in prison may wilfully behave in an exaggeratedly transgressive manner, including their use of language, as a defiant response to the moralistic labelling and generally harsh treatment they receive from authorities. If so, this might account for much of the denigration former prison staff direct at the memory of female inmates' behaviour, morals and language. There is historical precedent for this idea, all the way back to Australia's Convict Society and the days of transportation: Joy Damousi tells of convict women responding to the excessively moralistic and punitive treatment meted out to them by behaving, en masse and with clear premeditation, in ways designed to cause maximum offence to their colonial custodians.[42]

It is entirely possible that a combination of both of these factors is responsible for the proliferation of what many regard as "the worst word in the English language"[43] within spaces occupied by incarcerated women. In the final analysis I suspect that is the case. But none of this, of course, adds up to the sort of "ownership" feminist semioticians have in mind. The second scenario—wilful misbehaviour—posits the greatest degree of agency on the part of the women, but it is at best a *reactive* agency, and cannot, therefore, escape its inherent pathology.

*

Just as the special case of imprisonment adds a dimension to graffiti studies not normally encountered outside among the various graffiti subcultures, so too imprisonment as a radically abnormal variant of the human condition presents the feminist with special conceptual and methodological problems. It has, fortuitously, proved possible to turn the limitations noted above, regarding the restricted sample of women's graffiti available to me, to some advantage for the insights gained regarding the special situation of women in the transitional state prior to their entry into the main prison. But clearly, my study remains narrow in regard to women's prison graffiti generally, and draws attention to the need for a comprehensive gendered study of prison graffiti, both historical and contemporary. That narrowness also reminds us that women in Australian prisons have always been in a small minority.[44] Whether inside prisons or elsewhere, the historical study of minorities who have departed presents the researcher with special conceptual problems.

The graffiti of prisons constitute substantial aspects of the physical remains—the fabric—of those places. There is a sense, therefore, in which an examination of the graffiti, with a view to drawing meaningful inferences about the experiences of the inhabitants who drew them, stands as the beginnings of an historical archaeology of the prison,[45] and it is instructive briefly to consider some of the considerations that must be brought to bear on the special factors inherent in both gendered and minority studies in archaeology.

In defining the shortcomings of traditional methodologies in her field, archaeologist Elizabeth Scott posits a hypothetical culturally relativist archaeology, as a way of dramatizing the invisibility of certain cultures due to the priorities and prejudices of the prevailing cultural paradigm in which archaeology is usually practiced.[46] Scott's work draws on and elaborates Janet Spector's concept of "inclusive archaeology,"[47] which Spector developed while researching a tribe of Native Americans. Inclusive archaeology was her response to two related needs: her need for a holistic approach to her own investigations, in order to provide a coherent account of the subject tribe's culture;[48] and the need to render more visible the culture as a whole and, by extension, minority cultures in general that an archaeology centred on the hegemonic cultural paradigm tends to overlook or misinterpret.[49] This latter aspect led her to critique a further, and even more general, ramification of traditional archaeological myopia: the misinterpretation and/or neglect of women and their cultural significance in the archaeological record.[50] Importantly, as Scott points out, gender "cannot be studied in isolation," because it inherently connects to and is subsumed in class, race and ethnicity,[51] and is an indispensable component of human relationships within and, crucially, between, cultures and social groups.[52]

Such considerations highlight the fact that even in their gender-segregated areas, prisons are far from all-male or all-female environments. Overseeing prison officers, visiting relatives and various professional representatives may be of either sex, and inmates in certain circumstances have contact with inmates from the "other side." And yet the prevailing culture of assumptions, processes and perceptions in the prison, even the female prison, tends to be both heavily masculine and heavily gendered. Archaeologist Susan Lawrence, whose work has for the first time placed and comprehensively defined women's roles in the historical picture of the Victorian goldfields of the 1850s, acknowledges that her findings tend to confirm many gender stereotypes;[53] but as she points out, "one of the criticisms of feminist archaeology…[is] that it must be grounded in data,"[54] and in her work on the gold fields the data tends to reinforce traditional gender distinctions. She thus shows that the practice of simply "adding women," an approach viewed with universal disfavour by feminist theorists, can have some validity, and is at least better than nothing, when dealing with radically androcentric cultures.[55] This point is supported by my findings in the Watch House, where the women's graffiti stands as a rich body of data that does indeed tend to confirm those gender differences, but also offers new insights into women's experiences of incarceration.

As a public history site, the women's exercise yard presents a dilemma. Aside from issues to do with privacy (many of the "tags" provide inmates' full names and in some cases their home towns), much of the more uncompromising declarative material is sufficiently transgressive of social norms to warrant some thought of age-dependent censorship in the form of restricted entry, *à la* "15-plus" cinema admission. Yet if such access is to be made available to an adult general public, there is obviously much scope for the material itself to reinforce the moralistic stereotypes which the inmates endured. This is where the curators of the prison as a tourist site have an opportunity to challenge those stereotypes, however uncomfortable such challenge may make site visitors feel; by providing alternative narratives which do justice to the voices of those women who not only experienced incarceration, but who now find that the prison where they were once detained, and the record they left of themselves and each other upon its walls, have become part of Australia's prison tourist trade. As Dewar and Fredericksen point out, the prison museum must

> provide an inclusive history of [the] prison and its residents, a history that engenders public interest and discussion beyond that connected with the material fabric of the remaining structures...This can be [achieved] only by refocusing interpretation to the intimate details of the lives of the prison population, and bringing to light the various narratives contained therein. Here, history and archaeology have complementary roles to play.[56]

NOTES

1   Macdonald, *The Graffiti Subculture*, p. 127.

2   Carrington, "Girls and Graffiti"; Bruner and Kelso, "Gender Differences in Graffiti"; Green, "Writing on the Stall".

3   The courts themselves, which had occupied the building at the corner of Russell and Latrobe Streets since 1914, were relocated to new premises at the western end of the CBD in 1995. Magistrates Court of Victoria, http://www.magistratescourt.vic.gov.au/.

4   This applies also to a small number of graffiti among the genuine examples elsewhere in the jail, and I have had to discern at times, using internal textual evidence and/or comparisons with other graffiti, whether the occasional pithy interpolation or "reply" to what is clearly inmate graffiti is the work of subsequent inmate graffitists, or officers having

their say, post-decommissioning. Although the issue of graffiti created by staff or other police officers is of considerable interest sociologically and historically (and see also Chapter 6), it was beyond the scope of this study, for both practical and ethical reasons, to undertake a systematic investigation of the sort required to verify provenance and provide meaningful interpretation.

5   The Watch House curators' intentions on this matter were confirmed for me over numerous discussions concerning the interpretation of the site. Since I completed my fieldwork, they have made the site selectively available to a variety of groups such as RMIT architecture students.

6   In the mid-1980s women's corrections were complicated by a fire at Fairlea which for several years necessitated that some women be housed at Pentridge; in 1988 a twenty-four-bed minimum-security women's prison, Tarrengower, began accepting prisoners, and from 1990 a very small number went from Fairlea to serve their sentences in Barwon Prison, a maximum-security institution housing male and females. Emma Russell, *Fairlea: The History of a Women's Prison in Australia 1956–96* (Kew: CORE, 1998), pp. 27, 30; Corrections Victoria, Victorian Department of Justice, "Timeline / Chronology" (unpublished); Denton, *Dealing*, p. 188n.

7   This high figure was post-1994 when Barwon female division had closed, and Pentridge was no longer housing women. Corrections Victoria, Timeline; Denton, *Dealing*, p. 188n.

8   Denton, *Dealing*, p. 137

9   Ibid., pp. 134–5.

10   Woman and Imprisonment Group, *Women and Imprisonment*, Melbourne: Fitzroy Legal Service, 1995, pp. 1–4, 59–60.

11   Denton, *Dealing*, p. 135. Denton notes that although violence was always a danger in Fairlea, "Attacks and acts of extreme violence in the women's prison were considerably fewer than those reported in the corresponding male prison"; dominant inmates achieved their ends through "threats and standover tactics" (p. 154); cf. Pat Merlo, who worked in both Fairlea and Pentridge and confirms that in general "the men were definitely more violent." Merlo, *Screw*, p. 116.

12   Consistent with the nature of such a milieu and the social connections formed there, when inspecting the graffiti in the women's exercise yard I recognized several names, including that of my former friend/protector, among the tags.

13   Denton, *Dealing*, pp. 3, 136–52.

14   Ibid., p. 146.

15   Ibid., p. 145.

16   Amanda George, "Strip Searches: Sexual Assault by the State," in *Without Consent: Confronting Adult Sexual Violence, Proceedings of Conference 27–29 October 1992*, ed. Patricia Weiser Easteal, (Canberra: Australian Institute of Criminology, Conference Proceedings No. 20, 1993), p. 214.

17   Both the police officer's name and his squad location have been changed.

18   There are many reasons for finding the implications of this fragmentary narrative especially disturbing. The presence of minors in adult cells is an anomaly of the system for which there may be no satisfactory explanation, but which was known, by people on the

fringes of that system, to occur from time to time. During my State wardship, some Establishment agents such as social workers used the possibility of ending up in an adult jail, via (orchestrated) irregularities of the system, as a threat by which to coerce compliance from State wards they deemed unco-operative, including myself and others I knew.

19 The death rate for women, mostly due to suicide or self-harm, rose when they were transferred to various divisions of Pentridge after the Fairlea fire. Rikki Dewan, "In and Out of Prison," in *Women and Imprisonment* [discussion paper compilation] (Melbourne: Fitzroy Legal Service, 1995), pp. 59–60.

20 Susanne Davies and Sandy Cook, "Dying Outside: Women, Imprisonment and Post-Release Mortality," paper given at "Women in Corrections: Staff and Clients" conference, Adelaide: Australian Institute of Criminology, 31 October–1 November 2000.

21 Ibid.

22 Ibid.

23 Ibid.

24 Nancy Fraser,. *Unruly Practices: Power, Discourse and Gender in Contemporary Social Theory* (Cambridge: Polity Press, 1989).

25 Davies and Cook, "Dying Outside."

26 On the relative impotence of such benignly motivated individuals within the prison system, see, e.g., Merlo, *Screw*, pp. 43–4; also J. Smith interview.

27 Denton, *Dealing*, p. 158

28 Knapp interview.

29 This account is based primarily on the tour guide's presentation, which was closely congruent with various published accounts, including *An Australian Murder Almanac: 150 Years of Chilling Crime*, ed. Patricia Dasey (Adelaide: Nationwide News, 1993), p. 17; and "Wicked Mistress Hanged for Serial Killing," *Sunday Times* (Perth) 27 June 1993.

30 Anna Haebich, "Murdering Stepmothers: The Trial and Execution of Martha Rendell," *Journal of Australian Studies* no. 59, 1998.

31 Clemency from the State premier was her only hope of a reversal of the sentence, as Western Australia did not have a court of appeals until 1911. Also, on the questions regarding the conduct of Rendell's defence, see Anna Haebich, "Murdering Stepmothers", a substantially longer draft MS of the article with the same title, held at the Fremantle Prison archive.

32 A signal exception to this is the account of Elizabeth Woolcock's trial and execution, in 1873, at Adelaide Gaol; Woolcock's hanging was widely believed, even then, to have been unjust, and is so presented in the Gaol's presentation. See http://www.adelaidegaol .org.au/working.htm#History (accessed 10 March 2008).

33 The most comprehensive work on the etymology, social history and contemporary sociology of the word is Matthew Hunt, *Cunt: A Cultural History*, at http://www .matthewhunt.com/cunt.html (accessed 20 February 2008), an adaptation of his widely cited Coventry University MA dissertation, "Cunt: Taboo, Patriarchy and Liberation" (2000).

34 On this point I cite my own and my peers' linguistic development in underclass suburban Melbourne, where *cunt* is so ubiquitous one learns and becomes inured to it at an

early age as an everyday term. In that setting it remains on one level an abusive word, but is also used conversationally at times among peers, more or less in lieu of "mate," but with an undercurrent of suppressed aggression. This quasi-friendly usage, I believe, reflects both the reflexively defiant transgressiveness and the all-against-all ambience which are collectively never far from the surface in day-to-day relationships in that social stratum.

35   Rob Cover, "Some Cunts: Graffiti, Globalisation, Injurious Speech and 'Owning' Signification," *Social Semiotics* 12, no. 3, 2002, pp. 271–4.

36   Ibid., p. 275.

37   Ibid. (emphasis in original).

38   Ibid., p. 279 (emphasis in original).

39   Note that although I viewed and amassed a large number of images, I make no claim to having photographed *all* of the graffiti at either prison—due chiefly to the constraints recounted in Chapter 2 above—hence there may be instances of *cunt* among graffiti I did not see. I suggest, however, that the small number found among the extensive sample I did view justifies my present conclusions.

40   See, e.g., M.M., "One Day In Fairlea" in *Women and Imprisonment*, Women and Imprisonment Group (Melbourne: Fitzroy Legal Service, 1995), pp. 1–4.

41   George, "Strip Searches."

42   See Damousi, *Depraved and Disorderly*, pp. 59ff.

43   Hunt, *Cunt*, citing many sources paraphrasing this wording.

44   Australian Bureau of Statistics, Year Book Australia: Crime and justice: Women in prison, http://www.abs.gov.au/Ausstats/abs@.nsf/0/039E860CED15C3C6CA256F7200 832F17?Open (accessed 4 September 2005).

45   See, e.g., Dewar and Fredericksen, "Prison Heritage," for an account of the potential role of archaeological studies of historical prisons.

46   Elizabeth Scott, "Through the Lens of Gender: Archaeology, Inequality and Those 'of Little Note'," in *Those of Little Note: Gender, Race and Class in Historical Archaeology*, ed. Elizabeth Scott (Tucson: University of Arizona Press, 1994), p. 15.

47   Ibid., p. 14; Janet Spector, "What This Awl Means: Toward a Feminist Archaeology," in *Engendering Archaeology: Women and Prehistory*, ed. J. Gero and M. Conkey (Cambridge: Basil Blackwell, 1991), p. 394.

48   Spector, "What This Awl Means," pp. 392–4.

49   Ibid., p. 388.

50   Ibid., p. 404.

51   Scott, "Through the Lens of Gender," p. 4.

52   Ibid., pp. 7–9; also Suzanne Spencer-Wood, "Peeling the Androcentric Onion in Historical Archaeology," in *Redefining Archaeology: Feminist Perspectives*, ed. M. Casey et al. (Canberra: ANH Publications, 1998), pp. 26–7.

53   Susan Lawrence, "Approaches to Gender in the Archaeology of Mining," in *Redefining Archaeology: Feminist Perspectives*, ed. M. Casey et al. (Canberra: ANH Publications, 1998), pp. 131–2.

54   Ibid., p. 132.

55   Ibid., p. 126.

CHAPTER SIX

Hatred:
Race

As I noted earlier, during the 1970s and 1980s a number of Australian prisons became the subject of official inquiries into allegations of systemic abuse
of inmates by prison staff. Whatever the disposition of individual commissioners of inquiry, the issue of prison reform—especially when directly critical of the day-to-day practices of staff and perceived by them to be rooted in
public demonstrations or other outside "interference" in prison operations—
was regarded by many prison officers as reflecting a social politic broadly
typical of the Left-wing movements which had in some ways defined the
1960s.[1] Inevitably, then, an element of the "backlash" tended to take a politically reactionary form; in other words, there occurred among some prison
officers a move to the far Right.[2]

Several further factors exacerbated this politicization of prison staff:
perhaps the most significant was the rise in the 1970s of the incidence of
drug-related crime, with, as a corollary, a massive increase in inmate numbers and in illicit drug use in prisons. This, in the words of one former prison
officer I spoke to, "changed the place forever."[3] Those involved in day-to-
day inmate management had to contend with new behaviour problems, and at
the same time the inmate demographic was transformed, with a rise in the
social-justice awareness of new inmates; this led in turn to an unusually articulate strand of pro-reform inmate activism that paralleled the reform
movements occurring outside the jails, and hence further aggravated already
discontented staff and inmates.

Concurrent with these changes was an initiative, largely driven by academic departments in the universities, to improve the education of prison
populations overall. This led to influxes of visiting educators into prisons,

fuelling prison officer resentment of both the putative Leftism of the educators,[4] and the opportunities apparently being offered to inmates but not to staff.

Changes were also afoot in the social demographic outside the prison, but of a different kind: the advent of multiculturalism, both as social policy and as a burgeoning cultural condition of a number of Western societies including Australia and Britain, gradually became a catalyst for the rise of right-wing nationalism.[5] This reaction, exacerbated by the concurrent rise of globalization and economic rationalism, would culminate within mainstream Australian society as the quasi-respectable party-political phenomenon of Hansonism; less reputable, but more immediately appealing to a certain type of disaffected or isolated individual, was recourse to overtly racist, neo-Nazi activities. Hence the political complexion of inmate populations began to include a far-Right component, at the same moment that a section of the prison staff were moving toward a comparable position.

I mention Britain in this context for two reasons: Firstly, it happens that, just at the historical moment that the reforms and their outgrowths were occurring, Australian prison officers' numbers were being swelled by a wave of British-born immigrants with previous experience in prison management back home.[6] The exact implications of this are too complex to analyse in any detail here, but the fact should be borne in mind, especially as there is much anecdotal evidence from former staff and inmates to the effect that the British prison officers added a markedly conservative element to an already conservative group, and that they were particularly feared by prisoners for the harshness of their inmate-management styles.[7] It has also been credibly reported that sections of this group came to have inordinate influence over the prison officers' unions. This is a datum of some moment, as the abovementioned shift to the Right by prison officers in Australia was to a large extent sponsored and supported by their unions.[8] The Western Australian Ombudsman cites reports of a secretive power group at Fremantle Gaol and elsewhere known as the "Purple Circle," comprising British-born prison officers; this group was reputedly in control of the Western Australian Prison Officers' Union.[9]

Secondly, and perhaps more directly pertinent to the present topic, in 2003 the British Commission for Racial Equality (CRE) completed an inquiry into the incidence and nature of racism in English and Welsh prisons.

The Commission investigators collected oral and written testimony from current and former inmates and staff, studied internal and departmental reports, and conducted personal observations in the prisons. They concluded that aspects of the prison system in Britain fostered a "culture of racism," both among inmates *and* among staff.[10]

The latter finding—that there were staff members who exhibited racist attitudes and behaviour in their daily interactions with colleagues and inmates—many Britons thought unsurprising, given that the CRE's inquiry was prompted in part by a widely publicized instance of racist victimization of a prison officer by his colleagues, and given, too, that there were numerous reports of inaction by staff and management in cases of inmate-on-inmate racism. These included especially the racist murder of youth detention centre inmate Zahid Mubarek in March 2000. Mubarek, a 19-year-old Feltham Young Offenders Institute inmate of "Asian" descent who was serving a short sentence for a minor theft, was, inexplicably, bunked in a two-man cell with Robert Stewart, a notoriously violent and psychopathically racist young man who had made explicit threats against all non-whites. On the night before Mubarek's scheduled release, Stewart bashed him to death as he slept. The prison administration immediately became subject to intense criticism for apparently allowing the fatal situation to develop, through at least gross negligence or, by some accounts, actively racist agency on the part of prison officers.[11]

If systemic racism was not unexpected, what did come as something of a surprise to investigators was the extent of racism involving or at least tolerated by staff, and its modes of expression; the Commissioners reported that:

> Racist attitudes were often very obvious in prisons during the period covered by our terms of reference. Graffiti put up by prisoners—*and in some cases by staff*—along with the persistent racist taunting engaged in by some staff and prisoners created a background against which overt racial abuse and harassment became a persistent, unchanging feature of life for many staff and prisoners throughout their time working for HM Prison Service or in its custody.[12]

The British prison system Establishment was castigated in these and subsequent inquiries, and in the press, for their defensive and at times obfuscatory responses to allegations of toleration and even encouragement of this racist "background" and its consequences. Under sustained pressure of public opinion and consequent official investigations, that resistance has been somewhat eroded: "In its closing submission [to a government inquiry into Mubarek's death], the Prison Officers Association admitted that the Prison Service was institutionally racist."[13]

It is with the graffiti that I am centrally engaged here. According to the CRE Report's descriptions, the examples viewed were of similar tone and content, whether rendered by prison officer or inmate—that is, racist and extreme nationalist messages and images. Staff graffiti included, for instance, endorsements of the "KKK," and exhortations to, e.g., "PRESERVE WILDLIFE: PICKLE A NIGGER."[14] It must be acknowledged that examples of confirmed staff graffiti (that is, graffiti which appeared in staff-only work areas) were not as common as inmate-produced graffiti; but importantly, the Commissioners noted numerous cases of racist and neo-Fascist inmate graffiti being allowed to remain in place long after being reported to and/or sighted by staff.[15]

The fact that any graffiti at all, of any kind, was produced by prison staff—that is, by nominally responsible adult representatives of the non-transgressive social mainstream—might well seem astonishing on its face. The causes of such behaviour are likely to be complex; I would suggest that in broad terms much is accounted for by the point made earlier, that for the duration of every shift, every prison officer is confined, along with his/her charges, within the total institution. It is arguable, too, that aspects of this apparently incongruous behaviour may also be classed as a variation of the process of "capture," or "surrender," identified by Richard Harding in his study of prison privatization. Harding describes a phenomenon whereby outside representatives of regulatory bodies go native, as it were, and begin to conform to the norms and imperatives of the group they are supposedly overseeing, rather than to "the more remote and abstract public interest."[16] Although the particulars of role and relationship here are obviously not precisely what Harding has in mind—prison officers are not outside regulatory inspectors—it is clear that in general terms the social psychology involved may be similar.

I have made the point previously that the prevalence of inmate graffiti in operational prisons, and the persistence with which inmates revert to the practice despite threatened and/or incurred penalties, suggests an imperative intrinsic to the prison environment—that creating graffiti serves as a form of self-expression that is in some way "natural" for the incarcerated person by virtue of the condition of being incarcerated. Aside from the highly visible and extroverted examples I will discuss shortly, many are of a relatively mundane style and tone, and often seem to be intended as little more than statements of record. For instance, in the hours after his attack on Zahid Mubarek, having been removed to another cell, Robert Stewart documented his deed on the cell wall: "MANCHESTER [Stewart's home city] / KILLED ME PADMATE," followed by a crudely drawn swastika and a brief personal identification "tag."[17]

During my research in Australian former prisons I found a significant number of examples of racist and far-Right graffiti, in cells and inmates' common areas, bearing many similarities to their British counterparts as described in the Commission's report, in terms of affect expressed, terminology, and specific graphic texts. The apparent motivations of graffitists are also similar, including a sense of national dispossession, social disaffection and preoccupation with notional modes of self-empowerment.

   Typical graffiti of the type in question involve designs and/or messages constructed around swastikas, SS emblems and the like. These symbols, it must be acknowledged, are not, of themselves, always conclusive evidence of racist nor even of a strictly political sensibility. The occasional incongruous addition of the circumscribed "A" that signifies anarchist movements, or slogans referring to prisoners' rights movements, suggests that in some cases the Nazi symbols, especially the swastika, may have been depicted more in a spirit of undefined, dilettante rebelliousness than as ideological propaganda. Certainly in the 1970s and 1980s there was a tendency, among the more iconoclastic elements in both the punk and heavy metal movements, to employ imagery of the sort, often for little other than their shock value (the hyperbolical rock band Kiss, with their double-lightning "SS," are a case in point). Cultural theorist Dick Hebdige attributes a more socially responsible motive to the punks in his assertion that "Punks wear swastikas not because they are racist, but because they are not."[18] (But this optimistic notion is countered by more recent analyses of racism among the British punks of the 1970s, which show that there was undeniable anti-Semitism and pro-Nazi intent in the brandishing of swastikas and other Nazi symbols by some of the most prominent members of the punk movement.)[19]

   Such analytical nuances, however, have their limitations in considering the message actually communicated by these kinds of symbols in real-world prison settings. One is liable to find, accompanying graffiti which a sociological scepticism might deem "ambiguous," subsequent "reply" graffiti of a markedly *un*ambiguous bent, stating, for instance, that "NAZIS SUCK," and so on. Whether such replies are straightforward responses to the message perceived in the original text, or the product of the respondent's personal knowledge of the graffitist's beliefs, is generally impossible to say in any given instance; either way, the point stands that within the context of the total institution the practical consequence of drawing a swastika on a wall is to present a pro-Nazi stance. (It is notable, too, that the British CRE commissioners deemed the graffiti they found to be a significant contributing factor in providing the racist and abusive "background" they decried; there is no suggestion in their accounts that they felt it could plausibly be interpreted as innocuous.) In any case, many of the artists have made their agenda very clear: on a cell wall at Melbourne City Watch-house, for instance, a tattered Nazi flag has been drawn with some skill in marking pen, with the caption "KEEP THE FAITH." Likewise, combinations of neo-Nazi symbols and specifically racist texts may, I suggest, be taken at face value.

The political aspect is of course not always prominent; racist terms commonly occur without elaboration, and they can also be aligned with expressions of purely "moral" revulsion. It will be recalled that in Chapter Four we encountered a forcefully rendered graffito exhorting a paedophile to hang himself; it is worth noting that a later graffitist crudely interpolated the word "black" into the original text to precede the epithet "kidfucker."

My fieldwork in Australia took me into few of the types of staff-only areas in which the British CRE investigators found racist graffiti (and those areas I have seen generally show signs of having been freshly repainted); hence I am not in a position to say what might be found there. But as I will show, other signifiers, of the sort identified in the CRE report, imply a degree of complicity among some staff in Australian prisons.

Emblematic of my theme is an image that adorns the interior of a cell in Boggo Road. On the wall immediately above the doorway is a vampire bat, drawn, with considerable attention to anatomical detail and nuances of shading, in black and red marking pen. The animal glares, fanged jaws agape, straight at the viewer. Its symmetrical outstretched wings span almost a metre from wing-tip to wing-tip, and it is perched atop a large Nazi-style swastika. The overall design, in its juxtaposition of the vampire bat and the swastika, is starkly redolent of violence and coercive dominance. The bat, as a Gothic archetype of evil, has obvious connotations of the occult or the mystical (as does the swastika, of course, in its pre-Nazi incarnations); but it is worth noting that, whether by intention or due to the inmate's artistic limitations and even perhaps some unconscious evocation of his cultural milieu, the bat's countenance shows traces of pit-bull terrier—also a potent icon of violence, but manifestly earth-bound, and lending to the image a signally *un*-mystical hint of buzz-cuts and "bovver" boots.

In the assurance of its draughtsmanship, the Boggo Road bat is somewhat unusual (although, as we have seen, not unique) among prisoner graffiti. Its uncompromising malevolence combined with the skill of its rendition make it a highly assertive piece of work; but its assertiveness inheres not only in the image. The artist, apparently harbouring no anxieties regarding self-incrimination, has signed his work with the name "Cliffy."

As mentioned above, the swastika was adopted by certain groups and individuals in the 1970s and 1980s as a spiteful but largely thoughtless symbol of their version of "anarchy," and it is not categorically certain from the bat graffito alone, rancorous though it clearly is, whether Cliffy was a neo-Nazi, a peculiarly angry "Goth," or simply a frustrated tattoo artist (his signature, in fact, is accompanied by a small anarchist symbol). However, he did not confine his artistic efforts to that one locale. Elsewhere in the prison he left rather more of a manifesto, so to speak. In a different cell, covering much of the door and part of the wall and once again sporting a clear, confident signature, is a kind of textual montage in coloured media, comprising a variety of slogans and symbols of the general rebellion type (including an anarchist symbol and a spike-adorned fist captioned "FIGHT THE SYSTEM"), but dominated by a large red swastika and the words "UP THE NAZI PARTY." Below that, the further message "SIEG HEIL BABY" effectively dispels all ambiguity.

Physical evidence indicates that this work may be tentatively dated to the mid-1980s; it is reasonable to infer that the Bat was probably created about the same period. I noted above that as graffitists go, Cliffy seemed markedly unconcerned with preserving his anonymity; in fact, as this image makes clear, he was apparently intent on unabashed advertisement of his philosophical position, and seems to have had little fear of the sort of official repercussions that might have been expected to result from repeated, brazenly offensive defacement of government property. Such disregard for potential consequences might have been a function of a delinquent personality; but in fact it may well be that Cliffy had reason to believe there would *be* no consequences—that in fact he was acting with at least the tacit approval, and perhaps even explicit permission, of the prison's custodial staff.

As I observed in previous chapters, authorities at a number of prisons, including Boggo Road, allowed favoured prisoners to graffiti their cells during the late stages of the prison's operational life. It seems very likely that Cliffy was among those given carte blanche in this way, and therefore that he set to his artistic endeavours believing, correctly, that the normal rules had been set aside in his case.

We cannot know why this particular prisoner was one of those so privileged, and it would be presumptuous to suggest it was specifically because of his beliefs; but there is reason to regard his artwork as receiving a marked degree of toleration. Former Boggo Road staff told me that the pre-decommissioning graffiti was subject to post-facto censorship after the prison's closure, with a number of works being expunged on the grounds that they were too "filthy" or "offensive" to be allowed to remain. Yet swastikas, racism and barefaced promotion of Nazism were, apparently, not deemed "offensive" enough to warrant removal.

An extreme, but entirely plausible, implication of the simultaneous advent of racist, far-Right inmates and prison officers posits an environment in which a degree of collaboration occurs between the two groups on the basis of shared ideology, or at least shared attitude. Such a situation has obvious potential for the subversion of normal inmate-staff relations.

It is known that prison officers have at times enlisted favoured prisoners who display propensities for dominant behaviour to help facilitate inmate management, at which point the "collaboration" can amount to a kind of symbiosis.[20] Far-Right ideology might not be thought intrinsic to such a relationship; however, there does seem to be a tendency for one to go with the other. In "Chopper" Read's first book, published in 1991 while he was serving time in Pentridge, there appeared a snapshot of two prison officers happily posing with an anonymous inmate wearing a Ku Klux Klan hood.[21] Read, who claims to have been allowed to go about the prison armed and to have helped enforce discipline, identifies himself as the person wearing the hood, but avers that it was all "just a joke"—albeit, as he acknowledges, "a joke in poor taste."[22] Yet he also states that he was a "registered" member of the "international brotherhood of the KKK."[23] Read is ambivalent on the subject, making light of his involvement with such groups—an involvement which he states is purely pragmatic in the prison context—while warning that the "anti-Jewish, racist, neo-Nazi and National Action type groups are very active in prison," engaging in aggressive recruiting campaigns from outside.[24]

Joke or not, an image such as Read's "KKK" tableau does prompt questions about the mindset of prison staff who apparently felt comfortable with the creation of a permanent visual record of themselves consorting with one of the state's most dangerous men while he sported one of the most overt, potent and feared symbols of racism since the swastika. Nor, apparently, have they raised any objection to the picture's publication, with a caption identifying them by name, in Read's book (currently in its thirtieth reprinting). To assign to them attitudes that accord with the racism implicit in the hood is beyond what may be fairly undertaken in the interpretation of one photograph; but it may be said that in allowing the photograph to be taken, and to further allow its publication, the persons depicted—including Read—are effectively endorsing a general perception that the culture of laissez-faire masculinism prevalent in prison legitimates not only racism, but the freedom to express it.

Read's assertions are supported by Melbourne neo-Nazi Dane Sweetman, who tells of collusion between inmates and prison officers in forming a violently racist group inside Pentridge known as the "Pentridge Guard."[25] A number of former prison officers have informally confirmed his story to me. None, however, would break the "code of silence" and go on the record on this topic. This points up a problematic aspect of racism in Australian prisons, analogous to the problems barrister David Heilpern was responding to when he began his research in the early 1990s into Australian prison sexual violence—although notoriously prevalent, a lack of formal evidence renders it almost devoid of any forensic standing.[26]

*

Not all of the race-related graffiti found in prisons is right-wing; some may be categorized as "resistance narratives." These are the images and messages rendered by, or in sympathy with, proponents of "Black Power" and Indigenous rights. As Sylvia Kleinert says, "Far from passively acquiescing in the prison environment ... Aborigines occupy, manipulate and coopt the space of the prison for their own purposes." [27] One of the ways in which they do this is through graphic self-expression, in the form of both officially sanctioned murals, and conventional graffiti. A particularly striking example of this is a pencilled cell-wall mural in the Melbourne City Watch House—the only large-scale art work in that entire jail—that sums up the artist's views on the political and legal regimes which have incarcerated him. An Aboriginal man, drawn almost life-size, brandishes traditional weapons as he breaks free of chains; the caption, in large block letters, runs: "OUR LAND—YOUR LAW / PRISONER OF WAR." Here we glimpse the dreadful ironies inherent in the experience of incarceration for Indigenous people, in that the inmate regards the site of the prison itself as rightfully belonging to his own people, and himself as outside the moral jurisdiction of the laws that have placed him in that cell.

At Boggo Road and Fremantle Prisons the red, black and yellow Aboriginal flag, a key symbol of Aboriginal nationalism and resistance, is found in various forms on cell walls, in common areas, and even carved into sandstone walls, along with various slogans that challenge familiar signifiers of Australian identity. One large flag, on the wall of a Boggo Road cell, is notable for its depiction, in the central "sun," of Torres Straight Island land rights campaigner Eddie Mabo as an iconic figure in the Indigenous land rights cause. The date incorporated into the image (1988) is four years before the High Court's decision made the name Mabo a household word throughout Australia.

The creation of such images and, importantly, their survival beyond the institutions' decommissioning must be accounted for, in terms of the theme I am pursuing, of staff collusion in the propagation of pro-White racism. At first glance, they seem to suggest a counterpoint, an actively *anti*-racist element among prison officers intent on Aborigines being allowed to have their say. This may well be true, and I am not suggesting that there were no prison officers sympathetic to Aboriginal causes; however, interviews I have conducted with former prison staff and observations of tours operated by former prison guards tend to reveal something else at work. In a significant number of cases, it seems, prison officers facilitated Aborigines' aspirations to "do their art" for paternalistic reasons which are themselves subtly racist, in that they express and perpetuate the patronising undertone of vestigial colonialism which in the outside world can result in Aboriginal works adorning corporate boardroom walls while their authors languish in poverty.[28] The ironies of this issue have a certain arid banality: during fieldwork at Fremantle

Prison I observed a tour guide extolling for visitors the virtues of the site's Aboriginal murals, whilst outside the walls, local destitute Aborigines begged neighbourhood passers-by for money.

The very high per capita proportion of Aborigines in jail[29] must inevitably encourage correctional staff—even those of broadly sympathetic disposition—to be numbered among the many people in White society who think and speak in terms of the "Aboriginal *problem*," oblivious to the demeaning and depersonalizing connotations of such phrases.[30] The trend among prison officers to encourage Aborigines to "do their art" as a socially positive "outlet" reflects just such an attitude: typical of comments I have heard that reflect such a sensibility is the former prison officer who, while bemoaning to me the putative feckless dissoluteness of the Aborigines (both in and outside jail), pointed out an elaborate mural painted by an Aboriginal inmate and said, "If they would only channel themselves into that sort of thing."

*

A question remains regarding the degree to which race relations—and hence issues regarding the social implications of racist utterances and/or behaviour—within Britain and Australia are equivalent. It is beyond dispute that significant sections of British society today are beset by severe racial tensions.[31] Are Indigenous Australians subject, at least notionally, to comparable levels of hostility, persecution and/or oppression at the hands of their non-Indigenous fellow-citizens as are the various forms of "Asians" and other non-white peoples in Britain? Do immigrants or visitors to Australia from the Middle East, Africa, or Asia have reason to fear the rancour, perhaps even the violence, of extremist Australians of the far Right? Does a swastika daubed on an Australian wall, accompanied perhaps by a declaration of white superiority, provoke a justified sense of dread in a non-white or Jewish person approximately equivalent to that felt by a British counterpart? More to the point, how does such a sign affect an Australian prison inmate of Aboriginal or Middle-Eastern or Asian or African or Jewish origins, when they see it on a wall within the total institution?

No doubt many Australians would dispute the idea that our society has reached, or is even approaching, the sort of dire pass Britain is enduring. Clearly, our cities do not share with the urban areas of Britain the population characteristics of sheer numbers or high density that tend to exacerbate all forms of social tension. However, this optimistic perception, while undoubtedly accurate in much of Australia, overlooks the growing race-related problems focused in certain geographical areas—urban and rural—in which high concentrations of either Indigenous people or non-white immigrant groups have, since the 1970s, been accumulating alongside the traditional "Anglo"-Australian populations, and in which there has been a concomitant rise in racial violence. Events at certain Sydney beach suburbs such as Cronulla in 2005 tend to confirm this, but the situation has a longer history than many Australians realize. A 1989 study concluded that the incidence of racist violence in Australia had in fact grown to a level comparable to that of Britain,[32] and more recently, a 2004 Australian Institute of Criminology (AIC) study of areas of high migrant concentrations reported that 38 per cent of assaults on people of migrant groups were perceived as racially motivated, more than three times the rate for the general population.[33]

A crucial aspect of this multi-cultural clustering is that such enclaves are in many cases located in the same low-income areas which have historically provided a disproportionately high percentage of the prison populations. With the advent of this ethnic clustering has come increasing numbers of Middle-Eastern and Asian inmates into Australian prisons.[34] A high proportion of migrants were among the influx of drug offenders mentioned above who had, in the eyes of many staff, contributed to undesirable changes in the prison culture. One former prison officer, whom I will not identify here but who had made the transition to tour guide, told me candidly, and with some intensity of feeling, of his own and other officers' depth of resentment toward these new inmates, for their part in irrevocably altering the overall tone of the prison with which he was associated. He stated that the decline of "standards" all began with "Vietnamese inmates getting their own rice cookers." (He then announced that he was a member of Pauline Hanson's One Nation Party, and proudly showed me his firearms collection stored in his garden shed. He also (off the record) confirmed the KKK-prison connection, as, too, did a former prison welfare officer who identified a group of racist prison officers as having links with the KKK.)

Further, in recent decades the remainder of the Anglo-Australian populations of the new migrant areas produced most of the young, under-employed and radically disaffected "skinhead" foot-soldiers of neo-Nazi groups such as White Australian Resistance and National Action, which were increasingly active from the early 1970s into the 1990s.[35] (There has been a marked decline in the number of such groups in Australia since they were effectively made illegal by the introduction of the *Racial Discrimination Act* 1995.)

Little more than a generation has passed since Australian schoolchildren were being taught that the Aborigines were a "stone-age" people with no future; during much of the period under discussion here, pre-Mabo, the legal concept of *Terra Nullius* still conferred a quasi-legitimacy on whites' sense of proprietorship over the continent as found, which in turn fuelled profound resentment in some quarters at concepts such as Indigenous land rights. Also, the various effects of globalization, and the mass movements of African, Middle-Eastern and Asian refugees (the so-called "Asian invasion") have produced very similar responses from the disaffected extreme Right in Western societies throughout the world. Certainly, the parallels are sufficiently close to be apparent to the members of that alienated sector: Zahid Mubarek's murderer wrote a letter to a friend, in which he enthusiastically told of having watched and closely identified with the Australian film *Romper Stomper*, about rampaging skinheads in western-suburban Melbourne, two days before going on his own catastrophic rampage.[36]

As the graffiti examples already discussed indicate, not all, nor even most, prison graffiti is racist. Many of the texts one finds on cell walls are humdrum; many are sexual; many are straightforwardly aggressive and/or vengeful toward other prisoners or hated staff members, and some are surprisingly solicitous. But race has long been a problem in prisons—the nature of the total institution inevitably intensifies incipient social tensions, and this is exacerbated among incarcerated populations by the perennial over-representation of certain ethnic groups such as Aborigines. As the British CRE report rightly concludes, it is incumbent on staff at all levels, and on the prison system overall, to ameliorate rather than exacerbate such conditions. The AIC study on racial violence in Australia noted above identifies graffiti as one of the aspects of racism in need of further investigation; I would make the further point that there has not been any substantive analysis of race-motivated graffiti in Australian prisons—historical or contemporary—and suggest that such an investigation could well begin there.

*

The images I have examined in this and the previous two chapters present problems for both social scientists and museum curators, but in different ways. The latter tend to be guided by the presumed standards of the (paying) public regarding "vandalism" and what is "decent." As I have said, in historical prisons operating as tourist sites, most graffiti is obliterated from surfaces destined for public viewing, with an active pretence maintained in some cases that there never was any graffiti. The examples I have been granted access to are, in the main, sequestered from the public eye. On the other hand, researchers, for whom such texts stand as latent narratives of the total institution, must deal with questions of privacy equivalent to those encountered when accessing archival material, such as personal files, on persons still living.[37] Some of the authors of the texts mentioned here created those texts with a knowing eye to future audiences; some, on the other hand, produced what they believed were private expressions of despair, frustration or anguish. Discerning between these extremes is highly problematical, and their exposure in the public forum of scholarly investigation must therefore be done with caution. But the preservation and study of such material is essential if we are to understand the archetypal othered of our society, and the implications of that othering for our current prison system.

NOTES

1   Grabosky, *Wayward Governance*, ch. 2; Knapp interview; Armstrong interview; Forbes, "Prison Officers Offered $10,000."
2   The term "far Right" is, admittedly, rather broad, and also has been the subject of rather scant and sporadic study in the context of Australia's relatively temperate polity. Andrew Moore, "Writing About the Extreme Right in Australia," *Labour History* no. 89, November 2005. Here it refers to the range of political stances and attitudes from outright neo-Nazism all the way to the legal and quasi-respectable "Hansonism" of the "One Nation" party at what might be termed the "moderate" end of the spectrum. Pauline Hanson, the party's populist founder, developed a strong following in the mid-to-late 1990s among certain sections of middle Australia. Michael Leach, "Hansonism, Political Discourse and Australian Identity" in *The Rise and Fall of One Nation*, ed. Michael Leach, Geoffrey Stokes and Ian Ward (St Lucia, University of Queensland Press, 2000).
3   Armstrong interview.
4   Ibid.; Hoffman interview.
5   See, e.g., Hans-George Betz, *Radical Right-Wing Populism in Western Europe* (New York: Martin's Press, 1994), Ch. 4; P. Fray, "Might of the Right," *Sydney Morning Herald*, 27 April 2002.; Leach, "Hansonism."

6   Tony Vinson, *Wilful Obstruction* (Sydney: Methuen, 1982).

7   Knapp interview; Smith interview; M. Clarke (former Pentridge prison officer), interview 30 March 2001; R. Gill (former Pentridge prison officer and governor), interview 30 March 2001; P. Riley (former Pentridge prison officer and governor), interview 30 March 2001; Paul R.M. Wilson (former Pentridge inmate), personal communication to author, 1989. Former staff at Fremantle and Boggo Road spoke to me in similar terms, but declined to go "on record" on the subject.

8   Vinson, *Wilful Obstruction*; *idem*, "Reforming Prisons: A 1970s Experience," conference paper, History of Crime, Policing and Punishment, Canberra: Australian Institute of Criminology, 9–10 December 1999; Harding, *Private Prisons*.

9   Ombudsman WA, *Deaths in Prisons*, pp. 18–19.

10 CRE, "Racial Equality in Prisons, Part 2"; *idem*, "The murder of Zahid Mubarek" (news release), 2003, http://www.cre.gov.uk/media/nr_arch/2003/nr030709.html (accessed 24 March 2005).

11 CRE, "Murder of Zahid Mubarek"; see also Dominic Casciani, "The Murder of Zahid Mubarek," BBC News, 18 November 2004, http://news.bbc.co.uk/1/hi/uk/3198264.stm (accessed 24 March 2005); Laura Smith, "Inmate Killed 'in gladiator fight set up for staff bet'," *The Guardian*, 4 March 2005; *idem*, "Mubarek 'could have been saved 15 times'," *The Guardian*, 29 April 2005; D. Batty, "Youth Jail Officers 'resisted equality training'," *The Guardian*, 28 February 2005.

12 CRE, "Racial Equality in Prisons," p. 47 (emphasis added).

13 Smith, "Mubarek 'could have been saved 15 times'." The Mubarek inquiry itself, finally instituted five years after the killing, was the product of repeated appeals by his family and their supporters (including the CRE) through the courts all the way to the Law Lords, who ordered the Home Secretary to conduct a public investigation into the prison system's role in the affair. Ibid.

14 CRE, "Racial Equality in Prisons," p. 51.

15 Ibid., pp. 50–3.

16 Richard Harding, *Private Prisons and Public Accountability*, Buckingham: Open University Press, 1997, pp. 33, 43.

17 Casciani, "Murder of Zahid Mubarek."

18 Dick Hebdige, *Subculture: The Meaning of Style*, London: Methuen, 1979 (cited in Macdonald, *The Graffiti Subculture*, p. 43.)

19 Roger Vadim, "'I Won't Let That Dago By': Rethinking Punk and Racism," in *Punk Rock, So What? The Cultural Legacy of Punk*, ed. *idem* (London: Routledge, 1999), pp. 207–11.

20 Heilpern, *Fear or Favour*, p. 86; Knapp interview; Read, *Chopper: From the Inside*.

21 Read, *Chopper: From the Inside*.

22 Ibid., p. 125.

23 Ibid.

24 Ibid.

25 John Silvester and Andrew Rule, *Underbelly: True Crime Stories* (Smithfield NSW: Floradale, 2001), pp. 199–203

26 See Heilpern, *Fear or Favour*.

27 Sylvia Kleinert, "Revisiting the Prison: Museums in a Penal Landscape", Round Table No. 15, History and the Museum: New Narratives?, 20th International Congress of Historical Sciences, Sydney 3–9 July 2005.

28 R. Neill, *White Out: How Politics is Killing Black Australia* (Sydney: Allen and Unwin, 2002), p. 176; .

29 See Australian Bureau of Statistics, Year Book Australia: Crime and Justice: Indigenous Prisoners, http://www.abs.gov.au/Ausstats/abs@.nsf/0/11d3d2aeb026b334ca256dea000 53a79?OpenDocument (accessed 20 September 2005); Australian Human Rights and Equal Opportunity Commission, Aboriginal and Torres Strait Islander Social Justice, "Aboriginal and Torres Strait Islander People in Australia" [Indigenous Peoples and criminal Justice Systems], http://www.hreoc.gov.au/social_justice/statistics (accessed 20 September 2005); Kleinert, "Revisiting the Prison."

30 Jacqueline Wilson, Review of *Dumping Ground: A History of the Cherbourg Settlement* by Thom Blake, *History Australia* 1 no. 2, July 2004.

31 For an overview of the British problem, see CRE Homepage at http://www.cre.gov.uk and links.

32 Stephen Nugent, Meredith Wilkie and Robyn Iredale, *Violence Today: No. 8: Racist Violence* (Canberra: Australian Institute of Criminology, 1989).

33 Holly Johnson, "Experiences of Crime in Two Selected Migrant Communities," *Trends and Issues in Crime and Criminal Justice* no. 302, Australian Institute of Criminology, http://www.aic.gov.au./publications/tandi2/tandi302.pdf (accessed 10 October 2005).

34 Satyanshu Mukherjee, *Ethnicity and Crime: A Report Prepared for the Department of Immigration and Multicultural Affairs* (Canberra: Australian Institute of Criminology, 1999), pp. 48–67.

35 On the links between poverty, male youth disaffection and "hate" crimes, see Stephen Tomsen, "Hate Crimes and Masculinity: New Crimes, New Responses and Some Familiar Patterns," paper to the 4th National Outlook Symposium on Crime in Australia, "New Crimes or New Responses", Canberra: Australian Institute of Criminology, 21–22 June 2001; more generally on the geographical, socio-economic and cultural aspects of disaffection among under-class whites in Australia, see Jacqueline Z. Wilson, "Invisible Racism: The Language and Ontology of 'White Trash'," *Critique of Anthropology* 22 no. 4, December 2002.

36 Casciani, "Murder of Zahid Mubarek."

37 Dewar, "Forgotten Fragments."

PART THREE

Fame

The Adelaide Gaol, which first held prisoners in 1841, has operated as a prison museum since 1988. On the History page of its website there appears a short list of "some famous names associated with the Gaol."[1] These include Sister Mary MacKillop, for her pastoral work with inmates, and, in contrast, a handful of particularly infamous prisoners. Included among them, and the only one widely known outside South Australia, is the early-twentieth-century Melbourne gangster Leslie "Squizzy" Taylor. The website visitor learns that among the site's historical artefacts is an elaborate horsehair-and-mother-of-pearl "necklace ornament" supposedly made by the notorious Taylor "while he was being held in Adelaide Gaol."[2] The Gaol, we are told, "acquired" the item in 1991, but no details are given as to how this occurred, nor to support its alleged provenance. The reader *is* told, rather unexpectedly, that

> While there is no official record of Taylor ever being in Adelaide Gaol it is possible that he was held while using an assumed name....He was known to have been in Adelaide several times but only convicted once when fined £5 for theft.[3]

In other words, on the slim chance that "Squizzy" Taylor was at some stage arrested, appeared in court and then served time there, all under an alias despite his nationwide notoriety and being known to Adelaide police, the Adelaide Gaol chooses to feature him prominently among those "famous names associated with the Gaol."

Two interrelated things are happening here. Firstly, those responsible for promoting the prison as a tourist attraction have, in keeping with the routine practice noted earlier, installed an array of "markers" on the website; yet in the case of Squizzy Taylor, as presented, the marker they have put up is puzzlingly equivocal—analogous to a sign in a Massachusetts inn saying, "George Washington *might* have slept here." Put in these terms, such a display looks rather slight, even a little desperate. Secondly—and this provides the motive for the practice—in presenting this infamous name as having an association with the former prison, the site is employing a staple device of prison museum representation, which is to make prominent mention of any particularly well-known inmates—"celebrity prisoners"—whom the prison may have ever contained or even simply have some connection with, however distant. Thus at sites everywhere, tour presentations almost invariably feature anecdotes, artefacts and/or other "relics" of particularly notorious characters such as Ned Kelly (and his mother, Ellen), the aforementioned Squizzy Taylor, or Chopper Read—and if they are not mentioned, visitors can be relied on to ask about them.

NOTES

1   http://www.adelaidegaol.org.au/working.htm (accessed 10 March 2008).
2   Ibid, http://www.adelaidegaol.org.au/working.htm#taylor (accessed 10 March 2008).
3   Ibid.

CHAPTER SEVEN

The Celebrity Prisoner Confined:
Relics of a Desperate Act

A theme very commonly featured at former prisons, and one which holds great interest for both visitors and tour guides, is that of escapes and escape attempts. As historical episodes in the life of the prison, escapes embody inherent elements of both drama and novelty. Further, insofar as they seem predicated upon a universal motivation—the desire for freedom—they have the potential to provide a museum experience with which the visitor may be able to empathize more readily than representations of other out-of-routine dramas such as, for instance, floggings or periods of solitary confinement.

There are certain abiding characteristics in the way escapes are treated as fragments of public history—characteristics which exemplify the euphemization noted earlier. Except in those cases where escape attempts have resulted in unequivocally tragic consequences (such as the death of Prison Officer Hodson when Ronald Ryan and Peter Walker forced their way out of Pentridge in 1966, and Ryan's subsequent execution for the murder),[1] there is, I have found, a marked tendency for escapes to be recounted or depicted pretty much as "comic relief"—an opportunity for curators or tour guides with reputations to uphold as vivacious raconteurs to present and exploit the more "entertaining" aspects of life inside.

A prime example is the escape attempt depicted at Old Dubbo Gaol in east-central New South Wales, which I visited in January 2003. This display, which visitors observed from the open doorway of a cell, comprised a pair of life-sized animatronic mannequins costumed as colonial-era inmates, semi-frozen in the act of decamping from their cell through a hole in the ceiling. As a visual entertainment, the tableau was, as these things tend to be, rather stiff and kinetically limited; the chief "hook" lay in the accompanying audio presentation, which, one was left to assume, purported to reproduce dialogue typical of men engaged in such a pursuit. This dialogue, however, reflected virtually none of the terrible anxiety, nor the common-sense discretion, one might expect to inhere in a highly secret, physically difficult and extremely hazardous enterprise on which depended both desperately desired liberty and perhaps life itself. In fact, to judge from the giggling euphoria of their incautious banter as they laboured toward freedom, the two would-be escapees were engaged in little more than a risible jape—a rather jolly, and by implication inconsequential, antic.

In keeping with this tone, as one proceeded about the Old Dubbo site's external spaces, a further selection of "escapees" could be spotted here and there—static mannequins perched atop the exterior walls in mid-escape. These fragmentary displays were devoid of interpretative commentary and essentially contributed nothing more than occasional moments of innocuous visual amusement. The overall impression given was of something of a silent epidemic of absconders which could at any moment give rise to a "Keystone Kops"-style hue-and-cry. (I should mention that the curator at Old Dubbo Gaol, who had put in place there some fine and properly thought-provoking displays on a variety of topics, inherited the dummies and animatronics from her predecessor, and at the time of my visit had been trying for some time, in the face of stiff local opposition, to dispense with them.)[2]

But my purpose here is not to discuss at any length the notional colonial-era escape attempts depicted at Old Dubbo Gaol, however emblematic of my theme they may be; rather, I wish to consider the representation of a real escape attempt that occurred well within living memory, at an incarceration site of a rather different type, in rural Victoria.

A couple of hours' drive west of Melbourne, in the town of Ararat, is a nineteenth-century bluestone edifice, originally built in 1861 as a goldfields county prison but converted in 1886, under the authority of the then Lunacy Department, into a twenty-eight-bed institution for the "criminally insane." In this capacity it was reopened in 1887 as "J Ward," an annexe of nearby Aradale Psychiatric Hospital. Aradale subsequently became the State of Victoria's Centre of Forensic Psychiatry, with J Ward as its main high-security detention centre for mentally ill criminal offenders. J Ward would retain this role for over a century, until its final decommissioning in 1991.[3]

In his first book, Chopper Read succinctly characterized J Ward as "a dark legend…in the minds of the men who have been in it."[4] Read himself was not detained there; but as a resident of Pentridge he was well placed to gain some insights into the experience of those who were. For much of its career, J Ward had a close relationship with Pentridge. Home at times to over 1,200 inmates,[5] Pentridge had its own discrete, on-site sub-prison for emotionally or psychologically disturbed prisoners, known as "G Division," and a staff of forensic psychologists; it was not, however, adequately equipped to deal on a long-term basis with prisoners suffering full-blown mental illness or florid psychotic episodes, nor with those deemed by the courts to be unsuitable for conventional imprisonment for their crimes on the grounds of insanity. The latter category—the "criminally insane"—were in general consigned directly to J Ward, in whose care they would live out the duration of their illnesses—which in some cases, of course, meant the duration of their lives. (The centre's present heritage administrators report that in at least two cases elderly inmates passed away, still incarcerated, after spending upwards of six decades under J Ward's jurisdiction.)[6] The former group—prisoners of Pentridge who, for one reason or another (including, in many cases, simply the experience of imprisonment), became too disturbed for G Division— were transported, on an ad hoc basis, the 200 kilometres to the Ararat centre, as and when they were deemed to be in need of its superior facilities (and, like any hospital, subject to availability of beds). There they would spend anything from a few days to many weeks, undergoing whatever psychiatric treatment was judged necessary to render them fit to return to conventional imprisonment.

It is important to understand the criteria by which the mental and emotional health of Pentridge inmates was assessed, and with that the systemic assumptions underpinning their consignment, or otherwise, to Ararat. Unsurprisingly, there were inmates in Pentridge whose temperament, circumstances while incarcerated (such as suffering repeated rape or assault), or disordered personalities rendered them uncontrollably emotional, prone to suicidal or para-suicidal behaviour, or intractably unruly or violent. In keeping with the low priority routinely given to individual inmate welfare, such inmates could find themselves in G Division not necessarily because they needed help, but because their mental or emotional state made them a *management* problem. And it further follows that if their condition could not be successfully dealt with in G Division, then a period in J Ward might well be indicated, and in at least some cases this decision would occur "less on clinical grounds than as a respite for the correctional system."[7]

Given such an operative norm, it would be no surprise to find that many custodial staff tended toward generally indifferent, even derisory, attitudes to the distress suffered by inmates so unable to handle life inside that they found themselves in G Division or packed off to J Ward; nor that elements of the colloquial workplace language of those officers came to reflect such attitudes. This was brought home to me when, in the course of interviewing a former Pentridge Governor of Security, I asked him what he thought about G Division and the inmates "who couldn't cope with the stress of prison life." His response I found rather startling in both its uncompromising forthrightness and linguistic tenor: "They're real weak guys," he said, "their lives were hell—borderline, inadequate people; they were the butt of the joke. It's very hard with these borderline mental defectives."[8] I was further struck by his use of what I later learned was the standard term among Pentridge staff for the transfer of a prisoner to J Ward: in reference to the fact that it involved a two-to-three-hour road trip in a prison vehicle, consignment to the Ararat centre was known derisorily as "van therapy."[9]

There is more than mere callous sarcasm expressed here; over and above the plainly dismissive implications of such a phrase, the word *therapy* itself, as used by prison insiders, has darkly ambiguous overtones not obvious to those outside the system, for, as we have seen, aside from its clinical meaning, "therapy" also stood as a euphemism within prisons for premeditated violence inflicted on an inmate by prison officers. While I am not suggesting that the word literally signified anything of the kind in the case of the J Ward "transportees," its usage in the expression "van therapy" certainly carried connotations of coercive power, and in the process furthered the contemptuous othering of those members of the prison population who possessed the least power of all.

*

J Ward is now open for regular guided tours, with the tour guides, who are drawn from the volunteer group "Friends of J Ward," schooled in anecdotes and information supplied by the institution's former custodial staff. Unlike Dubbo, tours of J Ward are fully guided; visitors receive a fairly tightly structured and rehearsed exposition of selected portions of the jail, including a nineteenth-century gallows (legacy of the centre's pre-psychiatric days as a county prison), the chapel, various items of paraphernalia such as straitjackets, and the "shock-treatment room" (about which, more later). The latter part of the tour takes in what is termed the "old building"—a part of the original structure utilized, in its modern incarnation, as the jail's high-security division. Once inside the three-storey building and after traversing various rabbit-warren corridors, the tour pauses in a ground-floor cell, where visitors' attention is directed upward to a large discoloured area of brickwork high on a whitewashed wall. That, the guide announces with a certain jovial relish, is the visible evidence of an escape attempt made by Garry Ian Patrick David (1954-1993), the institution's most notorious prisoner—and by tacit suggestion in some ways its "maddest," although he was not formally diagnosed as "mentally ill." Changes in the mid-1980s to the legal definition of mental illness and its relationship with the Crimes Act rendered the forensic status of David's mental state problematic.[10] David (who was also known, against his will, as Garry Webb)[11] was one of Pentridge Prison's most emotionally volatile, violent and unstable inmates, and as such was a frequent beneficiary of "van therapy."[12] The cell with the discoloured bricks was his, and the decor in the corridor outside it consists chiefly of press clippings recounting his infamous career of violent crimes, threats against persons and society, profound emotional instability and the single-minded campaign of self-mutilation that eventually killed him.[13]

In 1990 Garry David became the only prisoner in Victoria's penal history to be consigned, by special Act of parliament, to indefinite imprisonment after completing his original sentence, not on the grounds of mental illness—which would have justified his detention "at the Governor's pleasure"—but on the grounds of the presumed threat he posed to society if released. This unique legal status was imposed on him after a routine search of his H Division cell in Pentridge unearthed a written plan to perpetrate a massacre on his release. David claimed that he had merely been following his psychiatrist's advice and putting his thoughts and feelings on paper, with no intention of ever following through with the objectives expressed.

The special legislation brought down expressly to cover David's case was extremely controversial, and gave rise to a complex and highly charged public debate over issues relating to civil liberties, prisoners' rights, community safety, and forensic definitions of mental illness; despite his being deceased since 1993 the debate is far from over, and the literature is extensive, both in legal/criminological circles and, especially, the mainstream press. The press was divided approximately along broadsheet-versus-tabloid lines: the latter took a fairly firm "community safety" stance that advocated continued detention (interestingly, in the process of siding against him, the tabloids tended to refer to David by his bureaucracy-imposed aka of "Webb," which he hated); the broadsheets offered a generally more measured discussion taking in, among other things, the prisoner's viewpoint, and most especially the civil liberty implications.[14] It is not my intention here to argue the wisdom or otherwise of the authorities' reaction to David's manifesto; but it should be noted that *if* he really was doing what he said he was doing—simply indulging in a clinically-sanctioned cathartic expression of his feelings—then it is possible that his chief mistake was to put it on paper and not on his cell wall, for the document may be viewed as in some degree equivalent to much of the graffiti with which prisoners routinely adorn their living environment. Although generally neither as organized nor as articulate as the programme Garry David committed to notepaper, as we have seen, exhortations and aspirations to "kill all cops," "off the cunt who put me here," and so on (not to mention the ubiquitous racist and neo-Nazi signs and sentiments), abound on cell walls.

Whatever the veracity of his explanation, it was in large part on the strength of this "manifesto" that a psychiatric panel agreed that (a) although at times highly disturbed and harbouring a significant personality disorder, David was not "mentally ill" in any sense that would legally permit his indefinite detention; and (b) he would almost certainly re-offend if released, probably with extreme violence. Suddenly labelled, hyperbolically, "the most dangerous man in the Victorian prison system," David found himself the subject of the only individually "customized" Act the Victorian Parliament ever passed, the *Community Protection Act* 1990, which effectively ensured that he stood little chance of ever being released. ("Customized" is not figurative; the Act actually named David as its specific subject.)[15] Whether he really was the "most dangerous" man in the state, there is no doubt that by the time he died, at thirty-eight, Garry David was the most comprehensively and explicitly othered.

David was born in 1954 to a mother who has been described as "hopelessly alcoholic," and an extremely violent, paedophilic father. His first institutional placement, in an orphanage, occurred at the age of five; he would go on to follow an all-too-common trajectory as a ward of the State, enduring a succession of institutions and youth detention centres, until, at seventeen, he first arrived in Pentridge's C Division, convicted of stealing motor vehicles.

It happened that his father, Rupert, was already there, and made a serious attempt to resume the abuse he had inflicted on his son as a child.[16]

As the *Sydney Morning Herald* colourfully put it at the height of the debate about what to do with him, "Look at Gary [*sic*] David's deprived and depraved history for a moment—it's the closest thing you will find to a stir-and-bake recipe for a psychopath."[17] There is little reason to doubt that by the time he reached adulthood, Garry David was, in the fullest possible sense, "institutionalized." Between that ill-omened debut at seventeen into the adult prison world and his self-inflicted death twenty-one years later, he spent less than a year outside the correctional system[18] (and some who knew him suggest he did not really want to leave it).[19] His offences escalated in seriousness from theft to crimes of increasing violence, until at age twenty-eight, having developed a pathological hatred of authority figures, especially police, he resolved to kill a police officer in an ambush. This ambition (which he furthered by first shooting a complete stranger as "bait" to draw police into his trap) resulted in a fourteen-year sentence for attempted murder. It was in the latter days of that sentence that the Act was passed to keep him in Pentridge, and it was there, three years later, that he finally "went too far" at the culmination of an incessant, thirteen-year campaign of self-mutilation, and inflicted upon himself a fatal abdominal wound. He was thirty-eight.

And so today, having confronted the press clippings, visitors to J Ward are told that the discoloured patch on the cell's brickwork indicates repairs done where Garry David, the definitive "menace to society," breached the wall, removing enough bricks to admit his slight frame and allow him access to an adjoining stairwell. Having gained the stairs he ascended to the top floor, where he removed yet more brickwork from yet another wall and thence, by virtue of some considerable acrobatics, achieved entry to a small roof cavity. Once inside this space, he removed a number of the slate tiles above his head, and climbed out onto the steeply pitched roof. There, however, his ingenuity failed him. There was no way down from the roof save by returning through the hole to the stairwell, where he knew a welcoming committee would be waiting.

The tour guide by now is in her element. Having painted for her audience a picture of the infamous and desperate David, for all his toil precariously perched on the sloping tiles forty feet up with nowhere to go, she presents the denouement with a sort of jolly school-marmish pride:

> Garry climbed back into the roof space, and there he stayed. The staff were outside and had a meeting. They decided it was too difficult to go in after him, so they should leave him there to come out of his own accord. So he stayed there, in the roof, for three days. It was the chops that got him down. Every Sunday there was a roast dinner cooked for the prisoners, and this particular Sunday it was chops. The smell of the chops cooking went up to where he was, and he couldn't stand it, and out he came, for his dinner. So there you go; even Garry had a roast dinner.

Both the story and the manner of its telling imply an operational ethos in J Ward of benign institutional wisdom and good-humoured paternalism: *Good old J Ward, looking after even the maddest and baddest—they can get up to their little bits of mischief, their escapades, and what's the response? Chops.* And David in particular—or rather the public-history representation of David—is the prime example, in J Ward, of the celebrity prisoner.

Having been entertained by the story of Garry and the chops, the next step for the tourist visitor is to participate in his commodification. This occurs when visitors eventually arrive at a souvenir-cum snack shop on an upper floor, a quaint sort of "kiosk" run by volunteers. Prominent among various items for sale is a sizable stack of pieces of slate tile, priced at $2:50 each, every one stencilled in white with certification of authenticity. The tiles, we are told, are those very ones removed by "Garry" during his escape attempt. So the visitor is given the opportunity to come away with a notional "relic" of Garry David's "adventure in the roof." What the visitor is not made aware of is that the tile fragments on display actually come from a very large stack of tiles—an entire roof's worth, in fact—that lies outside in a non-public area at the back—the result of having the roof replaced some years ago. Again, one is reminded of Julia Clarke's point regarding the vital distinction that public historians need to make between a supposed "authenticity" and "integrity."

I suggest that in commodifying David's escape attempt, and by doing so in such a cynically pragmatic manner, the gatekeepers complete the process of euphemization and trivialization of his experience of J Ward—that is, the experience, or rather the accumulation of experiences, that prompted such a desperate act in the first place. This raises a question whose answer seems prima facie obvious: Why do inmates attempt to escape? Why, in particular, did Garry David try it?

The "obvious" answer is: To avert confinement—an uncomplicated quest for freedom. But whatever the principles nominally underpinning incarceration as a standard punishment for social deviance, the realities of imprisonment tend to include characteristic experiences of suffering that far exceed mere deprivation of liberty.

The violence inherent in the prison experience has long been notorious; and, as has also become notorious in recent years, in many prisons that violence has often been inflicted upon inmates as much by their custodians as by their fellow-prisoners. Of course, in civil societies such as ours, such systemic violence transgresses the laws and regulations upon which the penal institution is based and operated—in other words, it is illegal, and constitutes a form of corruption. The practice of punitively "managing" refractory prisoners by lawful, ritualized corporal punishment, in the form of flogging, was banned over forty years ago in Victoria, and this and other reforms of recent decades mean that, by and large, the troublesome prisoner can expect legitimate punishment oriented more toward isolation, or radical loss of privileges, than the infliction of tangible harm.

J Ward, however, was not an ordinary prison. It is notable that the tour guides refer to the former inhabitants variously as "inmates," "prisoners," "patients," or "criminals," depending, it seems, partly on context and partly on whim, and in this indeterminacy of nomenclature may be glimpsed something of the institution's ambiguous and rather peculiar nature as both a jail and a clinical venue.

As has been noted, jails are centrally concerned with containment—both preventive and punitive—and only secondarily with the welfare of their inmates; but as a clinical venue J Ward was premised on a moral and legal acknowledgement that its inmates were by definition mentally unfit to discern right from wrong, whatever their crimes may have been, and that they were therefore legitimately entitled to be treated as patients, with the standard entitlements of patients that their welfare be given a high priority, and that their (necessary) containment comprise no punitive component. That there is a tension inherent in such a situation is obvious. The manifold details of how that tension played out for the inmates is beyond the scope of this discussion;[20] but there was one aspect of J Ward's day-to-day operations that I suggest stood as a direct expression of it: the regular use of electro-convulsive therapy—"E.C.T." or, as it is colloquially known, "shock treatment"—as both a form of psychotherapy and as an inmate management technique.

As at Dubbo, mannequins abound in J Ward, although lacking Dubbo's animatronic dynamism. On the ground floor of the old building, in the latter part of the tour, the visitor to J Ward today is guided to a room containing a bed, an electrical apparatus, and two dummies, one standing, dressed in clinical white coat, the other—the "patient"— supine in the bed, with the E.C.T. wires attached to its head. The implication is that this room, or another like it, is where the "therapy" was administered—a suitably private place. But in response to a direct question from a visitor in the group, the tour guide rather awkwardly admits that the treatments were in fact carried out in the corridor *outside* the room. As to the treatments' purpose: while the official line is that E.C.T. really was used as *therapy*, in accordance with psychiatric wisdom of the day, when pressed the tour guide (who on the day I was last there was J Ward's former head nurse) confirms the alternative explanation: "The inmates very rarely acted up, because they knew that if they acted up, they'd get a dose of shock therapy."[21] Further, we are told, for many years it was standard practice at J Ward to administer E.C.T. *without anaesthetic.*

Yet the punitive nature of the treatment is still subtly euphemized for the visitor: as the tour group hears it, the selection of E.C.T. patients at least lay in the hands of the most responsible professional possible—the consulting psychiatrist: "The psych's orders were: 'him, him and him', and you had to drag 'em from the yards," from which one infers that such choices were the product of a clinical examination of the patients; but during a later interview with the guide I rather doggedly pursued this issue, and he admitted, with notable reticence, that it was in fact the senior nursing staff, that is, those concerned with day-to-day inmate management, who advised the psychiatrist whom to select ("The psychs were busy men, after all"), and that the selected inmates "would be dragged, kicking and screaming" to receive their "therapy." (It is also worth noting, too, that an even simpler selection process determined who qualified for a period in a strait-jacket; that particular behaviour-management decision was left entirely in the hands of the nursing staff, with no higher ratification required.)[22]

The key inference to be made from all this is that long after flogging was outlawed in the State of Victoria, J Ward uniquely retained the legal use of a punishment technique arguably as terrible, and as feared. And if we wish to guess at what sort of motive a man might have for attempting to escape such a place, one need look no further than the existence of such a regime.

I briefly quoted Chopper Read earlier, on the subject of J Ward; in the same book Read, who has often spoken of the hard upbringing he endured, also had something to say about Garry David, with whom he was imprisoned in H Division at Pentridge:

> My old Dad used to say to me that we complain about having no shoes until we see a man with no feet. If I was born with no shoes, Garry was born with no feet....I don't feel sorry for many men, but Garry's hopeless situation makes me feel sorry. His life seems to have no answers.[23]

That Read takes this altruistic view of David is of some interest, in the context of the sociology of the total institution. Among the many instances of Pentridge prisoners during the 1970s and 1980s who felt, for a variety of reasons, that they had no recourse other than to inflict very significant bodily harm on themselves, two achieved a high degree of public notoriety: Read, for the self-amputation of his ears that led to a para-suicide "copy-cat" group in Pentridge known as the "Van Gogh club,"[24] and Garry David, who inherited Read's mantle as the leading "Van Gogh"[25] in the course of an unparalleled thirteen-year campaign of self-endangerment and self-harm that was wildly excessive even by Pentridge standards, and whose file by the end of his life recorded over eighty instances of self-mutilation.[26]

As I noted above, both men are examples of the celebrity prisoners that tend to feature in historical prisons' narratives and tourist promotion; Read, however, may also be counted among the "success stories" of the prison system—success in the sense of having had the necessary qualities to cope with, dominate and in large part control his circumstances and environment while in prison, and, through his writings and consequent prominence outside, to substantially transcend the system. The irrevocably institutionalized David, by contrast, is the antithesis of such a success story, by virtue of his extreme inability to cope with life inside the system—an inability rooted, according to accepted wisdom, in his inability to cope with life inside Garry David. For manifold reasons David had neither the inner resources nor the opportunity to prevent himself from fully identifying with the institution, and hence had no recourse for self-expression other than via an idiom intrinsic to that environment. As he himself put it in a letter: "If you are treated like an animal, you will start behaving like one."[27]

Melbourne journalist Alan Attwood, who had dealings with David in Pentridge, has this to say about his "hopeless situation":

If you wanted to mount a case about prisons being dehumanising, Garry David seemed to me to be proof of what could happen, if you treated individuals in fairly extreme ways; and it seemed to me to be a sort of never-ending cycle, you know, he acted badly, they treated him more harshly, he would act even worse, they would respond even harder. So it seemed to be a spiral there, you know, going on to its inevitable conclusion....

How should he be remembered? I think as a very extreme example of what can happen with any institution; but I don't believe it's appropriate to turn him into a tourist attraction.[28]

I cannot help agreeing with Attwood's final comment. An escape attempt is an act of desperation. It is manifestly inappropriate to transform anyone's escape attempt into light entertainment, much less that of the infamously unwell Garry David. Given the profoundly damaged nature of his personality, David hardly needed yet another "dark legend in his mind," and he could hardly be blamed, nor is it appropriate for him to be satirized, for wishing to escape it. Whatever it was he was doing up in the roof that day, or thought he was doing, it wasn't comedy.

NOTES

1   On Ryan's escape and execution, see, e.g., Mike Richards, *The Hanged Man: The Life and Death of Ronald Ryan* (Melbourne: Macmillan, 2003).
2   Christine Raszewski (curator, Old Dubbo Gaol), interviewed 16 January 2003.
3   Friends of J Ward, "Frequently Asked Questions" (FAQ), http://www.jward.ararat.net .au/faqs.html. Aradale itself closed in 1997, to be succeeded in its forensic role by the new Victorian Institute of Forensic Psychiatry at Fairfield, in suburban Melbourne. Graeme Walker, "Aradale to Close as Work Proceeds on New Forensic Centre," http:// hnb.dhs.vic.gov.au/web/pubaff/medrel.nsf/0/e50f66f085869f4a2565a90022f07e?Open Document (accessed 25 January 2006).
4   Read, *Chopper: From the Inside*, p. 67.
5   Broome, *Coburg*, p. 295.
6   Friends of J Ward, FAQ.
7   Deidre Greig, "Shifting the Boundary Between Psychiatry and the Law: The Garry David Case Revisited," http://www.libertyvictoria.org.au/docs/psychiatry_and_the_law.pdf (accessed 29 Sept 2003).
8   Armstrong interview.
9   Ibid; see also Greig, "Shifting the Boundary."

10   See *Mental Health Act* 1986 (Victoria); also, e.g., Bryan Keon-Cohen, "Dilemmas for the Law", http://libertyvictoria.org.au/docs/garry%20david.pdf; Deidre Greig, "The Politics of Dangerousness," http://www.aic.gov.au/publications/proceedings/19/greig.pdf.

11   Although he was legally, by usage and personal preference Garry David, he acquired the "aka" of Webb, his stepfather's surname, through an error on a special police report compiled in 1989, and thereafter, despite his insistent protests, he was never able fully to shake the name. Ben Hills, "The Deadly Dilemma of Australia's Most Unwanted Man," *Sydney Morning Herald* 5 May 1990.

12   Greig, "Shifting the Boundary."

13   For a succinct summary of David's career, see Hills, "Deadly Dilemma"; also Gary Tippet, "Garry David: A Lifetime of Lashing Back," *Sunday Age* 20 June 1993.

14   For a comprehensive social and criminological analysis of the case including an exhaustive survey of the relevant press coverage, see Deidre Greig, *Neither Mad nor Bad: The Competing Discourses of Psychiatry, Law and Politics* (London: Jessica Kingsley Publishers, 2002); see also Keon-Cohen, "Dilemmas for the Law"; Melinda Hinkson, "Goliath Wins," *Arena Magazine* August–September 1993; Paul Ames Fairall, "Violent Offenders and Community Protection in Victoria—the Gary David Experience," *Criminal Law Journal* 17 no.1, February 1993; Christopher Slobogin, "A Jurisprudence of Dangerousness," *Northwestern Law Review* 98, no. 1, 2003; Ron Merkel QC, "'Dangerous Persons': To Be Gaoled for What They Are, or What They May Do, *Not* for What They Have Done," http://www.aic.gov.au/publications/proceedings/19/merkel.pdf (accessed Sept. 2002).

15   *Community Protection Act* 1990 (Victoria), s. 1(a), 1(b); see also Greig, "Shifting the Boundary."

16   Tippet, "Garry David"; Read, *Chopper: From the Inside*, p. 174.

17   Hills, "Deadly Dilemma."

18   Tippet, "Garry David."

19   Alan Attwood, interviewed 2 October 2003; also Hills, "Deadly Dilemma."

20   For an informed glimpse of certain of those tensions, see Frederick Stamp, "Psychiatric Treatment of Violent Offenders in Prison," in *Serious Violent Offenders: Sentencing, Psychiatry and Law Reform: Proceedings of a Conference Held 29-31 October 1991,* ed. Sally-Anne Gerull and William Lucas (Canberra: Australian Institute of Criminology, 1993).

21   Robert Aston (former J Ward head nurse), interviewed 23 September 2002.

22   Ibid.

23   Read, *Chopper: From the Inside*, p. 174.

24   Hills, "Deadly Dilemma."

25   Read, *Chopper: From the Inside*, p. 174.

26   Hills, "Deadly Dilemma"; Alan Attwood, "Garry David, and the Deeper Darkness Within," *Age* 14 June 1993; Brett Quine, "Tortured Life Ends," *Herald Sun* 12 June 1993; Tippet, "Garry David."

27   David cited in Hills, "Deadly Dilemma."

28   Attwood interview.

CHAPTER EIGHT

The Celebrity Prisoner at Large:
The Case of Chopper

Supermarket magazines are well-known for their practice of sensationally revealing that "glamorous" persons such as film stars and other celebrities actually wake up with bed-hair, go shopping without their make-up on, argue with their lovers, and so on; in other words, there is a mundane side to their lives incompatible with the presentation of their public selves. That a market exists for such banal exposé presumably indicates a desire among the general public for evidence that famous people are at base not so different from themselves—combined, perhaps, with the perennial fascination with the hidden aspects of people's identities that drives routine gossip.[1] The celebrity's preoccupation with maintaining an appropriately splendid public image, and his or her concomitant preoccupation with concealing what goes on behind that façade, constitute a personal dichotomy innate to everyone—albeit writ large, in the case of the celebrity or public figure. Social psychologist Erving Goffman explicates this dichotomy in terms of a "dramaturgical" model of the human self comprising internal "regions" of self-construction.[2] These comprise "front regions" in which are performed those activities the self considers acceptable for public consumption, and "back regions," or "backstage" areas, where the less presentable activities occur. Goffman suggests that the functional public self involves a "performance" analogous to the operation of an establishment such as a restaurant, where the mode of table service and presentation of food are aimed primarily at meeting certain public expectations of convenience and aesthetics, while the unsightly or purely utilitarian preparation area is segregated from public view.[3]

It has been remarked that "Goffman's work has no systematic relationship to abstract academic theory and provides no encouragement to attempts to advance such theory";[4] but his central aim, as an "ethnographer of the self,"[5] was to characterize. In this capacity his dramaturgical model has proved of enduring value, providing as it does a metaphorical vocabulary with which to conceptually frame and illuminate the subject. In this chapter I intend to utilize that vocabulary of dramaturgy to examine perhaps the best-known celebrity prisoner in Australia: the career criminal-turned-writer Mark Brandon Read, known to the world as "Chopper."

*

Chopper Read (b. 1954) acquired his evocative nickname as a child after a cartoon character, Chopper the bulldog, in the early 1960s *Yogi Bear* series.[6] The epithet later gained a certain appositeness, within his milieu, from his trademark use of a pair of bolt-cutters as a coercive weapon while earning his living as a young stand-over man.[7] He first emerged from conventional underworld anonymity in 1978 to become briefly infamous by taking a Melbourne County Court judge hostage in his court at gunpoint, in an effort to "spring" James Loughnan, a friend and partner-in-crime, from J Ward.[8] The attempt, predictably, was futile, and for his trouble Read served nine years in jail. Within months of his release in the mid-1980s he was convicted of further crimes of violence and re-imprisoned, for another five years.

The County Court kidnapping that originally brought Read to general notice was in some ways spectacular for its audacity, and may be seen, in hindsight, as signifying a personality with an inclination toward the overt gesture (as he puts it, "a bit of a show pony"); this proclivity was confirmed later in the same year when, with a cellmate's help, he razored off his own ears, an action calculated to effect his removal from H Division.[9] But the notoriety arising from such acts was ephemeral; it hardly equalled true fame, and during the bulk of his incarceration the public largely forgot he existed.

Read re-emerged to public view in the early 1990s, to achieve this time a bona fide, if somewhat coarse-grained, celebrity status, via an irreverently candid autobiography penned in prison. This book, which would turn out to be the first in a series, was compiled from over three hundred letters written from his Pentridge cell to a Melbourne crime journalist[10] and published under the title *Chopper: From the Inside*. In it he recounted, in tones alternating rather chaotically between remorseful and brashly unrepentant, various crimes of his own and others, and described, in iconoclastically colourful and at times poignant terms, a number of his underworld and prison associates, both friend and foe.

Ten years on, in a review article on Read's *oeuvre*, Simon Caterson would borrow from Orwell to characterize *Chopper: From the Inside* as a "good bad book," on the grounds of its combined qualities of memorable readability and complete lack of "literary pretension."[11] A defining trait of books fitting the "good-bad" category is their robust and enduring popularity in the face of erudite criticism,[12] and Read's literary debut was no exception. By virtue of the clearly authentic insights it afforded of criminal life (an authenticity undiminished by Read's frequent admission that not everything he writes is strictly truthful), combined with a "disarmingly intimate and confessional prose style,"[13] *Chopper: From the Inside* became an instant bestseller, and at this writing is in its thirtieth print-run. A highly successful film adaptation was released in 2000 (about which, more in due course).

Chopper: From the Inside neatly established Read's persona as a darkly jocular perpetrator of violence both in and outside jail, widely feared and hated within the underworld as a "head-hunter," but with an avowed "Robin Hood" side, in that (as he stated then and maintains today) he only ever killed or maimed other criminals—especially drug dealers—thereby making society safer for ordinary citizens.[14] In creating such an image of himself, centred, not insignificantly, on the edgily ambiguous connotations of his nickname, Read presented himself as the embodiment of a kind of living myth. Caterson argues that this "Chopper" myth is analogous to the iconic Australian outlaw myth of Ned Kelly: "Like Kelly, Read seems to be regarded by many people as a 'good criminal'…but, more than this, he created an image that is larger than life and is the stuff of legend."[15] At the height of his career, Ned Kelly famously promulgated a lengthy and highly political manifesto-cum-apologia, the "Jerilderie letter."[16] Both Read and Kelly, Caterson says, in their writings "manifest an irrepressible urge for self-expression"—an "urge" that gained its original expression in their shared "flair for the dramatic," exhibited in the manner and choice of certain of their criminal activities.[17]

Caterson might be thought by some to be going a bit far in drawing such a parallel with any seriousness: the roots and motivations of Kelly's and Read's respective careers may well be too disparate to withstand the comparison, and Kelly, it should be noted, became a "legend" *during* his escapade, gaining wide contemporaneous renown within broad sections of the civilian community primarily through his transgressive acts (which always had a socio-political dimension entirely lacking in Read's "toe-cutting" adventures), rather than through witty literary self-reconstruction. Kelly's "Jerilderie letter" and defiant speechifying at his trial served to consolidate for history an image already well established "in the field." Nevertheless, however incongruous the Kelly comparison might seem, for almost any criminal or ex-criminal who identifies to a significant extent with Australian cultural memory the allure of such a notional link with our iconic outlaw hero is almost irresistible; and it is a fact that favourable, even reverential, verbal and graphic references to Ned Kelly may be found among graffiti in jail-cells literally across Australia. (I have observed this as far afield as Fremantle Gaol, almost 3,000 kilometres from the geographical theatre of Kelly's life and career.) Unsurprisingly, then, Read himself seems to have taken Caterson's idea to heart; having extended his creative repertoire to painting, he held a sell-out exhibition in August 2003 that resulted in the State Library of Victoria buying a "Chopper" self-portrait, *Tast Ful Old Criminal* [*sic*], which in its visual design alludes directly to the iconic imagery of Sidney Nolan's *Ned Kelly* series.[18]

This "good criminal" self-interpretation—clearly a "front-region" aspect—is bolstered, paradoxically, by Read's escapade with the judge—or at least by his telling of it: his motivation in undertaking such a foolhardy and manifestly doomed venture was, it seems, derived from a sense of chivalrous honour toward his friend Loughnan, based on a long-ago promise to that individual which no reasonable person would have expected to be fulfilled. In recounting the episode, Read fosters such an interpretation with two apparent aims: to justify his sense of grievance over the subsequent betrayal he suffered at Loughnan's hands (in 1979 Loughnan stabbed Read almost to death in jail);[19] and, not insignificantly, to reinforce his desired image as one benignly disposed toward the innocents of civil society, even when he has palpably wronged them:

> [A]fter [the kidnapping] was all over I wrote to Judge Martin [the victim] and said I was sorry and he wrote back to me. ...He was very concerned for me and wished me all the very best for the future. I thought that was very nice of him. I had no ill will towards him. It was all to try to get Jimmy Loughnan out of J Ward.[20]

A countering facet of the Chopper myth, and one which Read has also explicitly fostered, is that of the harder-than-hard man—the man of implacably and utterly ruthless violence who will stop at nothing because, ultimately, he fears nothing. The auto-amputation of his ears highlights what is perhaps his most disturbing attribute: an extraordinary emotional resistance, almost imperviousness, to physical pain—his own and, one inevitably infers, other people's. This, along with his habitual perverse wit, presumably contributed to his underworld reputation as a "psycho," which in turn facilitated his ascendance to power among prison populations wherever he was incarcerated. In his own words, "there's nothing more frightening in jail than a psycho."[21]

In and out of prison for much of his adult life, Read has been free and apparently reformed since 1998. In 2000 the motion picture adaptation of his story was released, entitled simply *Chopper*.[22] This did very respectable business at the box office, both in Australia and internationally, won critical acclaim, and launched the international film career of Melbourne comedian-cum-actor Eric Bana. Among the more striking of the film's promotional accoutrements was a poster image in which Bana adopted the armed-to-the-teeth pose of one of the more notorious illustrations in Read's first book. This picture, a black-and-white photograph of the author captioned "Dressed to Kill," was taken in his criminal heyday; he is stripped to the waist and "tooled up," as the argot has it, tattooed forearms crossed over his bare chest and sporting a large pistol in each upraised hand plus two tucked into his waistband, a shoulder-holster, and what appears to be a flick-knife hanging from a belt-loop.[23]

A brief comparison between the Bana image and the prototype is instructive. In the original photograph, taken indoors at the height of Read's criminal career—and hence well before he became an active publicity-seeker—neither personality nor passion are visible; a clean-shaven, slightly pudgy and manifestly unsexy Read gazes at the camera with a flat, vaguely belligerent lack of expression. The picture is, essentially, little more than a display of the tools of his trade, a snapshot presumably taken as a mere memento. By contrast, the image that graced cinema display cases has lost the drab banality of the original; Eric Bana's full-colour "Chopper" is literally aglow with potency and threat, but now the danger emanates at least as much from the man as from his weapons. Bana-Chopper has taken on the sunglasses and defiant, head-up posture of another of the book's black-and-white illustrations (which also graced the cover), added a flamboyant moustache that appeared in later years, and combined these with the crossed-arms pose. All visible distractions from the flesh have been minimized. The encumbering shoulder-holster has gone, and, more significantly, the balance between man and metal has shifted: his arsenal has diminished. The knife has vanished altogether, and, contrary to Hollywood's custom of endowing its protagonists with maximum firepower, Bana flaunts only three guns, compared to the real Chopper's four: the two handguns in his waistband have been replaced by a single small-bore sawn-off shotgun with a customized pistol-grip; a "Python" .357 Magnum revolver in the original's left hand has become a visually more modest and smaller-calibre semi-automatic; and, presumably for the sake of symmetry and to avoid any distractions from Bana's face, a Colt "New Frontier" revolver in his right hand, although of similar pattern to that in the original photograph, has been somehow— perhaps digitally—reduced in size, almost to toy-gun proportions.

As representations of masculinity go, the Eric Bana poster clearly is intended to combine danger and sexuality—not just a killer, but a sexually potent killer. And such an image clearly has patent appeal in certain quarters. A few months after its theatrical release the film arrived in the video rental stores, where, as part of the accompanying promotion campaign, life-sized stand-up cardboard versions of the poster image went on display. Staff at my neighbourhood video store told me that shortly after the stand-up appeared in the window, a female police officer walked in and asked, in all seriousness, if she could buy it.

It is, of course, impossible to divine the police officer's precise motivation in making such a request. Given the pop-cultural confluence between movie ersatz and the real, we cannot even know, ultimately, whose image she was subjectively buying. Nor do we know whether she intended the stand-up to adorn her home or her work-place—police stations, too, have "back regions," and it is not hard to imagine such an item being viewed with a certain ribald irony by those privy to such regions.

The reality-and-movie confluence had other, supposedly more substantial effects: in April 2002, career criminal Keith George Faure, a one-time foe of Read in Pentridge who had been portrayed in *Chopper* as "Keithy George," tried to use the film's treatment of himself as mitigation for a serious traffic offence for which he was on trial: the character intended to represent him is violently killed in the film's opening minutes, and Faure claimed to have been so upset after viewing his onscreen "death" that he drove a motor vehicle while unlicensed and hit a pole. (The magistrate was apparently unconvinced, and recorded a verdict of "guilty.")[24]

To judge by the real Chopper Read's public support for the film—in particular for Eric Bana's portrayal of him[25]—and the fact that the Bana poster image featured prominently on what long stood as the closest Read had to an "official" website (a somewhat confrontational site apparently posted on his behalf by confidants and since shut down), it is clear that the image was one of which he approved.[26] In thus endorsing a radically "Hollywoodized" representation of himself, Read effectively appropriated that representation as his own "front region," or at least as a defining portion thereof—a step arguably analogous, in the embracement of a counterfeit self, to the common celebrity practice of staving off the encroachment of back-region manifestations by resorting to cosmetic surgery. That appropriation subsequently gained a further dimension: Read eventually took responsibility for his own website[27]—a crucial front-region development for the modern celebrity—and among the promotional "memorabilia" offered through its "products" page is a photographic collage that includes the Bana image—but with Bana's head replaced by Read's, superimposed atop the actor's shoulders.[28]

Read is nothing if not complex, and his self-presentation is not confined to the crude "glamour" associated with displays of brute power; there are signs, too, that he has to a degree "moved on" from his wholehearted endorsement of his film persona. His public career now includes regular tours with various show-business and/or former underworld associates,[29] and he has embarked on a sporadic musical career, with a number of recordings to his credit. As noted above, he is at pains, in his memoirs, to leaven the "head-hunter" image with one of proper, if unorthodoxly constituted, concern for society's "civilian" (that is, non-criminal) population. It may be inferred from various sentiments expressed in his writings that he has hopes for some degree of "respectability"—some understanding and acknowledgement in the general community that, even given his proclivity for dark joking about his past career, he is, nevertheless, a reformed character.[30] His new website is markedly less lurid than its unofficial predecessor, more pragmatic in its promotional aspects, and rather more equivocal in its support for the film *Chopper*.[31]

From the moment of the publication of his first book, with its apparent aspiration to such recognition and its sometimes sage reflections on the inherent futility of his radically deviant life-course, Read had the potential to become what J. David Brown terms a "professional ex-"—that is, a person who provides themselves (wittingly or otherwise) with a mode of "exiting the deviant career" by taking up a role of service, or quasi-service, that depends on their deviant past for the core expertise and/or credentials necessary to fulfil that role.[32] In terms of front- and back-regions, the professional ex- is of some interest, because of his or her propensity to take what were once personal and, crucially, reprehensible back-region features and re-present them as front-region attributes, via a process of simultaneous affirmation and disavowal of those features—a kind of self-othering, as it were, by which the rehabilitated (or "recovering") deviant legitimates his or her new role.

Brown's discussion concerns itself primarily with the most common instance of the "professional ex-" phenomenon: alcohol- or drug-abuse counsellors;[33] there is no reason, however, to limit the category to this group, and it would certainly fit a former career criminal whose change of heart extended not merely to going straight but to constructing a whole new career, based on his former activities, as a public figure avowedly committed to law and order and the public good. Indeed, certain aspects of Read's public persona as it has evolved to the present are highly consistent with the "professional ex-" model—not least the fact that he is often consulted by news media for his views on "gangland" stories,[34] and that he performed in a series of road-safety television advertisements in which he explicitly invoked his prison experiences.

In 1995, while imprisoned in Tasmania's Risdon Prison for malicious wounding, Read married a Tax Office employee who had been visiting him in prison, and on his release moved with her to rural Tasmania, where he became a father and attempted to settle down to family and farming life. By his own admission, however, the marriage was, at least in part, a pragmatic undertaking motivated by his desire to get out of jail,[35] and although he seems to have genuinely immersed himself for a time in the attendant bucolic domesticity,[36] in the end the venture proved too alien to his nature and too much at odds with certain imperatives from his past.[37] Hence he returned to Melbourne in 2001, freshly divorced and announcing that he intended to marry his girlfriend of almost twenty years.

The wedding duly took place in January 2003, and was attended by an assortment of minor celebrities, several law-enforcement and prison officers,

and, importantly, a journalist and photographer from the supermarket magazine *Woman's Day*. In keeping with occasional celebrity wedding practice of
recent years, the groom and best man wore Scottish "Highland" dress—that
is, kilts and sporrans.[38] Largely on the strength of this lamely trendy eccen-
tricity, *Woman's Day* flagged the wedding in its cover-line as "outrageous"
and "wacky"; but in the report itself it reverted to a more conventionally
populist agenda by focussing heavily on the bride, and entitling the article
"Chopper Weds his First Sweetheart."[39] Thus the magazine account effectively encompasses the spectrum of social redemption necessary for the former violent criminal to qualify as a cheekily likeable rogue—or, to employ
the peculiarly Australian catch-all for such masculine characters: he may
now be regarded as a *larrikin*.[40]

The implications of Chopper's larrikin status will be further explored in
a later chapter. Suffice it here to note that a number of social advantages
more or less automatically accompany an individual's elevation to such
standing. "The larrikin has the license, denied his more reserved mates, to
subvert conventional mores."[41] As a mandated fun-loving rule-bender, he is
likely to be judged with considerable leniency if he chooses to venture into
fields of endeavour outside his customary expertise; hence Read's paintings,
which are of interest chiefly due to their creator's notoriety and at best might
be deemed "good-bad" art *à la* his books, can attract a critical rationale sufficiently potent to defend their purchase, with public funds, by the State Library of Victoria.[42] One hardly needs to look beyond this event for evidence
that Read has successfully shaken off the vestigial stigma of his deviant
past—notwithstanding the paradox, typical of the professional ex-, that it is
precisely that past which provides the credentials and at least some of the
dynamism for his present triumphs.

NOTES

1   On the nature of gossip see, e.g., Jack Levin and Arnold Arluke, *Gossip: The Inside
    Scoop* (New York: Plenum Press, 1987); Jörg Bergmann, *Discreet Indiscretions: The
    Social Organization of Gossip* (New York: Aldine De Gruyter, 1993); Ralph Rosnow
    and Gary Fine, *Rumor and Gossip: The Social Psychology of Hearsay* (New York: El-
    sevier, 1976).

2 Erving Goffman, *The Presentation of Self in Everyday Life* (New York: Anchor Books, 1959), pp. 106–13.

3 Ibid., pp. 116–19.

4 Eliot Freidson, "Celebrating Erving Goffman," *Contemporary Sociology* 12 no. 4, July 1983, p. 359.

5 Ibid.

6 Read, *Chopper: From the Inside*, p. 54; Mark Read interviewed on *Andrew Denton: Enough Rope*, ABC Television, broadcast 4 August 2003. But cf. Read's personal website, where he rather implausibly contradicts himself, dismissing his own account as "various theories," and attributing the nickname to his notorious lack of ears. http://www.chopperread.com (hereafter "Read personal website") (accessed 1 Sept 2006).

7 Read, *Chopper: From the Inside*, pp. 77–8.

8 Ibid., pp. 74–5.

9 Ibid., pp. 54–5.

10 Ibid., editors' note, , p. iv.

11 Simon Caterson, "Chopping into Literature: the Writings of Mark Brandon Read," *Australian Book Review* no. 236, November 2001, p. 19.

12 George Orwell, "Good Bad Books," in *The Penguin Essays of George Orwell*, London: Penguin, 1984.

13 Caterson, "Chopping into Literature," p. 20.

14 Read, *Chopper: From the Inside*, pp. 6–7, 52–3, 77–86; Read personal website.

15 Caterson, "Chopping into Literature," p. 20.

16 Ian Jones, *Ned Kelly: A Short Life* (Port Melbourne: Lothian, 1995), Ch. 14.

17 Caterson, "Chopping into Literature," pp. 19–20.

18 Jeremy Kelly, "State Library buys Chopper art," *Herald Sun* 26 August 2003; see also Heather Gallagher, "'Chopper' exhibition almost sold out after two days," *Age*, 1 August 2003.

19 Read, *Chopper: From the Inside*, pp. 71–5.

20 Ibid., p. 75.

21 Mark Read, interview appended in Andrew Dominik (director), *Chopper*, motion picture, video recording © Twentieth Century Fox Home Entertainment, 2001; see also Read in *Australian Story*.

22 Dominik, *Chopper*.

23 Read, *Chopper: From the Inside*, illustration opposite p. 100.

24 Elissa Hunt and Christine Caulfield, "Chopper Movie Upset Blamed for Crash," *Herald Sun* 6 April 2002.

25 C. James, "Chopper Weds His First Sweetheart," *Woman's Day* 17 February 2003, pp. 14–15.

26 Unofficial "Chopper" website, http://members.tripod.com/~Chopper_Read/ (accessed 2002, now removed).

27 See Read personal website.

28 See ibid., link to: http://www.chopperread.com/Memorabilia%20pages/Hab007.htm (accessed 1 Sept. 2006).

29 Ibid.
30 Read, *Chopper: From the Inside*, e.g., p. 75; also Read interview, *Enough Rope*.
31 Read personal website.
32 J. David Brown, "The Professional Ex-: An Alternative for Exiting the Deviant Career," *The Sociological Quarterly* 32, no 2, 1991, pp. 219–30; *idem*, "Preprofessional Socialization and Identity Transformation: The Case of the Professional Ex-," *Journal of Contemporary Ethnography* 20, no 2, July 1991, pp. 157–78.
33 Brown, "Professional Ex-."
34 See, e.g., Padraic Murphy, "Bulgarian Nick Dies in a Flurry of Shots, Victim of Suspected Underworld Hit," *Age* 17 April 2003; John Silvester, "Why Gangland's Bloody Code is Hard to Crack," *Sunday Age* 20 April 2003.
35 Read interview, *Enough Rope*.
36 See Read interview in Dominik, *Chopper*; also Read on *Australian Story*.
37 Read personal website; Read interview, *Enough Rope*; Read on *Australian Story*.
38 James, "Chopper Weds."
39 Ibid.
40 John Rickard, "Lovable Larrikins and Awful Ockers," *Journal of Australian Studies* no. 56, March 1998.
41 Ibid.
42 Kelly, "State Library Buys Chopper Art."

CHAPTER NINE

Front Regions, Back Regions:
The Celebrity Prison

Erving Goffman developed his dramaturgical model to explain the self; but as his "restaurant" metaphor suggests, it may equally be utilized to discuss the non-personal, corporate or institutional entity. In this chapter I will apply the concept of front and back regions to the total institution in which Chopper Read was confined when he first achieved celebrity, and with which he is most famously associated. That institution was Pentridge Prison, where Read was incarcerated when he did away with his ears, and in which he was again resident while writing his first book.

Due to the sequestered nature of their function, operational maximum-security prisons, although physically located in public spaces, are among the few types of entity which in the normal run of things are largely lacking in any form of persona that makes the concept of "front regions" meaningful. This lack is, of course, deliberate. Unlike people, and the organizations such as commercial dining-rooms with which Goffman models his theory, the prison is not centrally in the business of *presentation* of itself. In fact its officials are likely to avoid such presentation as much as possible, leaving its visible image to remain a forbidding blank—literally so in many cases, in the form of emblematic high, featureless walls. This is not to say, however, that Goffman's idea has no application here; rather, we should think in terms of a gross imbalance toward "back regions," with the front region radically mini-mized. (It is useful, and not significantly inexact, to think of the average inmate's life as divided into, say, 1 percent front region and 99 percent back region.) The front-region manifestations resulting from such minimization typically stand as exceptions that prove the rule, and a brief discussion of their characteristics is therefore worthwhile for the insights afforded into the operational prison and, by contrast, into the historical prison operating as a tourist site.

To the extent that the operational prison does go in for the unequivocal construction of front regions, the presentations associated with them tend to be public expressions or performances of existing inmate activities of the type Goffman describes, in his study of total institutions, as "removal activities": "Every total institution," he states, "can be seen as a kind of dead sea in which little islands of vivid, encapturing activity appear...Removal activities [are] voluntary unserious pursuits...[designed to] mercifully kill [time]."[1] These may include solitary hobbies such as crafts or artwork, team sports, ensemble dramatic presentations, debating societies, and so on—in other words, recreational or other diversionary pursuits undertaken primarily to gain relief or distraction from the experience of imprisonment. To those engaging in them, such pursuits are unlikely to be intended, in the first instance, as contributions to an institutional "front region," even given their potential for adaptation for "public consumption"; there is little reason for inmates to have any personal stake in providing a "storefront" for the institution per se. They do, however, have reason to welcome opportunities to interact or simply make contact with members of the public, and this desire is open to exploitation by officials who *are* concerned with the institution's image.

An abiding characteristic of such exploitation is that it imbues inmates' removal activities with implicit connotations of redemption—of the inmates' notional fitness to resume some degree of participation in civil society. This in turn reflects favourably upon the prison itself, in terms of its rehabilitative role and as an exemplar of orderly prisoner management. And inmates, as individuals, of course have their own front regions, which in many cases encompass aspirational presentations as socially redeemed persons.

A typical example would be for sporting events to be arranged against groups invited into the prison grounds from the surrounding neighbourhood. On such occasions, whatever the scale of the event, it is in the inmates' interests not merely to compete, but to demonstrate socialization appropriate to the occasion.[2] In Pentridge in the latter decades of its operation, football matches were played on a semi-regular basis between inmates and teams of senior students from a nearby high school. George Thompson, a veteran of one of those school teams, recalls that in 1977, as a "robust" 17-year-old, they chucked me into the footy side and we went in [to Pentridge's grounds] and played a game on their oval....We were all young sorts of blokes, we were pretty intimidated, but at the same time it was certainly our own little Gallipoli, it was a big adventure for us...there was that curiosity element...It went quite well. The guys [inmates]...were pretty comical, they were big sorts of blokes, and they—they won.[3]

Thompson's reminiscence evokes an encounter conducted in a spirit of good humour and sportsmanship befitting the youth and relative innocence of the inmates' opponents, and as such affirms the success of the exercise, from the institution's point of view, as a front-region performance. The encounter was typical of most prison–public front-region interactions, with a small number of outsiders permitted inside for a relatively brief, tightly structured sporting event. An alternative, albeit rare, example has the competition occurring only between inmates, over an extended period, with the public admitted en masse, purely as spectators; such is the case at the Louisiana State Penitentiary at Angola, which holds an annual rodeo on its farmland, attracting thousands of people for two weeks each Autumn to take in what amounts to a gladiatorial spectacle.[4]

Of course, not all prisoners are inclined toward removal activities of such broad physicality; intrinsically presentable goods such as art and craftwork can lend themselves equally well to the prison's front region, and in fact the Angola rodeo is accompanied by a fair at which those attending may purchase various products of the prison's workshops.[5] Similarly, a Pentridge prisoner with a propensity for, say, woodcraft or textiles might have found himself encouraged to join the "Pentridge Toy Makers," a group founded in 1961 to produce toys for needy and destitute children. Products of the Toy Makers' labours (upwards of 6,000 toys and hobbies annually, at their peak) were ceremonially displayed and distributed at lavish Christmas events held in the jail, to which groups of children from refugee communities, orphanages, and so on, were invited. There they were treated to pantomimes and various other entertainments, including meetings with a "Santa Claus" long resident in E Division. (Whether the children noticed the word DEATH tattooed across Santa's knuckles I cannot say.)[6] For fifteen years the Toy Makers' annual display received consistent press coverage,[7] until their activities were ended in 1976 by a major fire in their storage shed.[8]

It may appear harsh to connote in the Toy Makers' works an "exploitation" of inmates' propensities, for the sake of the institution's image; the

Pentridge Toy Makers' endeavours were, in their charitable purport, undeniably worthy, and no doubt engendered much genuine satisfaction—perhaps even a degree of personal redemption—for at least some of the inmates involved in the intrinsic good of making children happy. It is thus arguable that in this particular front region project the institutional authorities' intent—to foreground the redemptive prison—was in accord to a significant extent with inmate motivation. But such endeavours are rare; the vast majority of removal activities are "privileges" granted on the pragmatic basis that the inmate is, while so occupied, orderly. If the activity lends itself to front-region presentation, so much the better.

There is one further form of public access to the operational prison: personal visits to prisoners. These in fact constitute by far the most common form of such access; Pentridge, for example, admitted on the order of 60,000 civilians a year on this basis.[9] Such a figure seems at first to contradict the notion of front-region minimization referred to above; yet it is here that we actually encounter that minimization in its most extreme form—so extreme that such visits have a markedly ambiguous standing vis-à-vis the front-region-back-region dichotomy. That ambiguity and its causes provide a glimpse, and hence a conceptual point of entry, into the institution's back regions.

The non-professional visit tends to occur in modes and physical conditions of austerely utilitarian and security-impelled regulation, to rigorously exclude "general" public access, and, crucially, to be conducted with apparent disregard of visitors' emotional comfort or welfare. Apart from the obvious security factors that influence some of these conditions, a less obvious but key aspect of the personal prisoner visit is the prison staff's moral perception of, and attitude toward, the visitor. In the outside world, in conventional front-region performances such as running a restaurant, a central, defining characteristic—in effect the *raison d'être* of such performances—is the tacit authority that inheres in the audience or clientele; a restaurant's customers must be catered to and satisfied, after all. This authority is almost entirely missing in the case of prisoner visits. Within the prison context the run-of-the-mill visitor, insofar as he or she constitutes any form of audience or client, is completely lacking in authority, and indeed may be argued to have taken on, by association, some of the prisoner's fundamentally negative moral status in the institution. Aside from whatever emotions attend the strictly limited period of communication with the incarcerated friend or loved one, the visitor's experience of the visit tends to be chiefly character-ized by subtle manifestations of the prison's back-regions: most especially sensations of arid confinement, official disapproval, and a devaluing of the visitor's comfort and wellbeing—sensations to some degree shared with the inmates, for whom these features of institutional life, in their most extreme form, constitute the matrix of daily existence.

Attitudes are significant in a closed environment. In the systemic relegation of inmates' welfare described by Goffman, and the concomitant radical indif-ference on the part of the institution toward the individual inmate, lies an essential ethos of the total institution that in many ways frames and defines the inmate's general experience of life "inside," from his or her first mo-ments of imprisonment.[10] Further, this ethos may be discerned, as a principal contributory factor, at the root of the manifold forms of coercive dominance that characterize the routine experience of incarceration.[11]

In its relationship to harm, institutional indifference per se does not equate with malign agency; it does, however, foster a tendency, even in be-nignly disposed persons, to do harm, in the form of wilful neglect and, as we have seen, even direct assault. Such assaults may be regarded as possible variations of the process of "capture" described by Harding.[12] But to estab-lish a causal link between indifference and violent mishap does not require instances of deliberate staff brutality towards inmates—even though history has recorded an infinitude of these, not least at Pentridge. In any high-security prison it is inevitable that a significant percentage of inmates, whether convicted of violent crimes or not, will incline toward violence as a ready, and often primary, mode of self-expression or social problem-solving. All that is needed, in a maximum-security prison, is for custodial staff to leave inmates relatively unimpeded to get on with the natural business of establishing and maintaining their "pecking order." This approach, taken to its logical conclusion, leads in some prisons to the inmate-management strat-egy of allowing and even actively encouraging the development of a radi-cally divided, "all-against-all" social regime among the incarcerated population.[13] As one inmate has put it,

> Everywhere, every minute—like the air that you breathe—there is a threat of vio-lence lurking beneath the surface...it permeates every second of everyone's exis-tence [and] there is no let up from it—ever.[14]

Such a "jungle-like" atmosphere facilitates control of that population, both on a straightforward "divide and conquer" basis, and also via unofficial strategic alliances between staff and favoured "warlord" prisoners.[15] It was in just such an environment, by his own account, that Chopper Read thrived. He states that while in Pentridge he was often permitted by prison officers to go about the prison armed, on the premise that the encouragement of his dominion helped to maintain order.[16] (Read's value as an inmate-management asset was confirmed for me by a former Pentridge prison officer, although he did not explicitly corroborate Read's claims regarding weapons.)

A further, and arguably the most egregious, ramification of the *laissez-faire* approach to prisoner administration is the proliferation of sexual violence—that is, rape. This phenomenon is extremely widespread (in some prisons affecting on the order of one in four young male prisoners),[17] it has a history perhaps as long as imprisonment itself, and of all prison experiences is among the most damaging, physically and psychically.[18] It is also, despite its notoriety, the problem whose severity or even existence is most consistently denied or ignored by officials at all levels—including, crucially, the judiciary[19]—and only in recent years has it begun to receive a degree of acknowledgement and serious study in social-science, legal and policy-making circles.[20]

Such studies notwithstanding, mass media reports or commentary on prison sexual violence are virtually nonexistent; hence despite it being "common knowledge," public awareness of the realities of the problem remains very low—and, where some public awareness of prison sexuality does exist, it is in fact skewed toward a tacit acceptance that rape is an "appropriate" part of the punishment of jail.[21] This sort of apathy or ignorance is much the preferred state of affairs as far as prison officials are concerned. Thus it is apparent that in discussing the phenomenon we are, by definition, dealing with the most remote and secret backstage areas of any prison—indeed, of the prison system—and that its backstage status has a significant role in its perpetuation. In his groundbreaking study of prison sexual abuse in Australia, David Heilpern quotes Dr Frank McLeod, director of the New South Wales prison medical services, who in a 1990 interview asked rhetorically, "What do you say if a bloke tells you he fell backward on a broom handle…?"[22] McLeod went on to recount a further, even more grisly example; of note is his concluding disclaimer:

[O]ne bloke…was being stood over and used as a repository for everyone's excess semen to the point where his mouth was full of ulcerations and infections. How do you record that? I know it's there. They know it's there.[23]

In his "How do you record that?", McLeod comes as close as he dares to stating outright, "You *don't* record that." Which raises the irresistible question, Why not?

*

The aspects touched on above, as back regions, are of course kept hidden from public perception as far as possible; equally obvious is that they are light-years distant from the prison's "public face" as evinced by the occasional football match or children's Christmas party. Much changes when the prison is decommissioned. Once it becomes an historical entity, and especially when that history is to be exploited by opening the site to the public on a profit-making basis, the relevance of the established front regions diminishes, and their moral resonance as signifiers of the redeemed inmate comes to have little more than anecdotal status. A transformation of purport is now underway, for the public face of the historical prison is generally far more concerned with displaying a redeemed *institution*. A new front region must be invented, and as the tourist appeal of the historical prison's interior rests almost entirely on an expectation of back regions revealed—"What's it like to be in jail?"—the re-invented front region must cater to that expectation. (I make no claim that this re-invention is consciously conspiratorial; more that it is a concordance of individuals' and stakeholder groups' motivations.)

For those with a stake in this invention, two issues immediately arise: firstly, the secret nature of the functional prison leaves the public expectant, but with little clear idea of precisely what to expect; secondly, and a corollary to the first point, there is much in those back regions—the many dreadful realities of maximum-security incarceration—to cause entrepreneurs, site managers and tour operators to fear that the ordinary person will find the tour experience too negative to be entertaining, too disturbing to be tolerable, and/or too morally ambiguous to be readily assimilated. Hence the task of tour operators and their like is to euphemize the back regions, while somehow convincing the visitors that they are receiving an authentic account of those regions.

As we have seen, in the case of Pentridge, the proprietors adopted a solution common to many historical prisons around the world, in that the pres-

entation is largely informed, controlled and conducted by former prison officers, a group with a strong motivation to propagate a palatable, entertaining
and uncontroversial rendition of the back regions. And as we have further
seen, the utilization of retired prison officers in key roles promotes the tendency, prevalent in the media, to throw a jocular light upon serious, even
harrowing, subject-matter.[24] It is at this point that Chopper Read, in his post-
prison incarnation, is in his element, and becomes a significant asset to those
with a stake in the made-over institution. A natural wit, with a vast fund of
highly believable tales drawn from personal experience, he is one of the few
ex-prisoners deemed suitable for a place in the "official" history of Pentridge
that is developing. Although not directly involved in the tours, his "larrikin"
persona and status are integral and perfectly fitted to the invented Pentridge
front region, and it is significant that many former prison officers express
respect and some fondness for him. (It will be recalled that a number of them
were included among his wedding guests.)

Nor are front region manifestations necessarily confined to conventional
on-site presentations; they can take diverse forms, and so too the involvement of the celebrity prisoner: in 2001, Melbourne radio station Triple M ran
a "reality" competition, "Escape from Pentridge," in which contestants spent
nineteen days and nights "imprisoned" in the cells, undergoing a series of
"challenges" and "punishments." Read was recruited by Triple M for the exercise, and among the "punishments" contestants were encouraged to fear
was spending "a night in a cell with Chopper."[25]

Read's role as a celebrity prisoner in this context is fully consistent with
the standard practice of historical prison presentations, and in fact his connection with the prison barely needs promotion. While Pentridge was briefly
open for tours in 1997 immediately following its decommissioning, one of
the questions most commonly asked of tour guides was, "Which cell was
Chopper's?"[26] Of no small significance, too, is the fact that the prison interiors depicted in the film *Chopper* were shot in the authentic locations within
Pentridge. But although Read's example is to some degree true to type, it
also has certain unusual aspects of particular significance for the historical
representation of Pentridge.

Goffman notes that the typical inmate's primary experience of the total
institution tends to be symptomatic, in one way or another, of "a loss of self-
determination"[27]—a condition discernable at the heart of much of the "back
regions" matter discussed above, and which a great deal of inmate activity is

designed (whether wittingly or otherwise) to overcome. For the vast majority of prisoners, however, who for reasons of background, character, ill-fortune and institutional pressure can attain only tenuous or no control at all over their circumstances (in many cases a continuance of their experience of life before prison),[28] such activity is largely ineffectual; beyond instances of relatively little moment, self-determination remains essentially unattainable. The reason for this is simple: within the "jungle" of the total institution, individual autonomy is, in the final analysis, almost exclusively a consequence of personal (physical) power, and this is, perforce, the province of a small number of inmates peculiarly fitted for such status—the prison's "elite." By all accounts (not least his own), Chopper Read was precisely such an inmate.

The elite prisoner sets the bar impossibly high for the run-of-the-mill prison population, both during the period of imprisonment, when the stakes concern coercive dominance of the closed social environment, and, more subtly (and of course far less urgently), afterward when the central issues become historical ones of remembrance and representation. Put simply, the celebrity prisoner's prominence vis-à-vis the remembered prison effectively overwhelms the voices of the vast majority of the institution's former population, in the process helping to radically skew the overall interpretation of the site as an entity of public history. In Chopper's case, a key aspect of this skewing is to reinforce the notion in the public mind that the experience of prison was at base funny—or at least sufficiently innocuous that humour constituted an effective removal activity.

But although the historical front region is premised on the entertainment imperative, there are limits to what may be presented with humour and retain any semblance of authenticity. Displays of confiscated weapons and judiciously selected anecdotes of violent episodes are used to imply the wickedness of the inmates (precisely opposite to the "redeemed inmate" discussed earlier) and hence invoke their otherness; this in turn legitimates and redeems the prison itself. Chopper is not without a role here, too: as we have seen, he has come to display many attributes of the "professional ex-," including the paradoxical "self-othering" that lends credence to that role; in the process of repudiating his former self, by implication he fosters the othering of the general prison population. Also, prisons at which executions were conducted often display the gallows; in such cases, terrible crimes of the executed inmates tend to be emphasized in tour guides' accounts.[29] And the note of apparent authenticity struck in stories and images of institutional cruelty or unjust treatment of inmates obscures the fact that they are almost invariably derived from the distant past—often the nineteenth century—thus distancing the modern institution from such events in more recent times.

Some topics remain firmly taboo. As I have said, prison sexuality is relegated to the cognitive back regions more thoroughly than perhaps any other aspect of life "inside." But if it is hardly ever publicly referred to during the operational career of any prison, it is *never* spontaneously mentioned by tour guides during tours of prisons once they have closed down. Violent rape and serial sexual assault are unlikely to get too many laughs, however engaging the story-teller. Even Chopper Read avoids the subject. I have heard tour guides at a number of prisons, responding to visitors' direct questions, flatly deny that "it" went on; the same guides privately admitted to me later that it did. (Some, however, prefer to maintain the denial even privately. Former guards at Boggo Road stated categorically that "it never went on here," even when I pointed out instances of explicit and violent homosexual cell graffiti.)

There is one more back-regions aspect which I have not previously touched upon, and which, although not outright avoided in tour narratives, tends to be only sparingly acknowledged: the very high incidence of deliberate inmate self-harm. Tour guides will sometimes mention individual suicides, presenting them as unavoidable and, by implication, relatively rare tragedies.[30] But in fact people harm themselves far more frequently in prison than outside.[31] In a study of the phenomenon, criminologist Alison Leibling found that "the causes expressed by prisoners describing their activities as suicidal are the same as those causes relating to less lethal types of self-harm"; she concludes that such apparently disparate behaviours stand on "a continuum of self-destructive behaviour."[32] It becomes meaningful, therefore, to refer to those "less lethal" acts as "para-suicides."[33] Apart from deliberate drug overdoses, the most common form of inmate para-suicide is self-mutilation, usually with edged weapons such as razor-blades—what prison parlance terms "slashing up." The slash-up may be viewed as an inarticulate and desperate attempt by the inmate to compel the institution to attend to his or her welfare, a reaction to the institutional indifference noted above. It is a testament to the harshness of the environment within Pentridge that there were far more suicides and para-suicides there, especially in the last two decades of its operation, than in any other Australian prison.[34] Yet it is in this regard, I suggest, that perhaps the most effective euphemization of all has occurred, in the process of re-inventing Pentridge's front region—and once again with the help of the celebrity prisoner.

Chopper Read carries a permanent, highly visible legacy of his years in Pentridge, in the form of his self-amputated ears—evidence that he, too, became caught up in what has been described as an "epidemic" of slash-ups. It says much, in fact, about the environment within Pentridge that the self-styled "king" of H Division, one of the most feared criminals in the State of Victoria, could be driven to such an act. But in the course of remaking himself he has turned his own para-suicide event into an integral part of his image, a paradoxical symbol of empowerment, and a direct source of humour, both through his anecdotes and, especially, a self-penned song he recorded, which sports the rousing refrain "C'mon, c'mon, get yer bloody ears off."[35] In 2005 he appeared in comedy sketches on the highly popular Melbourne television programme *The Footy Show*, playing a character named "Terry the Ear."[36] Thus he has converted a physical legacy of the former back-regions of his life into a personal and professional front-region asset which by association feeds into the reconstructed front region of the historical Pentridge. In the process, the corporeal significance of the para-suicide syndrome is, like so much else in the human history of the jail, diminished and effectively trivialized.

*

The phenomenon of Dark Tourism rests on disparate motives, and visitors to historic sites of death and suffering arrive with a range of expectations: some are there to pay homage, some hope for edification; for others the attraction is little more than ghoulish titillation; many simply want to be entertained. The dominant affect associated with a site may be sombre reverence, shock, or amusement, depending on the site's historical nature, on public perceptions of that history, and on the manner and style of its presentation. Even the soil itself upon which the site's structures are grounded may have multiple, and deeply contested, meanings; the significance of a prison site for an indigenous person, for instance, may reside not in the functional history of the institution, nor in its "dark tourism" appeal, but in the fact that it was originally built on misappropriated land which *already* had meaning.[37] Such an aggrieved view is, of course, compounded for the indigenous person imprisoned at the site during its operational years.

In smuggling his story out of his cell in the early 1990s, Mark Brandon Read was responding to a self-expressive impulse that would set him on the path to celebrity status, open up for him a career as a "professional ex-" (albeit one showing few signs of the typical professional ex-'s earnest sobriety), and render vivid and accessible the world within Pentridge Prison. Hence that world, despite its manifold awfulness, became legitimized as an entertainment setting, by virtue of its depiction, under Chopper's pen, as the domain of the larrikin. Of course, *Chopper: From the Inside* was not intended as an *advertisement* for Pentridge as a public history entity; but witting or not, it has substantially contributed to the front-region euphemization of the prison, and led directly to the question apparently uppermost in the minds of tour visitors: "Which cell was Chopper's?"

NOTES

1   Goffman, *Asylums*, p. 69.
2   Daniel Bergner, *God of the Rodeo: The Quest for Redemption in Louisiana's Angola Prison* (Ballantine, New York, 1998), pp. 1–4 and *passim*.
3   George Thompson (former Coburg resident), interviewed 15 April 2001.
4   Bergner, *God of the Rodeo*, pp. 1–20, 285–92; see also http://www.angolarodeo.com.
5   Bergner, *God of the Rodeo*, loc. cit.
6   The tattoo is visible in a photo of "Santa" with a young child, in a magazine-format publication which is itself a front-region adjunct, compiled by staff to present prison life in precisely the redemptive terms outlined above. Bert Buckley, *H.M. Central Sub Prison Pentridge: Life Behind the Bluestone Walls from 1800's –1900's* (Coburg: Pentridge Prison, 1981), p. 18.
7   See: *Sun* (Melbourne) 28 November 1970, 24 November 1972, 23 Nov 1973; *Herald* (Melbourne) 30 Nov 1973. On the Pentridge "panto," see *Age*, 29 November 1974.
8   *Sun* 29 January 1976.
9   Peter Lynn, *Inquiry into the Victorian Prison System: Instituted to Inquire into a Report on Allegations of Maladministration, Corruption and Drug Trafficking within the Victorian Prison System* (Melbourne: Victorian Government, 1993), p. 113.
10   See, e.g., Mooney, "Bluestone Shadows."
11   I. O'Donnell and K. Edgar, "Fear in Prison," *The Prison Journal* 79 no. 1, March 1999, pp. 90–9.
12   See Ch 6.
13   Anthony Scacco cited in David Heilpern, *Fear or Favour*, p. 86.

14 Inmate Rothenburg cited in ibid., p. 100.
15 Greg Bearup, "On the Inside No-one Can Hear You Scream," *Good Weekend* 19 October 2002; Read, interviewed in Dominik, *Chopper*.
16 Read, *Chopper: From the Inside*, pp. 65–7; also Read interviewed in Dominik, *Chopper*.
17 Heilpern, *Fear or Favour*, p. 68; Frank Dunbaugh, *Amicus curiae* brief to US Supreme Court in *Farmer v Brennan* (1993), "SPR—Stop Prisoner Rape", http://www.spr.org/en/farmer_ argument.html; Richmond, "Fear of Homosexuality."
18 Dunbaugh, *Amicus curiae* brief.
19 Heilpern, *Fear or Favour*, pp. 5–6, 44.
20 Richmond's 1978 study was the first of its kind in Australia; virtually nothing substantive was then undertaken until Heilpern, *Fear or Favour*, in the late 1990s.
21 Heilpern, *Fear or Favour*, p. 86.
22 McLeod cited ibid., p. 62.
23 Ibid.
24 See, e.g., "Minardi Boss in Clink in a Blink," *Hume Leader* (Moreland edition), 9 March 2004.
25 Promoted on Triple M's website at: http://www.mmm.com.au/promotions/2001/escape_pentridge/diaries/index.php (accessed 30 October 2001).
26 Knapp interview; Pat Burchell (former tour guide, Pentridge), interviewed 24 January 2001.
27 Goffman, *Asylums*, p. 44.
28 J. Smith interview; Hoffman interview.
29 A notable exception to this being Old Dubbo Gaol.
30 E.g., Rule, "Inside Stories."
31 Leibling, *Suicides in Prison*, p. 84.
32 Ibid., p. 63.
33 Richard Harding cited in Leonie Lamont and Bruce Tobin, "Prison Suicides in Victoria Top Other States," *Age*, 22 September 1990.
34 Richard Harding, *Review of Suicide and Suicide Attempts in the Custody of the Office of Corrections, Victoria: Report* (Melbourne: Victorian Government, 1990); also Lamont and Tobin, "Prison Suicides."
35 Chopper Read, *Get Your Ears Off*, Import Generic, 1998.
36 *The Footy Show*, Nine Network, broadcast 16 & 30 June 2005.
37 See, e.g., Strange & Kempa, "Shades of Dark Tourism."

PART FOUR

Identity

The last section of this book is centrally concerned with aspects of the Australian national identity. This is a multi-faceted topic, and rather more complex than it used to be. For a century and a half after the first convict settlement Australia was, unequivocally and pretty much unquestioningly, British—and a relatively simplified form of British, at that. The monoculture posited by observers of the emerging nation-state through the nineteenth century and the first half of the twentieth largely ignored substantial sections of the population, negating the continent's indigenous people, non-British migrant groups, women, and large numbers of its poor.[1] This has given way more recently to attempts at an inclusive concept of national identity. Australia has become a self-consciously multi-cultural society, bent on achieving reconciliation with its Aboriginal citizens (but dismayed and not a little confused by the scope of the task), and has embraced many (but far from all) of the tenets of feminism, while taking its first steps to negotiate a viable place in the globalized world.[2] Even the reflexive attempt to re-create a simplified national image produces its own complications and contradictions: the Australian military archetype, the Anzac, has been so apotheosized that for many people the focus of national identity is, paradoxically, an offshore Dark Tourism site on a foreign coast: Gallipoli.

Nor are such vagaries only the product of shifts in material historical events or processes; the national identity can vary in consort with a peacetime phenomenon of popular affect that might be thought of as the national "mood." This can itself influence the course of history—most obviously as a factor in the democratic overturning of entrenched socio-legal institutions (the 1967 referendum on the Constitutional status of Australia's Aboriginals, for instance), or, occasionally, in the dislodgement of long-incumbent governments (such as the 1972 federal election). At least as commonly, such tides and shifts in the national mood may fuel eristic conflicts over just what constitutes that history—hence the virulent "History Wars" of recent years that produced an unusual confluence of scholarly debate, political complicity and tabloid acrimony.[3]

The national identity has become, it seems, irrevocably tangled. A societal skein of disparate political dispositions, ethnicities, socio-economic circumstances, gender perceptions, personal narratives and personal stakes in the historical narratives combine to render consensual answers elusive, yet all the more necessary to pursue.

I make no claim to solving these problems. I can do no more than consider some of the salient aspects that intersect with the subject matter of this book. I intend to discuss national identity as a polymorphous manifestation of individual identity, in the light of issues raised in the study of Australia's historical prison sites.

To begin with, some clarification of terms and ideas is needed. Here it is worth briefly revisiting the succinct definition of national identity (or, as he prefers, "national character") provided in the early 1960s by historian Russel Ward, whose enduring conception in many ways typified and did much to promote the earlier "monoculture" paradigm. Ward's initial schema of the basic concept is as an intrinsically subjective image: "National character" he defines essentially as "a people's idea of itself." But this "idea," he argues, is grounded in reality:

> [T]his stereotype, though often absurdly romanticized and exaggerated, is always connected with reality in two ways. It springs largely from a people's past experiences, and it often modifies current events by colouring [people's] ideas of how they ought "typically" to behave.[4]

In Ward's characterization of national identity as a function of self image there is clearly merit; to his description of the link with reality, however, must be interpolated a crucial caveat, the need for which suggests that at base he may have taken too much on faith. The "stereotype," I suggest, emerges not merely "from a people's past experiences," but also, and often mainly, from *what a people are told* are those "past experiences." (The most obvious example of this selective retelling is perhaps the mythologizing of the iconic Anzacs, a process of reconstruction that began with the official war diarist Charles Bean, as he edited his accounts of the Gallipoli trenches to make them more palatable for his readership back home in Australia.)[5] Equally, as I will show in the final chapter, the people's self-image may spring from what they are told, or led to believe, those experiences are *not*.

In my Introduction I cited Jerome Bruner's model of the self as narrative—an evolving "autobiography," as he puts it. On the basis that national and personal identity are fundamentally analogous, Ward's latter point, regarding the influence of the "stereotype" on the people's behaviour and hence on "current events," is supported by Bruner's suggestion that the narrative itself, and more particularly the *form* of the narrative, has a potency that goes beyond the mere provision of motivational clarity:

> [T]he ways of telling and the ways of conceptualizing that go with [the life narrative] become so habitual that they finally become recipes for structuring experience itself, for laying down routes into memory, for not only guiding the life narrative up to the present but directing it into the future. ... [A] life as led is inseparable from a life as told....
>
> The heart of my argument is this: eventually the culturally shaped cognitive and linguistic processes that guide the self-telling of life narratives achieve the power to structure perceptual experience, to organize memory, to segment and purpose-build the very "events" of a life.[6]

These, then, provide the conceptual parameters of the discussion in the following chapters. I begin by revisiting a number of themes and issues discussed in earlier chapters, to show how the typical Australian prison museum tourist or consumer is actively encouraged, through the control of the narratives, to positively identify with aspects of former prisons and prison life in which reside the greatest agency, and that these centres of power are recognizable as intrinsic aspects of the Australian character. In the final chapter I will argue that the process is in some cases inverted to become one of disempowering exclusion—of othering—and that this, too, involves a central aspect of Australian identity.

NOTES

1   See, e.g., Anthony Trollope, *Australia and New Zealand* (London: Dawsons of Pall Mall, 1968 [1873]); W.K. Hancock, *Australia* (Brisbane: Jacaranda Press, 1966 [1930]);

John Pringle, *Australian Accent* (London: Chatto and Windus, 1961); Donald Horne, *The Lucky Country* (Harmondsworth: Penguin, 1964).

2   On reconciliation, see, e.g., Ann Curthoys, "Revisiting Australian History: Including Aboriginal Resistance," *Arena* no. 62, 1983; Bain Attwood and Andrew Markus, "The Fight for Aboriginal Rights," in *The Australian Century: Political Struggle in the Building of a Nation*, ed. Robert Manne (Melbourne: Text, 1999); Robert Manne, *In Denial: The Stolen Generations and the Right* (Melbourne: Schwartz Publishing, 2001). On feminism see, e.g., Marilyn Lake, *Getting Equal: The History of Australian Feminism* (St Leonards NSW: Allen and Unwin, 1999). On Australia and globalization see, e.g., Paul Kelly, *The End of Certainty: Power, Politics and Business in Australia* (St Leonards NSW: Allen and Unwin, 1994).

3   See Stuart Macintyre and Anna Clark, *The History Wars* (Melbourne: Melbourne University Press, 2004).

4   Russel Ward, *The Australian Legend*, Melbourne: Oxford University Press, 2003, p. 1.

5   D.A. Kent, "The Anzac Book and the Anzac Legend," *Historical Studies* 21 no. 84, April 1985; Geoffrey Serle, "The Digger Tradition and Australian Nationalism," *Meanjin* June 1965.

6   Bruner, "Life as Narrative."

CHAPTER TEN

Law and Order:
Jailers, Larrikins, and Penal Populism

American prison reform activists Angela Davis and Gina Dent have noted a seeming paradox in the fact that (as they see it) Australians evince "pride" in their convict ancestry, while they ignore and take virtually no interest in the conditions and day-to-day plight of contemporary inmates of sites of incarceration.[1] Davis and Dent expressed their puzzlement in the latter days before the terrorist attacks on New York's "Twin Towers"—the event the vernacular has dubbed "9/11." The subsequent radical shift in policy in a number of Western countries, including Australia, toward increased border security, with concomitant rises in the numbers of incarcerated non-Australians on the grounds that they are officially perceived and treated as "illegal" entrants to Australia, has arguably accompanied, encouraged and in turn reflected a shift in the national mood of the kind referred to above—in this case a mood of reduced tolerance toward those seen as a threat to the Australian "way of life."[2]

It is not within my scope here to pursue the many questions arising from the prolonged detention of Middle-Eastern and South-East Asian refugees; but on the basis of my encounters with tourists in the prison museums I visited, and with Davis and Dent's comments in mind, I can state that if any shift has occurred in the general mood regarding modern prisoners it has not been in the direction of increased concern for their "day-to-day plight." It is reasonable to suggest, in fact, that Australia, along with its closest allies the United States and Britain, is currently in the midst of a wave of what criminologists term "penal populism"[3]—a paradigm in which criminal justice systems, and especially sentencing authorities, are driven toward the harsher end of the punishment spectrum by legislators who see themselves as responding to popular sentiment in favour of longer terms of imprisonment and reductions in inmates' "comforts." In keeping with such simplism, it has been noted that "The central tool of penal populism is imprisonment."[4]

I noted in Chapter One that a striking number of tourists I observed at historical prisons evinced attitudes that effectively supported the suffering of the former inmates (an inversion, as I also noted, of the norm at Dark Tourism sites). This they did by expressing their regret at the closure of the older-style jails. At a number of the former prisons I visited, I distributed questionnaires to tourists, gauging various aspects of their perceptions and responses to the sites. Of the several hundred completed questionnaires I received, approximately six percent included written comments to the effect that the prisoners of today in modern facilities have it "soft"; "live in luxury"; live in "motel" conditions; and that "they should bring back the old prisons." This is not on its face a large percentage, but it is significant for two reasons: firstly, the remarks were gratuitous; they were not offered in response to any question or prompting beyond providing a lined space at the end of the questionnaire. Secondly—and most cogently—the written observations were the tip of an iceberg: a far greater number of oral comments along similar lines were directed to me (sometimes in the course of apologising for not writing it down due to lack of time), or spoken in my hearing, directed to companions or tour guides. At sites where I had opportunities to converse with tourists, I took to specifically asking their opinion on the topic, with a casually framed question such as, "What do you think about this as a place to lock people up?"; a *majority* of responses affirmed approval of the site, usually with appended comments to the effect that "they have it too easy in these modern jails," and often expressing a general sentiment that today's prisoner accommodation is akin to a stay in a "motel." I was told many times that prisoners now "get their own room with a TV and video," gym equipment, use of a pool and an en-suite shower. A number of tourists commented that their own homes were "not as good as what the inmates have got."

These responses were in accord with specific comments offered during tours by many of the tour guides, and with the general tone and underlying temper of the sites' interpretation and presentation. In this way it could be said that the tendency of visitors, either in response to or in spontaneous concurrence with those interpretations, is to actively identify with the "jailers." The attitudes, sentiments and explicit messages expressed by the gatekeepers at each site with regard to the site's former inmates were in almost all cases consistent with the othering that characterizes inmates' treatment during their incarceration, and the visitors to those sites echoed their views, despite being in a position to see at close hand the conditions in which those incarcerated persons had lived. The old prisons were viewed as "tough but fair," in the sense that their harshness was not an inappropriate consequence of having committed whatever crime warranted incarceration in the first place.

As I have discussed earlier, a significant aspect of many sites' interpretations involved the euphemization of the prisons' more brutal aspects, most commonly through humour and highly selective choices of representative narratives. Something of an exception, among the recently decommissioned sites I visited, was the Old Dubbo Gaol, where the curator, Christine Raszewski, was in the throes of revising the site's interpretation, with a commitment to restoring what she saw as a long-term imbalance by representing the inmates without undue jocularity or diabolising.[5] She was pursuing her goals incrementally in the face of strong and at times rancorous opposition from the previous "generation" of gatekeepers, a group with links to various local community organizations including the historical society, and also to the sheriff's office.[6] One of the areas in which she had been successful in making revisions was in the representation of executions.

Many tourists at various prisons spoke approvingly to me (in some cases with palpable nostalgia) about capital punishment. Like the more general comments supporting the older prisons, these comments were unsolicited (at no time did I canvas opinions on capital punishment), and they were as likely to occur at sites with no displayed history of executions. In prisons where executions were carried out, it is not uncommon to find gallows on display. The atmosphere among visitors in the site areas containing gallows tends to be somewhat uncertain, ambivalent; the sight of a noosed rope hanging from a beam can be disquieting, even though there is no pretence that that specific rope is "authentic," that is, it was never actually used. Where there is no active commentary such as occurs during guided tours, the sense of unease engendered by the place and its artefacts makes some visitors fall quiet; others manifest their discomfort with awkward jocularity. (I have seen this take highly insensitive and/or foolhardy avenues, such as people placing the noose around their own necks and leering at their companions; a gallows display at Fanny Bay Jail, Darwin, had to be closed because tourists were placing themselves at risk of accidental hanging in order to be photographed by friends.)[7] Visitors' unease is often dispelled in cases where a tour guide or equivalent source of information, such as automatic audio-visual equipment, provides a commentary on the gallows which locates the apparatus in a narrative sympathetic to the place and its purport. As I noted in Chapter Five, such narratives tend to dwell on the especially heinous crimes committed by certain of the prisoners executed—what I term the site's "Featured Hanging."

The Featured Hanging may be thought of as a category of celebrity prisoner. Most prisons at which executions occurred, and especially where the site's representation includes a gallows, incorporate such a narrative in presenting the implement of death. Thus the prison's darkest feature, the aspect most difficult to euphemize, is redeemed, and with it, by implication, is the prison—legitimized as an instrument of justice and society's righteous struggle against the Other.

At Old Dubbo Gaol, however, although there is a gallows in place (without commentary), the prison's eight executions are represented in a separate space, in a detailed, low-key interpretation gallery that invites the visitor to read a series of substantive texts mounted on life-size pictorial renderings of their subjects, recounting each executed prisoner's story. These accounts include, crucially, the stories of those now believed to have been innocent men. The gallery, designed by Raszewski in collaboration with Port Arthur curator Julia Clark, is poignant and arresting. The detailed conveying of the stories serves to personalize even those executed prisoners whom it is reasonable to regard as unequivocally guilty, and in the process the human implications of the death penalty are foregrounded. A large number of the visitors who entered that room while I was there stayed long enough to read the texts.

A further virtue of the Old Dubbo Gaol display is that it also highlights the racial element in many incarcerations and executions. Several of the inmates hanged were recent migrants or Aborigines, and to judge by the histories recounted, were clearly victims of their own linguistic and/or cultural ignorance, vis-à-vis the legal process they found themselves caught up in, resulting in literally fatal injustices. I have already touched upon the inherent racism of the total institution; it is worth making the point here that penal populism has been shown to disproportionately punish members of racial minorities— as was graphically demonstrated within the past decade in the course of the Northern Territory's and Western Australia's juridical experiments with "mandatory sentencing."[8]

The ethos of interpretation and mode of representation at Old Dubbo Gaol are, as I have said, unusual among the prison museums I visited, and this attempt to revise the traditional style has been met with active opposition. At most sites, large and small, that were operational prisons within living memory, the interpretation of the site, selection of narratives and management of the physical evidence promote a line that effectively perpetuates the othering of today's inmates by othering the inmates of the recent past.

It has been shown that penal populism, a political phenomenon by definition intended to reflect the majority's attitudes toward crime and punishment, is in fact often based on incorrect, usually exaggerated, readings of the public's punitive intent, due to unsound surveying methodologies.[9] The danger, however, is that the policies, once in place or even merely through their promotion, can in turn become self-fulfilling by themselves influencing people's perceptions of crime. In this regard the prison museum has the potential to play an influential role through the de facto endorsement of harshly punitive carceral regimes. So too, individuals who are widely identified with the prison system, and who are seen by the public as highly credible on the subject, can be disproportionately influential. Chopper Read is on record as advocating the death penalty and a variety of other "old school" punishment modes;[10] it is appropriate, therefore, to further examine his social role and credentials as a public figure in the Australian context.

*

In analysing Chopper Read's relationship with the post-operational prison and his role in its euphemization and commodification, I argued that he has sufficiently reconstructed his public self to warrant the status of "larrikin." The larrikin is an emblematic "Australian" type—not least because it in large part characterizes one of the defining national icons, the Anzac—and figures centrally in the masculine Australian identity. It is important to consider the nature of larrikinism as a facet of the national sensibility, and the implications of a person such as Chopper Read attaining such status.

Amused (or bemused) fondness for the brazen but essentially harmless rule-breaker is often thought (by Australians) to be a trait peculiar to Australia; but it may well be a trait of all strongly individualist, that is liberal, societies—especially if those rules are broken in the pursuit of individual freedom. But there are historical specificities to the etymology of the word used in Australia to define the phenomenon that may well give the Australian version a particular social and cultural texture. Although *larrikin* is today deemed an Australian word,[11] it probably originated in Britain as an English dialect variant of *lark* (as in "larking about").[12] It appears to have been transported to the Antipodes in the mid-nineteenth century, to appear in Australian (and New Zealand) English as a term for a type of youthful urban ruffian known for a distinctive style in clothing and a range of anti-social public behaviour that included, at its worst, unprovoked pack violence.[13]

There was, it seems, little that was amusing or likeable about the original larrikins. The first Australian appearance of the word in print, in 1868, paints an unambiguously negative picture of "gangs" of "hooligans";[14] but its consistent identification with youth (and perhaps the echo of *lark* in the background) made it ripe for a lighter re-interpretation, and some literary uses of *larrikin* emphasising the essentially harmless "roguish urchin" connotations familiar today are recorded within a year or so of that first pejorative appearance.[15] For some decades the two contrasting meanings were in direct competition, until in the decade prior to the Great War its cloak of disapprobation began clearly to be shed (much credit for which, according to John Rickard, is due to C.J. Dennis's *Sentimental Bloke*).[16] By the early 1920s, coincident with the first publication of the comic strip *Ginger Meggs*, the word had been largely re-established in the public mind with the connotations it holds to this day: incorrigibly mischievous but at base harmless, a rule-breaker evoking affectionate, perhaps admiring, toleration, even from those nominally wronged.[17]

The "harmless" aspect of the larrikin is not simple. Possibly because the label retains a distant imprint of its less savoury origins, it may be said, as Rickard does, that "[a]ggression, whether physical or verbal, is basic to the larrikin."[18] But this aggression is invariably tempered by such disarming brazenness and good humour that he "gets away with it."[19] To accomplish this feat, the larrikin must maintain a running tension between dangerousness and harmlessness, between notional threat and perceived trustworthiness. For the rule-breaker with a personable presentation and some wit, in a conventional social environment in which the stakes are relatively innocuous, the parameters of such a balancing act are relatively straightforward; Ginger Meggs, for instance, plays out his larrikinism "within a familiar, comfortable suburban environment and is, by definition, likeable."[20] For an individual with Chopper Read's history, however, the task is more complex.

Read's past is one of extremes, and for such a past to be translated into a present larrikinism, the persona must be stated and restated in extreme terms—as Caterson says, "an image that is larger than life and is the stuff of legend."[21] I noted in Chapter Eight that Read has been likened, and more to the point has likened himself, to Ned Kelly. In thus identifying with the archetypal bushranger, he effectively casts himself—or allows others to cast him—as a personification of a core aspect of Australian identity. And interestingly, it appears that a substantial section of the Australian public is prepared to grant him this status. Despite the fact that his notoriety derives centrally from his prison identity and from recounting his *un*bushranger-like criminal behaviour, there is no general outcry at the incongruity of such a notion.

For Read to be thus indulged required him to be accepted as socially redeemed: he has had to demonstrate a return to innocence; he has had to prove, above all, that he is *harmless* to the general population. This has two main dimensions: humour and domestication. Rickard argues that a vital component of what might be termed the "classical" larrikin —the Sentimental Bloke being the exemplar—and what makes him "lovable," is his vulnerability to the domesticating power of a "good" woman—such as the Bloke's Doreen.[22] Rickard cites the further example of Ginger Meggs's "prim and proper girlfriend, Min, [who] is surely destined to domesticate him." In showing himself, however distantly, open to such taming, the larrikin reassures the public / audience / "victim" that there is a limit to his wildness, that the socially innocuous, "harmless" side will ultimately prevail. Read, as we have seen, has taken this crucial step twice in the last decade.

The other aspect, humour, comes naturally to Read, but that is not to say that he can tell any jokes he likes, in any way he likes. His audience is too aware of the visceral dangerousness in his background to feel comfortable and safe without some reassurance. As a humorist whose style rests in large part on the type of dark ironies that abound in prison, and who speaks at times of matters of violence the average person can find very discomforting, he must define the moral parameters with some precision. The victims of his jokes, like the victims of his avowed violence, are invariably identified as (a) clearly someone the audience can recognize as the Other; and (b) clearly morally bad—which is, of course, the essence of (a).

This othering can include Read himself, in his former incarnation as a member of the underworld; the professional ex-, by definition, has elevated himself above and out of that transgressive former identity and milieu, and it is not uncommon for Read to make himself the butt of a joke or amusing anecdote, when that joke shows up his own formerly reprehensible, or (for the purpose of the tale) deranged state of mind and morals. The general thrust of the film *Chopper* (which he did not author, but which was a response both to his writings and his direct input as a consultant) consolidates this theme very effectively, in that it depicts him as a wittily engaging feral creature who is at times clearly bewildered by his own character traits and proclivities. Read has had to re-invent himself, transforming a profoundly knowing—in other words, the antithesis of innocent—denizen of the underworld into something more child-like—a good-hearted and at base little more than *mischievous* (former) killer who just wants to get on with his newly earned good life in peace.

And yet the audience, while reassured of its own safety, wants to retain a sense of Chopper Read's dangerousness, and the dangers of his world, which are, after all, the exotic core of his appeal. The raw, brute power—the archetypal hard man—that underpins Read's public personality is rarely far from view; and like his audience, for Read to get the jokes, his own jokes, he too has to feel safe, for in the final analysis he has spent a lifetime ensuring his own survival not through innocence but through knowing, and being feared for it. An example of how this knowingness translates into his current self-presentation is his famous story, invariably couched in wryly ironic tones, of an escape attempt in Pentridge, organized by his closest friends inside, which involved breaking out of H Division and climbing onto a roof. According to Read, he was an unwilling participant in the escape, believing it to be folly, and this was confirmed when he was ambushed, as he emerged from a manhole, by a prison officer with a baton. Read has it that the officer hit him on the head "between 15 to 20 times before [the baton] broke."[23] A significant component of his jocular retelling of this beating is its ineffectuality upon him, in that even after the baton breaks on his head, he is still conscious and able to make threats. To maintain the innocent persona, he must depict himself in such situations as having (temporary) episodes of sheer stupidity, combined with an almost troll-like imperviousness to physical insult. (Consonant with this tone, in one version of the story the bashing with the baton "cured" him of recurring headaches he had suffered for a year since a previous beating with an iron bar.)[24]

Such a story, when juxtaposed with the story of Garry David's escape attempt, points up the degree to which the narratives of inmates such as David—and the multitude with even less agency than David's—are overshadowed by the narratives of the prison's elites, and hence are skewed, obscured and eventually lost. Even Read's ambivalence about escaping signifies his comparative imperviousness to the rigours of prison life, and in the process shifts the focus away from the other men involved in the attempt, and their motivation for making it. Read, of course, has a perfect right to recount his own experiences as he sees fit; where there is fault, it lies with those who would appropriate and re-present such accounts, or more commonly the *tone* of such accounts, in the course of euphemizing the experiences of people who find nothing at all to laugh about in jail.

In 2003 Read teamed up with former Australian Rules league footballer and professional zany Mark "Jacko" Jackson, and the well-known Sydney ex-detective Roger Rogerson, to tour the hotels and leagues clubs of (mostly) rural New South Wales with a spoken-word show based entirely on the trio's attractions as raconteurs. In an irreverent allusion to the iconic bushrangers of ballad and legend, the show was entitled *Wild Colonial Psychos*[25]— described by one observer as "somewhere between sportsmen's night and vaudeville, with a touch of freak show."[26] The show has undergone various mutations since it began, and for a while featured only Read and Jackson while Rogerson served a prison term for perjury; but Read's choice of touring colleagues is worth some brief examination.

Jackson, who is an old friend of Read, has been a credentialled larrikin since his football days in the 1980s, both for his eccentric antics at celebratory moments on the field, and for his "maverick" relations with coaches and other officials at the three clubs for whom he played.[27] Since retiring from football he has carved out a second life in the entertainment and advertising industries as a singer, actor and highly overt comedian. His contribution to *Wild Colonial Psychos* was the most conventional of the three, in that he is the closest to a "stand-up" comic, with a routine of football anecdotes, jokes and provocative remarks tailored to suit "pub" crowds. There is a sense in which his and Read's partnership in an entertainment context has a natural complementarity, in both their similarities and differences.

Roger Rogerson, however, has no longstanding relationship with either Jackson or Read, but was "recruited" to the venture, through mutual acquaintances in the liquor industry.[28] Like Read, he is seeking to redeem himself, although, as a former police officer accused of manifold forms of extreme corruption and convicted of conspiring to pervert the course of justice, he might be thought to have even more to overcome than Read in the quest for public respectability. But it is worth noting that at the time of the trio's first tour a slightly uneasy but markedly good-natured interview article appeared in the *Sydney Morning Herald* in which Rogerson was described as "a saloon-bar larrikin with a tobacco laugh and a blunt edge to his jokes."[29] The article struck a studiedly even-handed note, candidly summing up his career and painting his aspirations in optimistic terms. "Rogerson," it stated, "was a highly decorated police officer before he turned bad. He has been a hero and villain; now he seems poised to reinvent himself as a loveable rogue."[30]

Rogerson's quest for larrikin redemption suffered a temporary setback when he was jailed once more in early 2005, to serve a year for giving misleading testimony to a Police Integrity Commission hearing.[31] Given the unlikelihood of him establishing a "Robin Hood" image such as Read's, it would seem at first sight questionable whether he will be able to live down his notoriety to the extent of achieving "loveable" status. But it must be said that there is discernable in the *SMH* article an openness to the notion, plus, perhaps more significantly, there remains the public's perennial readiness to embrace those perceived as figures of power, however unsavoury their exercise of that power may be. Indeed, within days of his release from that latest prison term, he was back on the road with Read and Jackson, playing once more to enthusiastic crowds.[32]

Rogerson does not seriously attempt to present himself as a "Robin Hood."[33] During his policing days (before he "turned bad") he was known as an exceptionally effective enforcer of the law. He states that this success was through a "no-nonsense" policing style, an "old fashioned" approach based on striking fear into the "crims."[34] In his unrepentant espousal of that style by which he made his reputation, his persona is far more akin to the eponymous protagonist of the *Dirty Harry* films—to whom he was directly likened in a *60 Minutes* interview some years ago.[35] "You must create fear," he said in that interview. "Crims, be they tough crims, hard crims, they feared certain police officers and I was one of them."[36]

Clearly, such an approach to policing is congruent with the perceptions and attitudes associated with penal populism, and the espousal of such views on a top-rating television programme could be regarded as potentially highly effective promotion. And although Rogerson might be thought to have little credit with the public given his record, his views were effectively endorsed by *60 Minutes'* writers; the angle taken in the segment was that behaving towards criminals like "a real-life Dirty Harry" was not in itself a bad thing; Rogerson's fault was that he went too far and "finally crossed the line."[37]

Both Rogerson and Read, then, engender a fascination attributable in large part to their personal power—their notional dangerousness. Both avow that their propensities for violence were directed toward the Other. Both stress that those propensities lie firmly in the past. And both present themselves and their violence in at times confronting but ultimately palatable packages of humour. (Rogerson does not tell "jokes" in the manner of Read, having more the style of a straightforward raconteur, but there is an undeniably irreverent undercurrent in his delivery.) Both are explicitly labelled "larrikins." (And in the case of Read, some would have it that his status goes considerably beyond that: online advertising for a personal appearance tour promoting the release of the Wild Colonial Psychos' DVD styled him, apparently with no irony intended, as "one of Australia's most infamous characters and national icons.")[38]

To some extent, Jackson aids in the process of "legitimizing" the other two by association, on the strength of his longstanding "mainstream" audience, and having no criminal convictions in his past. And all three men, it should be noted, stand as emblematic spokesmen for an intensely masculinist subculture. This, as an incidental side-effect, cannot fail to further the othering of the women in the prison system and lend authority to the notion of women inmates as inherently difficult and transgressive.

*

It is arguable that the appeal of the "Wild Colonial Psychos" in some degree rests on the natural fascination and perverse pride many Australians have in their continent's peculiarly deadly landscape and wildlife—sharks, snakes, spiders and so on. But also visible, I suggest, is a rather less savoury extension of that fascination and pride: the quality George Orwell termed "bully worship"—a culture of uncritical admiration for society's exponents of "power and successful cruelty."[39] (Orwell was responding primarily to the broad support extended to the political evils of his day, but he equated this with a spectrum of cultural trends seen in business, the media and public life in general.) The sum result, in the case of Chopper Read and Roger Rogerson, as entities of the historical prison, as living embodiments of dark tourism, and as exponents of both penal populism and the favourite national trait of larrikinism, is a paradoxical conflation, or synthesis, of the jailer and the rebel—of the Establishment figure and the larrikin. Such a combination is highly potent as an influence on public perceptions of the correctional paradigm they effectively signify, and the people whose lives are, or were, intimately entwined within that paradigm.

NOTES

1   Angela Davis and Gina Dent, "Conversations: Prison as a Border: A Conversation on Gender, Globalization, and Punishment" (Panel Discussion), *Signs* 26 no. 4, Summer 2001. As I will show in Chapter 11, the "pride" Davis and Dent observed is becoming increasingly equivocal.

2   See Robert Manne with David Corlett, *Sending them Home: Refugees and the New Politics* (Melbourne: Black Inc., 2004).

3   See Julian Robert, Loretta Stalans, David Indermaur and Mike Hough, *Penal Populism and Public Opinion: Lessons from Five Countries* (New York: Oxford University Press, 2002), pp. 29, 64–6; also David Indermaur and Mike Hough, "Strategies for Changing Public Attitudes to Punishment," in *Changing Attitudes to Punishment: Public Opinion, Crime and Justice*, ed. Julian Roberts and Mike Hough (Cullompton, Devon: Willan, 2002).

4   Robert et al., *Penal Populism*, p. 5.

5   Raszewski interview; author observation on site.

6   Raszewski interview.

7   Dewar and Fredericksen, "Prison Heritage," p. 57.

8   Robert et al., *Penal Populism*, pp. 5–6, 56–7, 190nn 15 and 21.

9   Ibid., pp. 29ff; Ian Munro, "Public Softer on Crime than Judges, Study Finds"; *idem*, "Does the Time Fit the Crime?" both in *The Age* 30 September 2006; .

10 Read, *Chopper: From the Inside*, pp. 59, 65–7.

11 *Concise Oxford Dictionary.*

12 Frederick Ludowyk, "Aussie Words: Larrikin," *Ozwords*, June 1998, at: http://www.anu .edu.au/andc/Ozwords/June_98/5._larrikin.htm (accessed 7 December 2004).

13 Ibid.; also Rickard, "Lovable larrikins."

14 Ludowyk, "Aussie Words."

15 Ibid.

16 Rickard, "Lovable Larrikins."

17 Ibid.

18 Ibid.

19 Ibid.

20 Ibid.

21 Caterson, "Chopping into Literature," p. 20.

22 Rickard, "Lovable Larrikins," p. 81.

23 Read, *Chopper: From the Inside*, pp. 204, 72; also Read in *Australian Story*.

24 Read, *Chopper: From the Inside*, p. 204.

25 The NSW "country pub" chain known as "Pubboy" originally sponsored and promoted the tour, publicizing it at: http://www.pubboy.com.au/page/wild_colonial_phycos_tour _2005.html [*sic*] (accessed 10 March 2008).

26 Andrew Rule, "Telling It Straight," *Good Weekend*, 20 May 2006, p. 29.

27 See Australian Football League website: http://afl.com.au/default.asp?pg=aflrecord&spg =display&articleid=163360 (accessed 12 June 2005).

28 Mark Dapin, "'Jolly Rogerson'," *SMH* 14 November 2003.

29 Ibid.

30 Ibid.

31 Rogerson was convicted of perjury in late 2004 and sentenced in February 2005 to two years in prison, with a minimum of one year to be served. "Rogerson Jailed for Lying Under Oath," *Age* 18 February 2005.

32 Neil Mercer, "Rogerson's Roadshow," *Sunday Telegraph* 26 February 2006.

33 On Rogerson's personal aspirations, see Rule, "Telling It Straight."

34 Dapin, "'Jolly Rogerson'."

35 *60 Minutes*, "The Enforcer: Ruling By Fear" [Roger Rogerson interview], Nine Network, broadcast 9 April 2000.

36 Ibid.

37 Ibid.

38 Madman Entertainment, "Chopper's on DVD Again ...!", http://www.madman.com.au/ actions/news.do?method=view&newsld=45 (accessed 6 October 2005).

39 George Orwell, "Raffles and Miss Blandish," in *The Penguin Essays of George Orwell*, London: Penguin Books, 1984, p. 272.

CHAPTER ELEVEN

Cultural Memory:
The Convicts

In the previous chapter I referred to Angela Davis and Gina Dent's observation regarding Australians' "pride" in their convict past; it is time to examine that supposed affect more closely. In Chapter One I recounted a visit to my brother Paul in Pentridge, by way of explicating something of my personal stake in that prison and its subsequent reincarnation as a public history entity. Paul was in prison for approximately two years in the late 1980s. During that time, as I was, perforce, becoming increasingly acquainted with the jail, it happened that I was also re-establishing links with certain of my relatives. From one in particular, an aunt with an interest in genealogical research, I learned for the first time that my great-great grandfather on my mother's side, a Suffolk shoemaker named James Mauldon, was a convict—sent down in 1829 for larceny, and transported for life to the penal colony of Tasmania.[1] Several of his many years there were spent at the most feared place on the island, the special punishment centre at Port Arthur.[2]

James Mauldon was twenty-five when he was transported, and he left behind in Suffolk a wife and two children, whom he never saw again.[3] On his arrival in the colony he was put to work as an "assigned servant." Over the following twenty-five years, during which he several times earned, and then lost, his "ticket of leave," he alternated between periods of gainful employment and an assortment of penalties for crimes and misdemeanours, including inciting a strike among his "fellow-servants" (fifty lashes and three months on the chain gang); occasional minor and not-so-minor thefts (leading variously to fines, loss of employment, probation, ticket of leave revoked, and terms of imprisonment); allowing prisoners to escape while serving as a police constable (dismissed from the constabulary); and, most seriously, bigamy (seven years in prison).[4] In today's parlance, a recidivist.

With the exception of his bigamy conviction—a relatively unusual crime in a colony where the men outnumbered the women many-fold—such a career of misbehaviour is unremarkable among the convict records, and seems, like many of his fellows' records, to reflect more the transgressive opportunist than the "hardened criminal." I admit to feeling some relief at seeing no crimes of violence listed on my ancestor's record.

In 1855, now fifty years old and finally free with his last "conditional pardon," Mauldon married twenty-year-old Elizabeth Dunne, also a former convict. She was his fifth wife, and my great-great-grandmother. After living in Launceston for seven years, in 1862 they moved across Bass Strait to the port town of Warrnambool, on the south-west coast of Victoria. There he died of natural causes in 1867, leaving Elizabeth pregnant with their seventh child. She would remarry the following year and eventually move to Melbourne, but her son Robert would remain all his life in the area, as would his children and their children. In 1935, sixty-eight years after James Mauldon's death, his great-granddaughter, my mother, was born, also in Warrnambool.

My experience of becoming emotionally involved, as it were, with a maximum-security prison currently housing my nearest kin, and simultaneously discovering that my family history—at least the only line of it I knew anything about—had its Australian genesis in colonial penal institutions, affected me in a number of ways. Before discussing these matters, however, it is necessary to consider some more general aspects of the nature and meaning of convict ancestry.

In the first place, it should be noted that a significant number of Australians can count one or more convicts among their forebears. A survey conducted in association with the 1999 "Republic" referendum campaign found that 11·3 per cent of Australians, or approximately 2·4 million people (at current population figures), could, to their knowledge, answer "Yes" when asked if they were "descended from one or more of the convicts" transported during the settlement era, and a further 2·4 million would be likely to answer "Maybe."[5] Those who professed not to know amounted to 17·5 per cent, and 59·9 per cent said unequivocally "No."[6] Unsurprisingly, the percentage of "yes" respondents was higher (14 per cent) in the former "convict colonies" (New South Wales, Tasmania and Western Australia).[7] It follows that, if convict ancestry were confirmed for only half of the "maybe" respondents, the total would be very nearly 3·6 million Australians, or roughly the population of one of our largest cities. These figures—these people—should be borne in mind during the following discussion.

In a 1969 paper in *Historical Studies*, historian Henry Reynolds addressed a number of questions regarding the ongoing negative societal influence of intensive convict settlement.[8] Reynolds's discussion is confined to the special case of Tasmania, which "despite its restricted size and small population...absorb[ed] 42 per cent of all felons transported to Australia compared with 52 per cent sent to New South Wales."[9] He calls for wider scholarly recognition of the discrete nature of Australia's convict societies and their consequently disparate social legacies, noting that many of the geographical, socio-economic and political factors that served to imbue New South Wales and other mainland convict settlement areas with "specifically convict values like class solidarity, egalitarianism, [and] anti-authoritarianism"—qualities broadly identified as essential aspects of the Australian "legend"[10]—were so lacking in Tasmania that the colony's "largely emancipist working class...was probably the most dispirited proletariat in the Australian colonies."[11] He goes so far as to suggest that "the large ex-convict component in the population probably retarded the growth of radical and working class politics" in Tasmania, and that, in direct contrast to their mainland counterparts, the convicts of the island "were early exemplars of the submissive, unprotesting and a-political tendencies in Australian life."[12]

Implicit in Reynolds's analysis is the social stigma long associated, in Australian society, with convict ancestry (a stigma especially pronounced and enduring in Tasmania).[13] At the time he wrote, the tide of public sentiment across Australia was beginning to turn, with shame and denial gradually being replaced by a degree of acceptance and interest in the convict past generally, and with that, according to a number of commentators, an active pride among people who discover (generally via genealogical enquiries) a convict ancestor.[14] There are, however, complexities in this apparent shift in sensibilities, which I intend to consider in the light of two sociological studies undertaken within the last decade. The first is by Ronald Lambert, who in 1999 conducted a study of two "convict descendant societies" totalling approximately 1,000 members, and interviewed forty-six members of those groups on the topic of their own and others' understanding of and attitudes to their ancestries. He found that a significant number had directly experienced some form of stigmatizing over the issue. They reported numerous instances in which knowledge of their convict ancestry provoked reactions in others of manifest shame, embarrassment, stereotyping, and/or, especially among their own extended family members, outright denial.[15] Nor had this disapproval entirely faded as a social force; despite their general impression that such stigma "was largely a preoccupation of the past or confined today to older generations,"[16] some recounted recent instances of such reactions.

It is clear the respondents had managed individually to come to terms with the issue, but the process by which they did so is of interest. All, according to Lambert, had responded to the stigma—or expectation thereof—by employing a range of defensive narrative strategies in the stories they told about their ancestors. He discerned in their stories a range of rhetorically structured rationales via which they "argued against the convict stain,"[17] and found that one or more of five generic arguments underpinned their narratives, "each redefining convict ancestors as a category and assigning them more desirable identities in place of their historic master identities as convicts."[18] These arguments he characterized under the following headings:

(a) "[Convicts] as objects of quasi-professional interest"—the committed genealogist's avowedly objective "scientific" sense of the convict as primarily an object of study. Lambert notes that most were already engaged in genealogical research when they discovered their convict descent; he judged almost all respondents' narratives to fit this "scientific" category to some degree;

(b) "As nation-builders"—fuelling in the descendants a patriotic sense that tended toward republicanism, often including a somewhat resentful reaction against the predominantly "British" history received in their early education;

(c) "As a minority within a multicultural society"—an anchoring identity for white Anglo-Australians who feel outnumbered by immigrant groups able to claim "ethnic" status;

(d) "As collectibles"—a competitive pursuit of certificates of authenticity, proliferation of convict ancestors, and questing in hope of turning out to be a "First Fleeter";

(e) "As 'interesting stories'"—colourful, adventurous and/or titillatingly transgressive narratives, topics to dine out on, a source of "cool."[19]

The respondents also demonstrated a range of rhetorical strategies for the purpose of "redefining relationships" between the "respectable" modern descendant and the ancestral felon by: minimizing or euphemizing the transportee's offence(s); citing the historical distance from the present generation; empathizing with putative victims of injustice; or citing the ancestors' "redemption" gained through their own or, symbolically, their descendants' "respectable" lives.[20]

Lambert's study is of interest for a number of reasons. It is apparent that the avowed "pride" reported by his respondents is to some degree an artefact, constructed in the face of real or expected disapproval from other Australians (and in some cases from non-Australians, encountered in Australia or overseas).[21] To what degree the "stain" retains any social potency thus remains more open than either Lambert or his respondents seem willing to credit (I will return to this point shortly). The further question arises at once, to what extent is the "pride" in convict ancestry as felt by Lambert's group typical of the "pride" so widely averred among the convict descendants in the broader population—that is, to what extent is it, too, a defensive construct? A complicating factor in addressing this aspect is that as a sample of convict descendants, his respondents are themselves of questionable typicality (even within the demographic parameters he identifies), being members of groups ("societies") whose *raison d'être* is the search for and, in various ways, celebration of convict ancestry. They may be assumed not only to be more knowledgeable on the subject than the average person, but to have greater motivational resources in formulating the strategic narratives upon which their pride is based.

The typicality or otherwise of groups such as these is potentially of consequence for the prison museums that are presented as convict tourist sites, such as Port Arthur, Fremantle Prison, Hyde Park Barracks and a number of lesser-known sites. There is visible a growing tendency for genealogical societies to play a significant role in the construction of the narratives at some of these sites, with the imprimatur of curators. Little critical discussion seems to occur at curatorial level of the groups' credentials for such roles, and hence they are now effectively becoming the gatekeepers of convict narratives. This is particularly evident in displays or events in which explicit links between convict heritage and site visitor are invoked and/or exploited, such as the regular "Descendents' Days" which have been held at Fremantle Prison for some years, and which have strong links to genealogical societies.[22] Curators and tour guides at a number of sites I visited referred me to personnel of local genealogical societies for the "definitive" information on convicts associated with their particular sites. The terms in which such referrals were made almost invariably represented the recommended group or person as the best-resourced and most knowledgeable on the subject, and (at times it was stated explicitly) that there was no point in me even looking elsewhere for information. At sites which never housed convicts or where the convict era is a minimal factor in the history, I received similarly couched referrals to persons involved in local history societies. (During my early research on Pentridge more than one individual with personal experience of the site initially suggested that there was no point in my interviewing them, on the grounds that a former governor of security, who was, I discovered, also president of the Coburg Historical Society, had "written a book" on the place and could tell me "everything I needed to know." Unsurprisingly there is, I have found, often a conflation of genealogical and local history societies.)

There is no doubt that the resources and dynamism of genealogical groups and convict descendant societies have the potential to play an important adjunct role in the interpretation and presentation of such sites; but their increasing centrality in the process of informing visitors raises concerns similar to those raised by the centrality of any other stakeholder group. It is of some concern, too, that social scientists such as Lambert should look to groups such as these for examples of convict and convict-descendant narratives, apparently without taking into account how much or how little they have in common with the majority of convict descendants.

Definitive answers to the questions raised above as to the nature and veracity of "pride" in convict ancestry, as a truly emergent norm among the Australian population, are far beyond the capacities of this book; but some inferences may serve as a first step, and for these we must consider the currency or otherwise of the "stain," which I will suggest is more of a factor in twenty-first century Australia than many commentators have understood. This brings me to the second of the studies I wish to discuss. In a 2003 article in *Nations and Nationalism*, Bruce Tranter and Jed Donoghue analyse the Referendum survey data noted above, to derive a detailed, quantitative demographic breakdown of those Australians claiming convict descent.[23] On the premise that claims of convict descent constitute elements of personal and social identity, they draw on a number of theorists to distinguish between various forms of essentialist and socially constructed identity;[24] Tranter and Donoghue's stated position is that they "suspect that many of those who claim convict descent in the survey data are constructing an identity, rather than acknowledging an actual blood line."[25]

The data examined comprise respondents' demographic self-assessments of gender; age; education levels attained; income; occupation; religion; geographical location; urbanism; home ownership; marital status; ethnicity; political leaning; and class.[26] Further indicators such as attitudes to Australian achievements and interest in family history were factored in, and the data correlated against the Referendum Survey question on convict ancestry. (In their data compilations Tranter and Donoghue conflate the figures for "yes" and "maybe" respondents, tabling them under the single heading "Am or may be,"[27] a loss of distinction which they justify as statistically insignificant in the context of their methodology.[28] I am less than convinced, however, that this is an appropriate dismissal of the disparity of psychological nuance between those who claim convict ancestry as a fact and those who are prepared to entertain the possibility.) Tranter and Donoghue's analysis leads them to conclude that

> older, highly educated, higher income, large city dwellers are less likely to claim a convict ancestor, particularly if they happen to own their own home [outright]. On the other hand, less educated, left leaning, and working class Australians are most likely to say they are descended from convicts. The class, education and income effects suggest that lower status Australians—perhaps those with relatively heavy financial responsibilities—are most likely to identify with convicts. In a search for identity, they adopt a more "active" identification as they are more likely to claim their (alleged) convict ancestry.[29]

Further to the socio-economic factors, Tranter and Donoghue identify an

> "ethno-nationalist" / "nativist" [identity type] for whom being born in Australia was an important component of being "truly Australian" [and who] were more likely to claim convict ancestry.…
>
> Convict identifiers tend to be lower or middle ranking on a range of social indicators, such as education, class, housing tenure and income, even when age is held constant. One interpretation of these findings is that claims of convict ancestry are divided on the basis of achieved status.…Claiming to have convict ancestors may be a strategy adopted by some "white" Australians in order to make an identity claim of their own. Seen in this light, such claims from certain groups within the mythical "middle Australia," constitute a claim to a form of "white Australianness," that is neither indigenous, nor an "ethnic" identity associated with post World War II immigrants.[30]

In addressing the connections between convict ancestry, personal and national identity, and the demographic make-up of avowed descendants, Tranter and Donoghue raise a number of apposite issues; but I suggest that there are certain problematic assumptions underlying their analysis, and these have led them to draw some debatable conclusions. The most significant of these concern the motivation they ascribe to convict identifiers, and the nature and legacy of the convict "stain."

I take issue, firstly, with their reasoning that because a class divide is apparent between convict descendants and the more affluent class who tend not to claim descent, it follows that convict descent is "socially constructed," or at least a component in a constructed social identity. It well may be in some cases, but their evidence, which says almost nothing about individual motives, does not show this. Tranter and Donoghue in fact present the idea of socially constructed identity in a subtle but consistent pejorative tone; they seem, in fact, to be positing a kind of *mens rea* on the part of convict identifiers. The construction of identity has, in their analysis, a connotation of (not necessarily honest) *choice*, as though family history research, in particular when it turns up convicts, is viewed by many who pursue it as a kind of shopping trip in a market of identity signifiers. There is, of course, no reason to doubt that some claims to convict ancestry are spurious; one can always find a few people who value notoriety over veracity. But the implication in Tranter and Donoghue's discussion that any claim is suspect, as exemplified above in their parenthetical "alleged," seems to ignore the obvious fact that a large number of Australians—probably enough, as I noted earlier, to populate a major city—*are* descended from convicts, whatever their attitude to the fact.

A predominance of convict claimants in a particular demographic necessarily indicates a process of witting "construction," along the lines Tranter and Donoghue argue, only if one ignores (as they apparently do) the possibility that today's identifier demographic reflects a genuine preponderance of convict ancestors among that group—that is, the possibility that the original convicts' social status and class have remained "seated" across successive generations to the present day. I stated above that learning of my convict ancestry, concurrently with my involvement with Pentridge Prison as a regular visitor, affected me in a number of ways. The first and most enduring effect arose from an acute awareness, which I had had since my early years, of a peculiarly aggressive and transgressive style of socialization prevalent in my family, especially among my male relatives. (It was indirectly due to this characteristic of my family that I had spent periods of my childhood in various forms of "care" before becoming a ward of the State as a teenager, and for several years after that remained estranged from almost all of my relatives, close and distant.) This sense of what might be termed a deviant family ethos was combined with an equally pressing awareness of apparently enculturated poverty—try as we might, we had always existed outside the supposedly inclusive dominion of Australian affluence. On learning that I had convict ancestors, one of my first thoughts was, "That explains a lot." Suddenly, too, the towering presence of that epitome of neo-Gothic Victoriana, Pentridge, in our family's life at that moment seemed to fit. And as time passed and I learned more of the details of James and Elizabeth Mauldon's lives and those of their offspring, my feeling if anything increased that here, finally, was an *explanation* for the seemingly inevitable social, economic and legal trajectories followed by me and so many of my relatives. Even the fact that James had been flogged for organizing a strike among his fellow transportees accorded with my own uncles' heavily activist, fringes-of-legality style of trade unionism in the Builders' Labourers Federation, which had been a major cultural aspect of my childhood. (I can see it as nothing less than typical of my family that their industrial relations activism should have been bound up with a trade union so militant and anarchic it was destined to be de-registered and its leader jailed.)

Of course, in the context of an investigation such as Tranter and Donoghue's, a single anecdotal instance such as mine does not qualify as evidence of anything at all (nor, it should be noted, does it comfortably fit any of Lambert's narrative categories). To many, the idea that discovering convicts in the early Victorian recesses of one's family tree should plausibly serve to "explain" one's present-day experience of family, society and self hardly seems reasonable. "Oh come on," they say, "it was a long time ago." And yet, as I have taken to pointing out, only three generations separate James Maulden and my mother.

Like the story of my visit to my brother in jail, which I have included in this work because I have reason to believe it in some degree typifies such experiences, I present here my experience of discovering my ancestry because I believe it to be of a more general type than is immediately apparent. I had long suspected this to be the case, but had only minimal evidence—the occasional informal comment here, a fragmentary anecdote there—to support this notion, until I met and interviewed another convict descendant whose personal background, and whose account of learning of her ancestry, paralleled mine in certain significant ways.

Lyn McLeavy writes that her great-great grandmother, Jane Cook of County Tyrone, was transported at the age of twenty-six to Tasmania for "stealing a pot lid." She arrived at the Cascades "Female Factory" in Hobart with her 11-year-old daughter in 1850.[31] Jane's story is, like James Mauldon's, typical: re-imprisoned many times in conditions of infamous harshness, a life of seemingly habitual but unremarkable social transgression, ending anonymously in a pauper's grave.[32] What caught my attention, when I first read McLeavy's account, was the following passage, which suggested that she, too, had found in her ancestry an explanation of her own life:

> It took a long time and much effort for me to know this part of my background. At last I understood the urgency I had felt as a child to ask questions about my impoverished childhood on Melbourne's waterfront. Seems it had been a small journey from the Female Factory.[33]

When I interviewed her, McLeavy explained that the family's convict history had for several generations been "lost," not through shame, but through the kind of forgetfulness that comes out of a constant preoccupation, generation after generation, with the endless complications of simply getting by.[34] I knew immediately what she meant: had I asked my own mother about our ancestry (it never occurred to me to do so), I would undoubtedly have been met with a firmly worded enquiry as to why such things matter. I asked McLeavy if in finding Jane she had a better idea of her own origins:

> I think about finding Jane and knowing where I come from; when I told my aunties they said, "It fits," and what they meant was, it fits in our lives, you know, it made complete sense to us that, you know, we had this convict, because I think my family, well I know they do, my aunties feel that…their own childhood was really difficult and their parents were [in the same situation]…and so I think they've been living this really very working-class life for a very long time and so the fact that Jane was in the beginning in Australia, that made complete sense.[35]

She went on to describe a family life intimately involved with the lower-working-class community in inner-suburban Port Melbourne, bound by a reflexively "socialist" ethos, a "network of survival…which came out of all that hard living, you know, being at the bottom of the pile."[36] Upward mobility was, it seemed, perpetually out of reach; few of her relatives ever owned their homes. In such a milieu radical trade unionism was second-nature, and this tendency she also attributes in part to inheritance.

On the intractable recidivism of her convict ancestor, and on such "criminality" in the typical lower-class environment, McLeavy spoke with an insight that resonated strongly with me, mindful as I was of James Mauldon's crowded prison record, and of my own social background:

> [T]he Melbourne docks...was a bit of a terrible place,...a terrible place to work, and really bad conditions and stuff like that, and casual work[ers], they were just treated really badly and so they had to go on strike...just to get a bit of decency and dignity and safety; but also I think that because their economic existence was so insecure, and also from my own childhood, I know that a lot of people that I knew when I was a child, they'd been to jail, you know, that was part of life, people went to jail. I guess it's like being an Aboriginal person, you know, it just comes with the territory. And so when I was a child in the fifties, I'd always hear my father say, oh, So-and-So's getting out...and it wasn't that they were like how the press was always raving on about, I mean there were obviously criminals on the Melbourne waterfront that were, you know, serious criminals, but a lot of people were just ordinary people, say, like my father, who wasn't a criminal, but he would be in trouble with the police, because that was, you know, what happened if you grew up in Port Melbourne.[37]

Here is encapsulated one of the ways in which a familial connection with incarceration that begins with transportation is, or is at least perceived as being, perpetuated. Such an account embodies the sort of understanding of "lower-status" life that is essential for the social scientist aspiring to gauge motivation or affect with regard to personal/social identity, but which is, I submit, almost entirely lacking in Tranter and Donoghue's article. It is in fact hard to avoid the impression that they are reacting to the convict identifiers in the manner which they identify as typical of their own higher-income, professional demographic: "Claiming convict identity," they aver, "is less attractive to high status, highly educated, large city dwelling Australians who may appreciate that [as Robert Hughes puts it] 'eight out of ten convicts were thieves'."[38] I will return to the matter of "elite" opinion shortly.

The idea of a transgenerational seatedness of class, inherited from an underclass prototype, may seem to call for a return to some form of essentialism. It does not. It rests, rather, on the idea that the social forces impinging upon successive generations can be, or at least can be experienced as, ineradicable, when combined with the successive received narratives that form a familial culture.

There is of course a sense in which all family trees, pedigrees and lineage are constructed; that our feeling of kinship with an ancestor long dead is as "imagined" as is the sense of national "community" of which Anderson speaks.[39] In such cognitive distances lies the malleability of the ancestral stories that Lambert attempts to account for. And if it were about no more than "blood lines," about a solely genetic connection (and a highly attenuated one at that), or about mere connecting ink-lines on the "Family Tree," then one might be persuaded that the life, behaviour, experiences and fate of an ancestor bore no material relevance to one's own; but what must be taken into account is the linear ontology and transmitted social memory—the lived narrative—of successive consanguine households, and what for many is the irresistible potency of that narrative.

The assumption that in a land of opportunity everyone has equal access to that opportunity has been proven false too many times to need argument; let one example stand for the convicts: In 1851 the Victorian gold rush began. It is axiomatic, and uncontroversial, that not everyone struck it rich on the goldfields,[40] but equally, it is well known that the gold fields generated opportunities in other business or entrepreneurial areas, and that enormous prosperity ensued for the colony in general.[41] For years prior to the gold rush, former convicts unable to find work in Tasmania had been emigrating to the mainland;[42] but in 1852 the Victorian legislature, against the advice and wishes of the British government, passed the *Convicts Prevention Act*, which barred Tasmanian ex-convicts from even setting foot in Victoria.[43] Such was the public support for this law—such, in other words, was the depth of public feeling against former convicts—that when Britain moved in 1854 to repeal the Act (as it had the power to do), ten thousand citizens staged a highly vocal demonstration in La Trobe Street Melbourne, and the Act remained law.[44] By 1862, when James and Elizabeth Mauldon and their children made the crossing to Warrnambool, although the first full flush of the gold rush had passed and the Convicts Prevention Act was no longer enforced with such urgency, there remained widespread prejudice against "government men." This, then, is but one facet of the "convict stain" as a social force of the sort that engenders within families the kind of defensive, anti-establishment (or at least cavalier-toward-the-establishment) attitudes that are passed down and absorbed by the young of succeeding generations as nature's doctrine (even after the histories have been "lost"), and which can therefore continue to militate against upward mobility or even ordinary prosperity, long after the origins of such indigence are forgotten.

This brings me to my second point of disagreement with Tranter and Donoghue. On the basis of the relative youth of the convict identifiers, they declare the "stain" "senescent," and assert that it "should diminish with intergenerational replacement."[45] This conclusion is plainly hasty. They arrive at it without discussion, merely stating that, insofar as significantly fewer older respondents claim convict ancestry, this constitutes evidence that the stain remains a factor in older generations' outlook. I contend that the stain is (a) more diverse in form than Tranter and Donoghue realize; (b) active in modern Australia; and (c) more significant as a social force than is at first apparent.

The first point to consider is how, in today's society, the "stain" should be defined. I suggest that it takes three main, albeit overlapping and hazily bounded, forms:

1. *Traditional abhorrence.* This affect, which is closest to the abiding shame and stigma that underscores Reynolds's analysis, is the form that has reportedly been replaced by "pride" since the 1960s. It is presumably the motive of many of the "older generation" respondents who according to Tranter and Donoghue's analysis decline to claim convict ancestry. (Although here, once again, there is scope for some misunderstanding of the data; we cannot know how many histories have been "lost," in the manner of Lyn McLeavy's family.)[46] Lambert's respondents reported that their experience of the stain often stemmed from older family members.

The assumption that this form of the stain is fading into senescence rests on a further assumption that the older generation's influence on younger generations and on society at large is and will continue to be negligible, and that the social values that give rise to widespread attitudes toward crime and criminals will remain uniformly liberal indefinitely into the future. These are, I submit, big assumptions. A further factor vis-à-vis traditional abhorrence is geographical inconstancy—the example of 1850s Victoria referred to above clearly denotes public sentiment of a texture and consequence peculiar to that place, and although broad similarities could undoubtedly be found between the Victorian and Tasmanian examples (for instance), a particulate social history of each area would be necessary to gauge and define the extent of those respective examples. The attitudes in New South Wales would doubtless be different again. In Western Australia, the organizer of the Fremantle Prison Descendants' Day, a local genealogist, told me that she has become a "de facto counsellor" for people who, on discovering they have a convict ancestor, contact her in distress over the stigma they now feel. She expressed the opinion that in her view the stain is still very much a factor in Western Australia.[47] Such comparisons highlight, once more, the pertinence of Reynolds's call for comparative studies of the disparate convict societies.

2. *Exogenous stigma.* By this I mean the expressed or expected opinions of non-Australians, whether resident in Australia or outside it. This form of the stain is mentioned by Lambert as having been experienced by an unspecified number of his respondents.[48] Its prevalence is impossible to quantify from data currently available, but there is a significant body of anecdotal evidence to suggest that many overseas-born or overseas-resident observers of Australia retain and express negative or at least stereotyped views of the convict origins of our society.

It is not uncommon, for instance, for Australians to find themselves stigmatized whether they have convict ancestors or not, through ethnicity-based comments of the type that tar all Anglo-Australians with the "convict" brush. Such comments may be uncomplicatedly hostile and made without regard for their veracity; but some apparently arise from a genuinely mistaken idea that all Anglo-Australians are descended from convicts. (A recent, highly public example of this was Sheik Taj Din al-Hilali's misguided haranguing of non-Islamic Australians.)[49] A point to note is that even when remarks along these lines are not meant aggressively or disparagingly, they may be experienced as stigmatizing, due to what might be termed "residual stain anxiety" in the mind of the recipient of the comment. It is possible, in other words, that the stain may produce in some Australians, whether convict descendants or not, what psychologists term "stereotype threat"—a subtle form of negative (and insidiously debilitating) affect produced by the individual's expectation of others' negative views, whether expressed or not.[50]

3. *Disdainful indifference.* This is, I suspect, now the most prevalent yet least recognized form of the stain, and is also arguably the most influential today. The exemplar of this form was unknowingly witnessed by a television audience of several billion people. The Opening Ceremony of the 2000 Olympic Games in Sydney was a pageant of extravagant proportions, the purport of which was to celebrate before the world Australia's quintessential historical

events, characters and cultural themes.[51] The performance represented every major phase of our history, from the Indigenous Dreaming, through European rediscovery, the exploration era, gold rushes, the Kelly outbreak, wars, post-war immigration, to mundane suburban prosperity. Among the manifold historical national players characterized for the television viewers of the world, only one of any significance was absent—the convicts. None were depicted, none were mentioned. And in virtually none of the subsequent media reviews of the Ceremony was this omission deemed worthy of comment, much less complaint.

The exclusion of Australia's founding colonial population and the ancestors of perhaps one-fifth of Australians living today, in an exhibition designed to present to the world our image of ourselves as a nation, is an occurrence deserving of some discussion. That the organizers might have been swayed by national shame or embarrassment, that is, "traditional abhorrence," seems prima facie unlikely; and a fear of exogenous stigma, as a deciding factor in the design of an artistic presentation of such extraordinarily confident self-assertiveness, likewise looks implausible. It seems to me most likely that the omission of convicts was a choice made by the Ceremony's designers for the simple reason that the convicts were not considered particularly important—that they were, in fact, passé.

As noted above, Tranter and Donoghue found that highly urban, well-paid professionals tend not to be convict identifiers. This is consistent with an earlier analysis (2001) by Tranter in which he identified Australia's major-city "elites" as far more interested in finding *bushrangers* among their ancestors than convicts.[52] This change in "preferred" ancestor (which surely has connotations of the "shopping for identity signifiers" noted above) was presented as a shift in what the elites had come to regard as fashionable, or "cool." Tranter flippantly remarked that for this group, "a bushranger on the bookshelf is better than a convict in the closet."[53]

It is axiomatic that the designers and organizers of the 2000 Olympics Opening Ceremony fall into the "elite" demographic—as do the media commentators, op-ed columnists and public intellectuals who had every opportunity in subsequent days to note the Ceremony's lack of convicts, and yet made no mention of it. One must presume that they, too, thought the matter not worth the trouble. There seems to have arisen an unspoken consensus among the leaders of opinion that we as a nation have "moved on" from the preoccupation with convict heritage that became so "trendy" around the time of the bi-centenary.

Why is this important?

The issue, at its core, is about the nation *choosing to forget*. Paula Hamilton speaks of the "socially organized amnesia" that forms a key aspect of the construction of any national identity:

> Defining groups or nations always necessitates a dual process of inclusion and exclusion and remembering the past is a central mechanism of that process. Many have noted that forgetting is one of the most powerful forces that shape national remembering.[54]

If, as I am arguing, there is currently a tendency for such "exclusion" by "forgetting" about the convicts as a substantial component of Australia's history, it is occurring at the expense of the present and future generations of convict descendants—both in the sense of their disenfranchisement from the civic project of sharing in the formation of the national memory, and in the sense of the personal experience of being declared historically irrelevant. Indifference can be a potent social force; the negation of the individual's narrative context, of his or her place in the social memory, amounts, in its effective denial of a part of the self, to an experience akin to the stain.

A 2005 television mini-series, *The Incredible Journey of Mary Bryant*,[55] a major British-Australian production portraying First Fleet convicts and based on real events, would appear at first glance to contradict my argument. However, it in fact affirms it. In 1791 the eponymous Mary Bryant, a young Cornish woman transported in the First Fleet for the theft of a bonnet, decamped with her husband, Will, in the Governor's personal cutter, and sailed it, with a handful of other convicts, from Botany Bay to Timor—a seafaring achievement rivalling that of William Bligh after the *Bounty* mutiny.[56] The theme of the television story and the nature of its principal characters are entirely consistent with the typical mode of representation of historical prisons I have identified in previous chapters: of all the narratives of all the thousands of convicts who populated the earliest Australian colonies, the only one depicted on commercial television today, in *The Incredible Journey of Mary Bryant*, is that of an escape—and a spectacular one at that—by the convict equivalent of a celebrity prisoner. And here in the mini-series, as in the film *Chopper*, the celebrity prisoner is romanticized and gratuitously sexualized: the script has Mary Bryant becoming involved with Lieutenant

Ralph Clarke (the colonial officer whose heartfelt utterance at the sight of arriving convict women gave Anne Summers the "damned whores" of her celebrated title).[57] In a striking echo of much that we have encountered in this book, the producer justifies this invention on the grounds that the story must be "dramatic and entertaining."[58]

When discussing Bruner's schema of the self as narrative, I also noted Alasdaire MacIntyre's pronouncement that without such an inner self-telling, life is, in his words, no longer "intelligible." Elaborating on this point, MacIntyre implicitly equates intelligibility with potency, judging both to reside necessarily on narrative context. As he puts it, "I can only answer the question 'What am I to do?' if I can answer the prior question 'Of what story or stories do I find myself a part?'"[59] The question "What am I to do?", it is apparent, equally has the sense What *can* I do?—that is, What is the degree, form and nature of my own capacity for action? The search for historical context, in other words, may be read as a search for personal agency, and the denial of that place in history becomes a negation of individual empowerment. To put it another way, in the terms I have used throughout this book to refer to the inmates of the institutions under examination: the convict descendant is today being othered, as surely as he or she was fifty years ago. This process has disproportionate consequences on those affected, given that the population sector involved is, as we have seen, a stratum already burdened by a host of disempowering influences.

The convict stain may have faded, but it has also mutated. To what extent does it, in its various forms, retain its social force? What does it contribute to social tensions? In which geographical areas is it most strongly a factor, and among which groups of Australians? The further question, for the consideration of curators of convict prison museums, is, In what ways does the stigma then inform and shape the narratives emergent from the sites? To none of these questions do I have any definite answer. My chief point is that without further investigation, by researchers whose fundamental assumptions do not exclude the possibilities I have outlined above, all we have are isolated but evocative anecdotes of the kind recounted here. A combination of quantitative and qualitative methodologies is needed. Both Lambert's and Tranter and Donoghue's studies, more especially the latter, look rather like opportunities missed. Tranter and Donoghue appear at first to have heeded Reynolds's call (although they do not cite him) for a community-by-community, particulate study of convict societies' legacy; but having gathered the tools and material for such a task, they then make the critical error of homogenizing the disparate and discrete. Australian convict societies, which lasted and made their manifold marks on the emerging nation for over seventy years, were at least as complex and varied as any of the societal forms that eventually overtook them, as was the social legacy they bequeathed to their descendants, in the form of the "hated stain." This is, I believe, a fundamental aspect of Australian identity that is being overlooked.

There are intrinsic perils in the scientific attempt to quantify the component elements of social memory and identity, for it brings us up against the investigative limitations of reason. Identity, at its core, is not rational. Various things Lyn McLeavy speaks of, for instance, are utterances and intuitions that are all too easily dismissed as rather hare-brained. She writes at one point that she believes she is the reincarnation of Jane Cook; and that her "Irishness" tells her that a flock of seagulls overhead are "the souls of the convict women."[60] At a number of the prison museum sites I visited, tour guides told me (often in strictest confidence), or included as anonymous written comments on survey questionnaires, that they had had unexplained and uncanny experiences on-site that could be interpreted as the activities of "ghosts." There was a time when I would have viewed such notions as merely fantastical, had I encountered them before mid-2002. But in June of that year I attended an historical conference, "Islands of Vanishment," held at the Port Arthur Historic Site. It was my first visit to the site, and to Tasmania.

  Port Arthur epitomizes for Australian tourists the romanticism of the neo-Gothic, in this case irresistibly enhanced by the happenstance of including a roofless ruin not unlike the medieval shells that dot the countryside of Mother England, set in the midst of one of the most visually beautiful landscapes in which anyone ever built a jail.[61] The site occupies approximately 100 acres around a perpetually placid inlet below densely wooded hills, and includes dozens of buildings of varying sizes, styles and vintages, in varying states of restoration. As a tourist site, it is deeply ambiguous—an archetypal Dark Tourism locale. The still, quiet beauty is juxtaposed in the visitor's mind not only with the convict history, but also the far more recent mass-murder that took place there in 1996, about which visitors are briefly informed (the website carries an account of the events), with requests not to question site personnel directly on the subject.[62]

On arrival the tourist first encounters a modern "Visitors' Centre," styled to complement (but thought by some to clash with) its archaic surroundings, and which includes an interactive interpretation gallery.[63] This incorporates the narratives of fifty-two selected convicts whose individual circumstances and legal experiences are synthesized into a deck of stylized "playing cards" which are singly "dealt" to tourists, who may then follow the variously presented episodes of "their" convict's story through the gallery. Also available, for purchase, is a compilation of the fifty-two narratives in the form of a book.[64] These stories are intended to personalize the convict population, to revise the traditional "simplistic views, which have depicted the mass of convicts as a pack of undifferentiated thieves."[65] Tourists have the option of declining a card, bypassing the gallery and proceeding directly into the grounds.

James Mauldon does not feature among the fifty-two "cards"; on reflection, however, I must assume he would have known some of the convicts they represent. I was, of course, conscious of his having been at Port Arthur, and arrived with some expectations; but they were undefined, and as I am not given to flights of either sentimentality or mysticism I did not expect anything epiphanic. I was unprepared, therefore, for the intensity of my feelings, and even more unprepared for the direction they took. A combination of the atmosphere of the site and the knowledge that my ancestor had preceded me there gave me a peculiarly assertive sense of legitimacy in the place—I felt (on no rational basis, I knew) that I had a *right* to be there, a right of a sort that I had not felt I had almost anywhere else in my life. Further, as I walked about the grounds, I had an irresistible impulse to actually speak to James Mauldon, to say a greeting, and tell him about myself, and my children. I got as far as saying "Hello," then stopped myself, a little embarrassed, but the sensation remained. It was as if the place itself was alive; as if it somehow embodied one's ancestors, even though they left the place and lived many years outside it free, and died in their beds hundreds of kilometres away.

Part of me—the rationalist—watched me, with a certain detached interest, conversing thus with ghosts; intrigued and (perhaps naively) enthusiastic, I later recounted the experience to an academic colleague at the conference. I was laughed at for my candour. Clearly, I had transgressed the professional reasoner's "flakiness" threshold, and I became a little more cautious thereafter about sharing my thoughts in that type of company. However, at a later discussion workshop after the main conference, convened by the Tasman Institute for Conservation and Convict Studies (TICCS), I was among those invited to speak about the role and significance of the personal stakeholder—the "descendant"—in potential interpretation outcomes for the site. I recounted a little of my own story, including my reaction to the site. The reception this time was less sceptical; the poet Margaret Scott, TICCS founder and one of the leading discussants, was especially interested, and it became apparent that she both understood such experiences and believed them to be meaningful in regard to the site's interpretation.

The perceived validity of reactions such as mine, when recounted to others, is dependant on a certain empathic capability in the listener and a willingness, born of commonality of experience or a facility of imagination, or both, to leave "common sense" out of the equation. Some people, in other words, simply understand. Margaret Scott—a poet—was clearly one of them. Another was a local bus driver with whom I struck up a conversation, who thought it quite reasonable to talk to one's ancestors. He knew what I meant. He told me that he had, after some searching, located his convict ancestor's grave, and then when his grandfather died he was buried in the same grave. "We're together now," he said. "The family's together."[66] It is worth noting that when Lyn McLeavy expressed her belief that she was her convict ancestor reincarnated, her interlocutor, also a convict descendant, "seemed to understand how I could say that."[67]

In reflecting now on my first reactions to Port Arthur, and on Lyn McLeavy's "Irish" whimsies, I am reminded of Peter Read's *Haunted Earth*, and his musings in a Sydney cemetery as he begins his exploration of Australia's "inspirited places":

> Paul Carter thinks that we Australians, rootless rationalists that we are, will have to bring something to our sense of belonging in this country beyond insecurity, technology and fear. We need a new conception of land and our relationship to it. All right, Paul, I think we're moving toward new and local spiritualities that begin to recognize the spirits of the living, the dead and the non-living in many forms and many places.[68]

Read retails an anecdote of W.B. Yeats discussing the fairy-folk with an Irishwoman who has a fund of traditional stories about them. In answer to his question she states that she does not "believe in the fairies"; but she then wryly reminds him that, despite her disbelief, "they're there, Mr Yeats. They're there."[69] Read continues:

> That's a starting point to realize that we don't have to rely on the evidence of our own senses as a final determinant. Although I have neither seen nor felt the spirits of the dead, I've felt for a time a kinship of shared place with them.[70]

*

Every society identifies itself and its essential qualities by recourse to what are deemed its generative historical narratives. Those narratives are the products of manifold processes of inheritance, mythmaking, remembering, forgetting and choice. As a nation-state still working through those processes, still making those choices, Australia is a society in transition, with individual citizens each conducting their own searches, whether diligently or sporadically or entirely subconsciously, for their sense of personal identity in relation to the nation. We are, in one way or another, engaged in the quest for a collective intelligibility. I contend that for that intelligibility to be any more than ephemeral, an illusion of coherence, it must arise from an *inclusive* spectrum of narratives. Australia's social memory must include, for better or worse, a wholehearted acknowledgement of its origins as a colonial prison, and the fact that it therefore has a unique historical relationship with the incarcerated population that comprised its first citizens, and with the successive generations of descendants of those first citizens. It is not a matter of pride, nor of shame; it is not a matter of trends or fashions in identity; it is simply a matter of not forgetting.

NOTES

1   Archives Office of Tasmania (AOT), record no. 746 (the record misspells Mauldon as "Maulden" throughout). My thanks to archivist Robyn Eastley for her help in accessing this record. The name "Tasmania" had been in unofficial use since the early 1820s (in preference to "Van Diemen's Land"), but was not officially adopted until 1856. National Archives of Australia, "Order-in-Council changing name to Tasmania 21 July 1855 (UK)" , http://www.foundingdocs.gov.au/item.asp?sdID=35 (accessed 2 October 2005).

2   AOT record no. 746.

3   These and certain of the following personal details regarding James Mauldon, aside from

data available in his prison record cited above, are derived from a privately compiled family history passed on to me by my aunt. Although this history has a noticeable tendency toward romantic glossing in matters of interpretation, it is based on sound and quite extensive primary-source research, and is therefore generally reliable on matters of data. In this it is consistent with Graeme Davison's remark that "Genealogy may be the last refuge of scientific history….The genealogists themselves are often formidable historical technicians, experts in the 'how' of history." *The Use and Abuse of Australian History* (Crows Nest NSW: Allen & Unwin, 2000), pp. 83–4.

4   AOT record no. 746.

5   Ronald D. Lambert, "Reclaiming the Ancestral Past: Narrative, Rhetoric and the 'Convict Stain'," *Journal of Sociology* 38 no. 2, 2002, pp. 114–15; see also Australian Social Sciences Data Archive (ASSDA), "Australian Constitutional Referendum Study 1999," Section C, Q. C7, http://assda.anu.edu.au/codebooks/acrs99/3vars.html. Lambert derives a figure of 2·1 million from the percentages quoted; my adjustment to fit current figures assumes that the percentages discovered by ASSDA have remained approximately constant, and on the ABS's estimate of Australia's population at this writing as just over 21.1 million. Australian Bureau of Statistics, "Population Clock", http://www.abs.gov.au/websitedbs/d3310114.nsf/Home/Popular%20Statistics, link to "Australia's current population" (accessed 1 Oct 2007).

6   Lambert, "Reclaiming the Ancestral Past," p. 114.

7   Ibid., p. 115.

8   Henry Reynolds, "'That Hated Stain': The Aftermath of Transportation in Tasmania," *Historical Studies* 14 no. 53, October 1969, pp. 19–31.

9   Ibid., p. 19.

10   Ibid., p. 31, drawing on Russel Ward.

11   Ibid.

12   Ibid.

13   Lambert, "Reclaiming the Ancestral Past," pp. 111–27.

14   Ibid.

15   Ibid., pp. 115–17.

16   Ibid., p. 115.

17   Ibid., pp. 117ff.

18   Ibid.

19   Ibid., pp. 117–21.

20   Ibid., pp. 121–23.

21   Ibid., p. 116.

22   Gillian O'Mara (Fremantle Prison convict genealogist), interviewed 25 April 2003.

23   Bruce Tranter and Jed Donoghue, "Convict Ancestry: A Neglected Aspect of Australian Identity," *Nations and Nationalism* 9 no. 4, 2003, pp. 555–77.

24   Ibid., pp. 557–8.

25   Ibid., p. 558.

26   Ibid., pp. 563–4.

27   Ibid., pp. 563f.

28   Ibid., pp. 561, 574 n. 13.

29 Ibid., p. 571. In thus using the term "active" the authors draw on H. Bradley's work on the nature of identity.

30 Ibid., p. 572. (The authors point out in a footnote that this interpretation is not intended to suggest a racist motive for such claimants.)

31 Lyn McLeavy, "Jane Cook and Me," *Age* 6 April 2002.

32 Ibid.

33 Ibid.

34 Lyn McLeavy, interviewed 6 Jan 2003.

35 Ibid.

36 Ibid.

37 Ibid.

38 Tranter and Donoghue, "Convict Ancestry," p. 571.

39 Benedict Anderson, *Imagined Communities: Reflections on the Origin and Spread of Nationalism* (London: Verso, 1983).

40 See, e.g., Christina Twomey, *Deserted and Destitute: Motherhood, Wife Desertion and Colonial Welfare* (Melbourne: Australian Scholarly Publishing, 2002).

41 Geoffrey Serle, "The Gold Generation," *Victorian Historical Magazine* 41 no. 1, February 1970, pp. 265–72.

42 Ibid., p. 267.

43 Geoffrey Serle, *The Golden Age: A History of the Colony of Victoria 1851–1861* (Melbourne: Melbourne University Press, 1963), pp. 126–30; Broome, "Stigma of Pentridge," p. 10.

44 Broome, "Stigma of Pentridge," p. 10.

45 Tranter and Donoghue, "Convict Ancestry," p. 568.

46 A further possible factor in the loss of such family histories may be the active official covering-up recounted by Babette Smith in her recent analysis of convict history and the "stain." Babette Smith, *Australia's Birthstain: The Startling Legacy of the Convict Era* (Crows Nest NSW: Allen and Unwin, 2008).

47 O'Mara interview.

48 Lambert, "Reclaiming the Ancestral Past."

49 Richard Kerbaj, "Hilali Ridicules nation of Convicts", *Australian* 12 January 2007

50 Claude Steele, "Thin Ice: 'Stereotype Threat' and Black College Students," *Atlantic Monthly* August 1999.

51 The world television audience was estimated at between 3·5 and 4 billion. ABS, Year Book Australia: The Sydney 2000 Olympic Games, http://www.abs.gov.au/Ausstats/abs@.nsf/0/e99215ff41ca7defca256b35001bacf9?OpenDocument (accessed 9 July 2005).

52 Mark Chipperfield, "Bushwhacker Breeding is Cooler than Convict Chic," *The Scotsman* 16 Dec 2001; Adele Horin, "Smart Set Losing their Convictions," *Age* 13 Dec 2001.

53 Tranter, quoted in both Chipperfield, "Bushwhacker Breeding" and Horin, "Smart Set Losing their Convictions."

54 Paula Hamilton, "The Knife Edge," p. 23.

55 Peter Andrikidis (dir.), *The Incredible Journey of Mary Bryant*, Television drama, Ten Network, broadcast 30 and 31 October 2005.

56 See, e.g., Jonathon King, *Mary Bryant: Her Life and Escape from Botany Bay* (Pymble

NSW: Simon and Schuster, 2004). The paucity of documentation regarding Bryant's life prior to transportation and after her eventual return to Cornwell has tended to result in accounts of rather uneven veracity. King's is the most recent substantive version purporting to be historical; his account of the New South Wales period and the escape are essentially sound, but on the Cornish denouement he becomes far less plausible and at times plainly fanciful.

57   Summers, *Damned Whores and God's Police*, p. 267.

58   Des Monaghan quoted in Jacqui Taffel, "Escape from the Colony," *Age Green Guide* 27 October 2005.

59   MacIntyre, *After Virtue*, p. 201.

60   McLeavy, "Jane Cook and Me."

61   On the aesthetics of Port Arthur, see Nicola Goc, "From Convict Prison to the Gothic Ruins of Tourist Attraction," *Historic Environment* 16 no. 3, 2002; Richard Morrison, "The Management of Paradox: the Archaeology of the Port Arthur Landscape," *Historic Environment* 16 no. 3, 2002.

62   A lone gunman used a high-powered rifle to kill thirty-five people at the site and nearby. Port Arthur Historic Site, "Sunday 28 April 1996: A Brief Outline of Events", http://www.portarthur.org.au/pashow.php?ACTION=Public&menu_code=400.300 (accessed 12 August 2005). For a detailed account of the massacre see, e.g., Margaret Scott, *Port Arthur: A Story of Strength and Courage* (Milsons Point, NSW: Random House, 1997).

63   Strange, "From 'Place of Misery'."

64   Hamish Maxwell-Stewart & Susan Hood, *Pack of Thieves? 52 Port Arthur Lives* (Port Arthur, Tas.: Port Arthur Historic Site Management Authority, 2001).

65   Ibid., p. 8.

66   Conversation (anonymity requested), Tasman Peninsular, 9 June 2002.

67   McLeavy, "Jane Cook and Me."

68   Peter Read, *Haunted Earth*, Sydney: University of new South Wales Press, 2003, p. 42.

69   Ibid.

70   Ibid., pp. 42–3.

CONCLUSION

Imagining the Prison

A former resident of the neighbourhood of Pentridge Prison tried to sum up for me his unresolvable sense of puzzlement about the place:

> You'd drive past it along Murray Road, you might go past it every day, and there'd be the lake and park on one side, and on the other this bloody great long wall. Twenty feet high. It was weird, 'cos you sort of knew that there were people in there, but you couldn't even begin to imagine what was going on in there. It was just a blank.[1]

Although it is not always obvious, the difficulties inherent in imagining what goes on in a prison do not end with its decommissioning and the opening of its doors to the public. And yet such a feat of imagination is precisely what we need seriously to attempt, if we are fully to acknowledge the essential humanity of those behind the "blank" walls, and in the process further our own societal understanding and the integrity of our social memory. Such a project does not automatically, nor necessarily, require a stance reflexively sympathetic to all prisoners, nor does it signify approval of their crimes; but it does presume a willingness in us to make distinctions between persons among the population of the jail in some ways equivalent to the distinctions we routinely make between citizens outside it. To do so requires a degree of moral imagination, a sensitivity to nuances of character, an openness to the narratives embodied in those persons, that is innately at odds with the process of undifferentiated othering.

In examining historical prison sites as entities of public history, I have pursued two main themes. I have identified and characterized some of the processes by which Australia's incarcerated—both historical and contemporary—are othered, and hence, through indifference, dismissal and disdain—exclusion, in a word—are rendered historically voiceless. And I have sought to restore those voices, where some trace of them can be discerned. The latter task I have undertaken both to redress the imbalance, in accordance with my commitment to writing "history from below," and by way of exploring avenues via which such a project might be approached by public historians and other persons who control or influence the representation of Australia's historical prisons.

The radical othering of inmates at those sites does a disservice to the collective memory; but it has more immediate social implications. It effectively promotes penal populism, which has obvious potential ramifications for current penal practice, for sentencing, and for the treatment of inmates after release. The othering processes take a variety of forms. Othering begins, naturally enough, as a function of the criminal's transgressive relationship with society. It is exacerbated in the first instance by the Gothic architectural style of the prison itself through its psychological impact on those outside the walls, for whom both the implied violence and radical separateness of the prison population are emphasized by the fortress façade and connotations of armed might. Once the prison becomes a museum, the outsider's sense of foreboding when confronted by the Gothic architecture tends to be overturned. Yet the aesthetic transformation in perceptions of the built fabric do not necessarily translate into a more benign attitude to the historical inmates, but rather to an affirmation of their othering—a seemingly paradoxical inversion of customary Dark Tourism response, as a corollary to the physical prison's legitimization as a setting of containment.

The strongest influence militating against an inclusive interpretation is the predominance, at any given site, of stakeholder groups. These groups have demonstrated a tendency to take on highly active roles in the prison's post-operational life, and can become gatekeepers committed to controlling access to the site, and to the narratives emergent from and associated with it. The most common and most influential gatekeeper group tends to be former prison officers, who combine a strong and abiding personal stake in the jail's narratives with high public credibility as interpreters of those narratives. They stand as exemplars of the prison's Establishment, and as such tend to reflect and actively propagate a persistently and indiscriminately negative view of the "crims" formerly in their charge. This both influences and is reinforced by the attitudes of many tour visitors, especially in the very common instances where the prison officers have become tour guides.

The prison officers also promote, as a spontaneous expression of deeply felt attitudes, a highly negative view of female inmates. And as with their general othering of inmates, their attitudes to those women are authoritatively transmitted to tourists. These perceptions are arguably the product of generically sexist views—to the point, I suggest, of outright misogyny in many cases—which are themselves a reflection of a profound masculinism that is the norm in most prisons, plus a broader societal abhorrence of the transgressive female. Within the system overall, it is widely believed that women are more difficult to manage in jail than men, and this belief, at once both oppressive and patronising, can in various ways add to the trauma inherent in women's experience of imprisonment.

There is a strong tendency for commercial considerations to directly conflict with inclusive interpretation of sites. This commercialism may take the form of private/entrepreneurial exploitation—Pentridge is the most extreme example discussed here—or, far more commonly, the perennial public history turnstile agenda. The prison museum's position as an historical entity is prone, always, to compromise due to the pressures arising from operating in a public-history "market-place," within which sites must contend for tourist dollars. The narratives and the quest for inclusive public history are easily compromised when the inherent problems arising from stakeholders' disparate and often opposing influences are compounded by the need to appease a tourist populace who are, or are expected to be, predisposed against such inclusivity. And such presumptions, of course, are all too likely to prove self-fulfilling. Populist, market-place public history tends to lead to the euphemization of inmate suffering, to a general normative inclination toward "infotainment" as the mode of representation, to the adoption and promotion of celebrity prisoners, and to the active suppression of narrative elements such as suicides and sexual violence, and aspects of the built fabric such as inmate graffiti. The influence of commercialism is most egregious in instances where the site becomes entirely a private-sector entity, as in the case of Pentridge (and, on a far more minor scale, Kilmore Gaol), at which point the phenomenon of historical entrepreneurism renders the possibility of any inclusivity at all a matter of random chance at best, due to the likelihood of the site's interpretation resting in the hands of individuals with *no* stake in the social memory of the prison.

The prison's elite inmates, as exemplified here by Chopper Read—who also stands as the archetypal celebrity prisoner—foster and perpetuate the othering of the prison's main population, by virtue of the elites' explicit or tacit disdain for the ordinary inmates whom they have reason to see as their inferiors, in the Darwinian context of the total institution. This disdain tends to be implied in their public self-representations, and is duly assimilated by audiences and the general public who are motivated by a broadly tolerant, perhaps even approving, sensibility toward the elite former criminal. The elite inmate often also has a propensity for euphemization of the prison experience. A key factor in many such cases is his or her capacity as an entertainer, in which regard Read, of course, excels, as he does also in his unwitting role as a "professional ex-," and, rather more self-consciously, as a mandated larrikin.

A broadly complicit agent in the othering process overall is the mass media, which in some cases (especially the tabloid press and the more populist of the electronic media outlets) reflexively takes the part of the prison Establishment, unless reporting corruption in that quarter. Even in the quality press, reports of prison activities, whether involving operational or historical prisons, consistently veer toward a "light entertainment" tone. And as I have shown, the media must share responsibility for the othering of Australia's colonial convicts, for instance through its wholesale neglect of the lack of any convict representation in the Sydney Olympics Opening Ceremony, and in its choice of historical narratives when depicting convicts for the purposes of dramatic entertainment.

The second theme noted above—restoring the voices of the othered via a gleaning of the sites' hidden narratives—has borne fruit in three main ways: by "reading between the lines" of tour guides' and curatorial representations on-site; through interviews and informal discourse with site personnel and others who, broadly speaking, represent the Establishment position; and, perhaps most emphatically, through a close reading of inmates' graphic ornamentation of the prisons' built fabric. An adjunct source which I have "sampled" is the personal account of an outsider—myself—with an emotional stake in a specific inmate's welfare.

Tour presentations, which as we have seen tend to reflect Establishment and/or broadly populist viewpoints, can imply much to the constructively sceptical tourist. Tour guides' choices of narrative and modes of delivery, elements omitted from their patter, and their responses to questions and attitudes to the inmates often imply more of a site's alternative narratives than they intend or realize.

Interviews and discussions with Establishment figures tended, as a matter of course, to prompt spontaneous expressions of othering toward inmates; in the process, much could be inferred regarding the experience of those othered. Aside from such inadvertent revelation, some individuals, prompted perhaps by the distance of years, or (as in at least one case) uneasy conscience, spoke frankly on a range of pertinent issues. Persons with inside knowledge who had always been placed somewhat toward the periphery of the Establishment— by virtue, for instance, of a professional concern for inmates' welfare—tended to be the most open, recalling, with at times disturbing candour, things seen and (wilfully) unseen.

Graffiti reveals much of the social dynamics within the operational prison, and with that the affect, preoccupations and aspirations of individual prisoners. Among male prisoners, variations on the theme of power relationships predominate as graffiti topics, expressed in terms of revenge, sexuality—which is clearly at least as much to do with violently coercive dealings as with lust—and pervasive rancour. Racism, too, is evinced on the walls of the jails. Yet the inmate's self-affirming impulse can also find voice in non-violent expressions of humour and friendship, celebrations of chemically-induced moments of relief, and artistic flights of fancy designed to avert the psychological arch-enemy, boredom.

Imprisoned women also produce graffiti in abundance, of which various aspects point up the fact that women inmates were othered in specifically gendered ways by the prison Establishment, by the penal system overall, and by society. The examples investigated here, rendered within the Melbourne City Watch House, indicate that although the women shared many of the men's concerns, thoughts of vengeance and other power considerations were complicated by a networking imperative arising from the near-monopoly of one female prison and the consequent need to establish and consolidate alliances, and to promulgate signifiers of individuals' pecking-order credentials. The relatively small number of female inmates overall is reflected in the sense of community expressed in their graffiti (which is not to say, of course, that it was necessarily a *harmonious* community), and in this regard, the women's graffiti is at variance in tone, content and general emotional candour from that of the men, whose asserted individuality is rarely subsumed in any perceptible collectivity. A fragment of this female community, and its response to other, darker aspects of women's incarceration, is glimpsed in expressions of grief for a deceased colleague.

*

There is an ethical dimension to the practice of public history. It is a core assumption of this book that those who inherit, purchase or otherwise acquire the capacity to interpret and represent the component narratives of social memory have a responsibility to do so, as far as possible, inclusively. Many public historians are, of course, well aware of these parameters, and operate as best they can within them, but the constraints upon them are significant. In an ideal public history paradigm, the narratives of an historical prison's former non-elite inmates would be supplied directly by those inmates, whether acting as tour guides (as is the practice at some sites overseas) or via pre-recorded oral presentations. Both of these options present legal and/or practical problems in Australian prison museums. In the absence of first-person testimony on-site, and given the dearth of published memoirs by non-elite inmates from which to draw textual representations, it becomes more than ever necessary to look to sources such as those I have drawn upon here, especially those involving an inclusive reading of the most readily available "text"—the surfaces and general form of the built fabric.

An appropriate yardstick, I suggest, in the interpretation and design stages of any prison museum representation—and which is at least tacitly observed at some sites I have identified—would be for the imagined audience to include a former inmate or two, drawn not from the ranks of the prison's elites nor from its "celebrity" cast, but from the myriad "average" prisoners who formed the overwhelming majority of the incarcerated population. The design criterion in such a hypothetical scenario would be for the knowledgeable insider to respond to the representation of the site of his/her former imprisonment with an affirming nod and the words, "Yes, that's how it was."

Given the intensity, persistence, and ubiquity of established public attitudes to the criminal other, it is apparent that, if left to their own devices, tourist visitors to prison museums are unlikely to spontaneously embrace an inclusive ethos—especially given that many of the museums provide very little material or informational basis for such an epiphany. The wholehearted adoption of an inclusive approach to site interpretation by curators must inevitably contend with—confront—the normative influence of othering, on the perceptions of the visiting general public. A radical shift in attitude must somehow be effected. Social theorist Harold Garfinkel states that:

> A society's members encounter and know the moral order as perceivedly normal courses of action—familiar scenes of everyday affairs, the world of daily life known in common with others and with others taken for granted.[2]

Further, he points out that the social environment always includes some "seen but unnoticed," expected, background features of everyday scenes:

> The member of society uses background expectancies as a[n unexamined] scheme of interpretation. ... For these background expectancies to come into view [that is, to be examined] one must either be a stranger to the "life as usual" character of everyday scenes, or become estranged from them. As Alfred Schutz pointed out, a "special motive" is required to make them problematic.[3]

But if, as I have argued, society's members identify themselves, and by extension their "world of daily life," in terms of narratives, it follows that a morally discomforting "background" aspect of that world may be dealt with by the manipulation or excision of certain of those narratives, which are hence placed among those the group "chooses to forget." In the context of the typical prison museum, where the endemic loss of narratives is of historiographical *and* social significance, it is incumbent upon the public historian in some way to induce that "estrangement"—to coax, cajole, challenge or guide the visitor toward what psychologists call "cognitive dissonance,"[4] and hence to the attitude change required to appreciate the validity of a somewhat less "entertaining" experience of the site.

*

Australia's historical prisons form a matrix across the continent. Without exception, they are products of the wave of prison construction that swept the British Empire in the early to mid-nineteenth century, and as such they stand today as tangible manifestations of British colonization. (This historical common ground, it should be noted, applies to all the prisons discussed, not merely the bona fide "convict" sites.) In their demise as operational institutions, it might be said that they symbolize the process of decolonization. But although united by history, functional purport and architectural heritage, the sites operate as museums independently of each other, and there is a tendency for them to view each other competitively—"This site is the oldest /

biggest / most isolated / most haunted," and so on—which arises inevitably from the need for each one to make its way in the marketplace of public history.

These perceptions must be noted as a problematic aspect of Australian public history, in that they are symptomatic of the commercialism which I have identified as a significant exclusionary factor in the sites' narratives, and also because they promote a fragmented public view of Australian penal history overall. The sites are located within a wider history of Australian incarceration, extending from convict settlement to the present, and as such need to be viewed both by the general public and by historians as landmarks on a continuum across that range. Nor do their individual histories end neatly with their decommissioning; aside from the considerations I have highlighted in this book, there is also the fact that a significant number of the sites' former inmates are still incarcerated, having simply been transferred to other jails. A study of historical prisons must be understood as inevitably a study, as much as anything, in current history.

This raises the point that most of the sites discussed here were decommissioned in recent years to be replaced in the corrections system by modern facilities. These new, operational prisons of course fall entirely outside the research scope of this book. But it should be kept in mind that it is not only *historical* inmates who are radically othered, and whose narratives are therefore excluded. The walls of the modern jail are no less opaque to the outsider's gaze than were their Gothic predecessors, and there are many reasons to suspect that the stories currently unfolding behind them are at least as worthy of attention. Ethnographer Loïc Wacquant laments the dearth of substantive research in modern prisons, noting that three decades ago, many prisons actually employed on-site sociologists, and that little more than the odd anecdote now emerges from the same institutions.[5] At a time of increasingly punitive responses to criminality and a broadening of the parameters by which we define criminality, and therefore escalating numbers in prison populations, such lacunae may have a significant bearing on the processes that will determine who is remembered and who is forgotten in the prisons of Australia.

NOTES

1   Mark Paton (former resident, Pentridge neighbourhood), interview, 5 May 2001.
2   Harold Garfinkel, *Studies in Ethnomethodology*, Englewood Cliffs NJ: Prentice-Hall, 1967, p. 35.
3   Ibid., pp. 36-7.
4   Cognitive dissonance—an experience of insupportable emotional tension between expectation (born of belief) and contradictory cognized reality. "The resolution of the conflict is assumed to serve as a basis for attitude change in that belief patterns are generally modified so as to be consistent with [reality]." Arthur S. Reber, *The Penguin Dictionary of Psychology*, Harmondsworth: Penguin Books, 1985.
5   Loïc Wacquant, "The Curious Eclipse of Prison Ethnography in the Age of Mass Incarceration," *Ethnography* Vol. 3 No. 4, December 2002.

APPENDIX ONE

Interviews

Armstrong, George ("Jim") (ex-Pentridge Governor of Security). 31 January 2001.

Aston, Robert (former J Ward head nurse). 23 September 2002.

Attwood, Alan. 2 October 2003.

Banks, John (former prison officer, Boggo Road Gaol). 20 January 2003.

Birmingham, Catherine (documentary film maker). 5 April 2001.

Burchill, Laurie (vice-president, Coburg Historical Society). 24 January 2001, 16 August 2002.

Clarke, Martin (former Pentridge prison officer). 30 March 2001.

Collins, Sally (Coburg resident). 10 February 2001.

Gammie, Graeme (Fremantle Prison site manager). 24 April 2003.

Gill, Robert (former Pentridge prison officer and governor). 30 March 2001.

Hoffman, Maureen (former Pentridge educator). 27 February 2001.

Knapp, Timothy (former Pentridge prison officer). 7 March 2001.

McLeavy, Lyn (convict descendant). 6 January 2003.

O'Mara, Gillian (Fremantle Prison convict genealogist). 25 April 2003.

Paton, Mark (former resident of Pentridge Prison neighbourhood). 5 May 2001.

Raszewski, Christine (curator, Dubbo Gaol). 16 January 2003.

Riley, Peter (former Pentridge prison officer and governor). 30 March 2001.

Snelling, Cr Leigh (Moreland City Council). 4 April 2001.

Smith, Jason (ex-prison welfare officer). 30 April 2003.

Smith, Roger (day manager, Video Ezy Glenroy). 6 September 2001.

Thompson, George (former Coburg resident). 15 April 2001.

Wilson, Paul R.M. (former Pentridge inmate). Personal communications to author, 1989.

APPENDIX TWO

Decommissioned Prisons Visited

Victoria

Pentridge Prison: Established 1850, decommissioned 1997. The chief maximum-security prison for the State of Victoria. The main buildings and iconic gatehouses were erected between 1857–1870. The entire site was sold by the State Government to a private developer soon after closure. Presently a burgeoning housing estate, offices, apartments, piazza and business precinct. Tours operate sporadically, run by former prison officers in conjunction with site owners.

Old Melbourne Gaol: Established 1864, decommissioned 1926. A prison museum owned and run by National Trust Australia (Victoria). Guided and self-guided tours are run by volunteers under the auspices of National Trust staff, and there are trained curatorial staff on site. The site has extensive links to educational bodies and conservation groups. Ned Kelly was hanged there, and this features prominently in presentations and exhibits. A kiosk on-site sells a large range of Kelly memorabilia.

"J Ward": Centre for the Criminally Insane: Established between 1857–1861 as a prison and acquired by the then Lunacy Department in the 1880s. Decommissioned in 1991, now a Museum. Guided tours are conducted by volunteers under the auspices of former senior staff.

Old Geelong Gaol: Established between 1849–1864, decommissioned in 1991. A prison museum operating guided and self-guided tours. Tours run by volunteers with links to former prison officers and Rotary.

Melbourne City Watch House: Established in 1892, decommissioned in 1994, with the closure of the Old Magistrates Court. Owned by the Royal Melbourne Institute of Technology University, who are working with National Trust Australia (Victoria) to adapt the site for tourism. The City Watch house is adjacent to the National Trust's most popular tourist site, the Old Melbourne Gaol.

Kilmore Gaol: Established in 1859 as a prison, closed and converted to a butter factory in 1891. Now a private residence and business which includes a restaurant, folk museum and antique shop.

New South Wales

Wentworth Gaol: Established between 1879 and 1881. Referred to as an "Australian designed" prison—the same design as Hay Gaol (see below). Decommissioned in 1927. Owned by the local council and at the time of my visit leased to a private operator who ran guided and self-guided tours as well as making the premises available for private social functions.

Hay Gaol: Established in 1878. Like Wentworth Gaol, an "Australian designed" prison. Put to various uses including maternity hospital, high-security institution for girls, prisoner of war detention centre, and a locked hospital for the insane. Now operated as a folk museum, with guided and self-guided tours. The site is run by volunteers drawn from a committee, and a professional museum curator was employed there when I visited.

Hyde Park Barracks: Established between 1818 and 1819, and used as a convict site until 1848, after which it served various functions, including female asylum, until 1886. Served as Law Courts until 1979. The site is now operated as a museum by Historic Houses Trust NSW, providing guided and self-guided tours. Trained curatorial staff on site. Extensive ongoing archaeological works may be viewed by the general public.

Old Dubbo Gaol: Established in the 1870s, decommissioned in 1966 and now a museum. Animatronic mannequins are featured at various locations about the jail; other displays include an outdoor gallows and full hangman's kit, plus a narrative account of each of the executions conducted there.

Guided and self-guided tours run by volunteers with links to the Sheriff's office. A professional curator was employed on-site when I visited.

Maitland Gaol: Established during the 1850s, decommissioned in 1998. I visited the site purely as a tourist, as access for fieldwork was denied me due to site works. Maitland claims in its promotional material to be Australia's "most haunted" jail, a status exploited in "psychic tours" and "sleepovers". There is much inmate graffiti extant.

Queensland

Boggo Road Gaol: Established in 1903, served as a women's prison until 1921, when it became a men's prison. Decommissioned in 1989. The site is owned by the Queensland Government and operated as a museum by former prison officers, most of whom are volunteers. At the time of my visit the site was available for social functions including overnight events, with party guests given untrammelled access to cell blocks after hours.

Tasmania

Port Arthur Historic Site: Extensive coastal site comprising many buildings and other features in various states of preservation. Established as a "secondary punishment" convict centre during the 1830s–1840s. It was used as an asylum during the 1860s, and closed in 1877. Owned by the Tasmanian Government, the site has benefited from significant financial support in the last decade. A large management and curatorial staff is employed on site, with professional, trained guides operating tours, including evening "ghost tours". Daytime tours are guided or self-guided. Links to various educational bodies and Tasmanian Convict Archives.

Port Arthur was the location of Australia's worst-ever mass murder by a lone gunman in 1996, with thirty-five people shot dead on site or in the near vicinity.

Point Puer Boys Prison: Less than a mile from the Port Arthur Site, but accessible to tourists only by boat. Established in 1834 and decommissioned in

1849. The British Empire's first juvenile reformatory for boys. An extensive archaeological site.

Sarah Island: Convict site and penitentiary established in Macquarie Harbour in 1822, closed in 1833. Located in Tasmania's west-coast "World Heritage Wilderness" region, the site operates as a tourist venue with guided tours run by Tasmanian Parks and Wildlife Services. The remains of the penitentiary are largely in ruins.

Ross Female Factory: Established as a female convict site in 1847, closed in 1854. Managed by Tasmanian Parks and Wildlife Services, the Factory is now predominantly an archaeological site, but is open to the public. The site has links to the University of Tasmania and the Queen Victoria Museum and Art Gallery. Volunteers and community members have assisted with archaeological excavations carried out on-site since 1995.

Cascades Female Factory: Established as a female convict centre in 1828, operated until 1856. The site has many links to community groups. The University of Tasmania is involved in a number of on-site projects with convict descendants. My visit was brief and did not include fieldwork, due to very bad weather. The Factory's website flags a range of new and innovative interpretation strategies.

Richmond Gaol: Established in 1825, closed in 1928. Billed as the oldest intact gaol in Australia, and run as a museum and souvenir shop with an extensive range of convict memorabilia. Possibly unique in having an intact female solitary cell on display. Tours are self-guided. The only staff present on the day I visited was the kiosk operator. The site is owned by the Tasmanian Government, and has links to educational bodies.

Penitentiary Chapel and Criminal Courts Hobart: Established in 1831. The last inmates were transferred out in 1961. A convict and post-convict site, owned by National Trust Australia (Tasmania), comprising extensive underground solitary confinement cells, a courthouse and a chapel in a three-storey configuration. The site also displays a gallows. It is operated as a museum on a sporadic basis by volunteers, with most tours run at night as "ghost tours." A substantial archaeological site is open to public viewing. The site has links to the University of Tasmania and other educational bodies. On the day I visited there were no tourists in attendance, and a tour guide present spoke of the site's struggle to remain viable.

South Australia

Adelaide Gaol: Established in 1841 and decommissioned in 1988. Formerly South Australia's main maximum-security prison, and the site of all executions carried out in the state from its opening to the early 1960s. Now a museum, owned by the state government and run by the Adelaide Gaol Preservation Society. Built to hold several hundred inmates, the prison's original layout is a radial, Pentonville-style semi-circle. The prison's castellated gothic gatehouse is featured on the museum's website. Owing to time constraints, I was unable to do fieldwork at Adelaide, visiting the prison only as a tourist.

Western Australia

Fremantle Prison: Established in the 1850s, decommissioned in 1991. Owned by the Western Australian Government. Guided tours operate under the direction of former prison officers. Although some professional guides are employed, many are former prison officers working as volunteers. The site has established links with local community groups including historical and genealogical societies, and runs regular "Descendant Days" catering to people with convict ancestry.

BIBLIOGRAPHY

Newspapers and Popular Media

The Age (Melbourne). Letter to the Editor. "Why Can't We Know the Price?" 5 May 1999.

———. "Rogerson Jailed for Lying Under Oath." 18 February 2005.

Andrikidis, Peter (director). *The Incredible Journey of Mary Bryant.* Television Drama. Network Ten. Broadcast (Melbourne) 30 and 31 October 2005.

Attwood, Alan. "Garry David, and the Deeper Darkness Within." *The Age,* 14 June 1993.

Bearup, Greg. "On the Inside No-one Can Hear You Scream." *The Age: Good Weekend Magazine,* 19 October 2002.

Bennett, Goya. "Walled City Hope for Site." *Moreland Community News* (Coburg, Vic.) 18 June 2002.

———. "Prison Yields its Terrible Past." *Moreland Community News,* 2 July 2002.

Border Mail (Albury, NSW). "Rogerson Jailed for His Lying." 19 February 2005.

Butcher, Steve. "Court Fears for Safety of Witnesses." *The Age,* 12 June 2004.

Childs, Kevin. "Pentridge: A Prisoner's View." *The Age,* 20 May 1972.

Critchley, Cheryl. "Recognition at Last for Ryan." *Herald Sun* (Melbourne), 4 Feb 1998.

Dapin, Mark. "Jolly Rogerson." *Sydney Morning Herald,* 14 November 2003.

Dominik, Andrew (director). *Chopper.* Motion picture, video recording © Twentieth Century Fox Home Entertainment, 2001.

Ellingsen, Peter. "Deconstructing Jeff." *The Age,* 4 September 1999.

Fray, Peter. "Might of the Right." *Sydney Morning Herald,* 27 April 2002.

Flanagan, Martin. "Preserving Memories We May Wish to Forget." *The Age,* 7 June 2002.

Forbes, Mark. "Prison Officers Offered $10,000 as 'Incentive'." *The Age,* 19 December 1993.

Gallagher, Heather. "'Chopper' exhibition almost sold out after two days." *The Age,* 1 August 2003.

Glancey, Jonathon. "Within these Walls." *The Guardian* (Manchester), 1 February 2001.

Gratten, Michelle. "Doing Business with Jeff Kennett." *Australian Financial Review Magazine,* March 1997.

Hawes, Rachel. "$250m Hard Cell for Des Res, Mod Cons." *Australian,* 30 April 1999.

Herald (Melbourne). "Restrictions on Jail Inquest: Pentridge Will Get 'Bash' Probe." 17 May 1972.

———. "Inquiry Told of Breakdown." 12 October 1972.

———. "'I Could Have Been Killed' says Ex-prisoner." 2 November 1972.

Hills, Ben. "The Deadly Dilemma of Australia's Most Unwanted Man." *Sydney Morning Herald*, 5 May 1990.

Hodgkins, Nerida. "Save Grave: Chaplain." *Moreland Courier*, 28 April 1997.

Horin, Adele. "Smart Set Losing their Convictions." *The Age*, 13 December 2001.

Hume Leader (Moreland edition). "Minardi Boss in Clink in a Blink." 9 March 2004.

Hunt, Elissa, and Christine Caulfield. "Chopper Movie Upset Blamed for Crash." *Herald Sun*, 6 April 2002.

James, C. "Chopper Weds His First Sweetheart." *Woman's Day*, 17 February 2003.

Kelly, Jeremy. "State Library buys Chopper art." *Herald Sun*, 26 August 2003.

Kennedy, Julian. "Jail Funds Gap." *Moreland Community News*, 19 February 2002.

———. "Going Green: 'Environmental Village' Plans for Pentridge." *Moreland Community News*. 6 August 2002.

Kerbaj, Richard. "Hilali Ridicules nation of Convicts." *Australian*, 12 January 2007

Lamont, Leonie, and Bruce Tobin. "Prison Suicides in Victoria Top Other States." *The Age*, 22 September 1990.

McLeavy, Lyn. "Jane Cook and Me." *The Age*, 6 April 2002.

Mercer, Neil. "Rogerson's Roadshow." *Sunday Telegraph* (Sydney), 26 February 2006.

Millar, Royce. "Planning Work at Pentridge Shuts Down." *The Age*, 4 January 2003.

Mooney, Ray. "Bluestone Shadows." *Sunday Age* "Agenda." 14 September 1997.

Munro, Ian. "Public Softer on Crime than Judges, Study Finds." *The Age*, 30 September 2006.

———. "Does the Time Fit the Crime?." *The Age*, 30 September 2006.

Murphy, Padraic. "Bulgarian Nick Dies in a Flurry of Shots, Victim of Suspected Underworld Hit." *The Age*, 17 April 2003.

Quine, Brett. "Tortured Life Ends." *Herald Sun*, 12 June 1993.

Read, Mark Brandon. Subject of *Australian Story: Inside Out*. ABC Television. Broadcast 3 May 2001.

———. Interviewed by Andrew Denton. *Andrew Denton: Enough Rope*. ABC Television. Broadcast 4 August 2003.

———. Appearance on *The Footy Show*. Nine Television Network. Broadcast 16 and 30 June 2005.

———. *Get Your Ears Off* [musical recording]. Import Generic, 1998.

Rogers, Douglas. "Extreme Theme Park." *Weekend Australian Magazine*, 31 August–1 September 2002.

Rogerson, Roger. Interviewed on *60 Minutes*. "The Enforcer: Ruling By Fear." Nine Network. Broadcast 9 April 2000.

Rule, Andrew. "The Inside Stories from a Man Who Should Know." *The Age*, 1 August 2002.

———. "Telling It Straight." *The Age: Good Weekend Magazine*, 20 May 2006, pp. 27–34.

Sunday Times (Perth). "Wicked Mistress Hanged for Serial Killing." 27 June 1993.

Sun News-Pictorial (Melbourne). "Lawyers to Probe Jail Complaints." 20 February 1972.

———. "I'm Afraid to Leave H Division—Pentridge Guard." 6 October 1972.

———. "I Wanted to Die After Beating: Prisoner." 12 December 1972.

———. "Jail Bash Men Needed Aid: Inquiry is Told." 12 October 1972.

Truth (Melbourne). "Grim Story in Prison Papers." 27 May 1972.

van Gronigen, John [former Director, Corrections Victoria]. Interviewed on *The National Interest*. ABC Radio National. Broadcast 8 October 2000.

Books, Journal Articles and Other Sources

Adelaide Historical Gaol. Website. http://www.adelaidegaol.org.au/.
————. "History". http://www.adelaidegaol.org.au/working.htm#taylor (accessed 10 March 2008).
Allom Lovell and Associates. *HM Metropolitan Prison Pentridge and HM Metropolitan Prison (Coburg Prison Complex): Conservation Management Plan*, Prepared for the Dept of Treasury and Finance and the City of Moreland, 1996.
Angola Rodeo website. http://www.angolarodeo.com.
Anderson, Benedict. *Imagined Communities: Reflections on the Origin and Spread of Nationalism*. London: Verso, 1983.
Anderson, Margaret. "Oh What a Tangled Web…Politics, History and Museums." *Australian Historical Studies* 33, no. 119, 2002.
Attwood, Bain, and Andrew Markus. "The Fight for Aboriginal Rights." In *The Australian Century: Political Struggle in the Building of a Nation*, edited by Robert Manne. Melbourne: Text, 1999.
Australian Bureau of Statistics. Year Book Australia: The Sydney 2000 Olympic Games. http://www.abs.gov.au/Ausstats/abs@.nsf/0/e99215ff41ca7defca256b35001bacf9?Open Document (accessed 9 July 2005).
————. Year Book Australia: Crime and Justice: Indigenous Prisoners. http://www.abs.gov.au /Ausstats/abs@.nsf/0/11d3d2aeb026b334ca256dea00053a79?OpenDocument (accessed 20 September 2005).
————. Year Book Australia: Crime and Justice: Women in Prison. http://www.abs.gov.au/ Ausstats/abs@.nsf/0/039E860CED15C3C6CA256F7200832F17?Open (accessed 4 September 2005).
Australian Football League website. "Mark Jackson." http://afl.com.au/default.asp?pg =aflrecordandspg=displayandarticleid=163360 (accessed 12 June 2005).
Australian Human Rights and Equal Opportunity Commission. Aboriginal and Torres Strait Islander Social Justice: "Aboriginal and Torres Strait Islander People in Australia" [Indigenous Peoples and criminal Justice Systems]. http://www.hreoc.gov.au/social _justice/statistics (accessed 20 September 2005).
Australian Social Sciences Data Archive (ASSDA). "Australian Constitutional Referendum Study 1999", Section C. http://assda.anu.edu.au/codebooks/acrs99/3vars.html.
Beeston, Roger. "Sandridge (Bendigo) Gaol, Victoria." *Historic Environment* 14, no. 2, 1999, pp.17–24.
Beilhartz, Peter. "The Prosthetic Fetish: Worlds We are Losing." Paper to Sociology Dept, La Trobe University Bundoora, June 2001.
Bennet, Tony. *The Birth of the Museum: History, Theory, Politics*. London: Routledge, 1995.

Bentham, Jeremy. *"Panopticon": or, the Inspection-House; Containing the Idea of a New Principal of Construction Applicable to Any Sort of Establishment, in Which Persons of Any Description are to be Kept Under Inspection.* London: T. Payne, 1791.

Bergmann, Jörg. *Discreet Indiscretions: The Social Organization of Gossip.* New York: Aldine De Gruyter, 1993.

Bergner, Daniel. *God of the Rodeo: The Quest for Redemption in Louisiana's Angola Prison.* New York: Ballantine, 1998.

Berrigan, Daniel. *Prison Poems.* Greensboro NC: Unicorn Press. 1973.

Betz, Hans-George. *Radical Right-Wing Populism in Western Europe.* New York: Martin's Press, 1994.

Biles, David, and Vicki Dalton. "Deaths in Private Prisons 1990–99: A Comparative Study." *Trends and Issues in Criminal Justice* no. 120. Canberra: Australian Institute of Criminology, June 1999.

Birmingham, Catherine (director). *Pentridge: Some Ghosts and Memories from the Big House.* videorecording © Pentridge Village Pty Ltd 2000.

Boggo Road Gaol. http://www.boggoroadgaol.com.au/pages/brg-page-tours.htm.

Bosworth, Michal. *Convict Fremantle: A Place of Promise and Punishment.* Perth: University of Western Australia Press, 2004.

Boyle, Ian. "The Sounds of Violence." *Arena Magazine.* October–November 1996.

Brodie, Allan, Jane Croom and James O. Davies. *English Prisons: An Architectural History.* Swindon UK: English Heritage, 2002.

Broome, Richard. *Coburg: Between Two Creeks.* Melbourne: Coburg Historical Society, 2002.

———. "The Stigma of Pentridge: The View from Coburg 1850–1987." *Journal of Australian Studies* no. 22, 1988.

Brown, David. Interview, *Four Corners*, Australian Broadcasting Corporation Television. Broadcast 7 November 2005.

Brown, J. David. "The Professional Ex-: An Alternative for Exiting the Deviant Career." *The Sociological Quarterly* 32, no. 2, 1991, pp. 219–30.

———. "Preprofessional Socialization and Identity Transformation: The Case of the Professional Ex-." *Journal of Contemporary Ethnography* 20, no 2, July 1991, pp. 157–78.

Bruner, Edward M., and Jane Paige Kelso. "Gender Differences in Graffiti: A Semiotic Perspective." *Women's Studies International Quarterly* 3, 1980.

Bruner, Jerome. "The Narrative Construction of Reality." *Critical Inquiry* Autumn 1991, pp. 1–21.

———. "Life as Narrative." In *Consumption and Everyday Life*, edited by Hugh MacKay. London: Sage, 1997.

Bryson, Bill. *Down Under.* London: Black Swan, 2001.

Buckley, Bert. *H.M. Central Sub Prison Pentridge: Life Behind the Bluestone Walls from 1800's –1900's.* Coburg: Pentridge Prison, 1981.

Carment, David. "Making Museum History in Australia's Northern Territory." *Australian Historical Studies* 33, no. 119, 2002.

Carrington, Kerry. *Offending Girls: Sex, Youth and Justice.* St Leonards NSW: Allen and Unwin, 1993.

———. "Girls and Graffiti." *Cultural Studies* 3, no. 1, 1989.

Caterson, Simon. "Chopping into Literature: The Writings of Mark Brandon Read." *Australian Book Review* no. 236, November 2001.

Casciani, Dominic. "The Murder of Zahid Mubarek." BBC News. 18 November 2004. http://news.bbc.co.uk/1/hi/uk/3198264.stm (accessed 24 March 2005).

Chipperfield, Mark. "Bushwhacker Breeding is Cooler than Convict Chic." *The Scotsman*, 16 December 2001.

Clark, Julia. "Talking with Empty Rooms." *Historic Environment* 16, no. 3, 2002.

"Chopper" [unofficial Chopper Read website]. http://members.tripod.com/~Chopper_Read/ (accessed June 2002).

Coburg Historical Society. "Response to Pentridge Piazza Proposal." Correspondence to B. Kosky. 5 July 2002.

———. "Interpreting Pentridge: Sound and Light and Other Options." Prepared for CHS by Carol Atwell and The Shirley Spectra, n.d.

———. "Coburg Historical Society: Interpretation Concept", paper prepared for CHS by The Shirley Spectra, 1999.

Commission for Racial Equality [UK]. Website Homepage. http://www.cre.gov.uk.

———. "Racial Equality in Prisons: A Formal Investigation by the Commission for Racial Equality into HM Prison Service of England and Wales, Part 2," London, 2003. http://www.statewatch.org/news/2003/oct/crePrisons.pdf (accessed 14 February 2004).

———. "The murder of Zahid Mubarek" (news release, 2003). http://www.cre.gov.uk/media/nr_arch/2003/nr030709.html (accessed 24 March 2005).

Coroner, State of Victoria. Inquiry into Fatal Fire at Jika Jika. File nos 4771–75/87, Public Records Office, no. 24P7, Box 79. [1987].

Corrections Victoria, Victorian Department of Justice. "Timeline/Chronology" (internal document, unpublished).

Concise Oxford Dictionary of Current English (9th edition). Oxford: Clarendon Press, 1995.

Conover, Ted. *Newjack: Guarding Sing Sing*. New York: Random House, 2000.

Cooke, Pat. "Kilmainham Gaol: Interpreting Irish Nationalism and Republicanism." *Open Museum Journal* 2, Aug 2000. http://amol.org.au/omj/volume2/volume2_index.asp (accessed 23 Mar 2004).

Cover, Rob. "Some Cunts: Graffiti, Globalisation, Injurious Speech and 'Owning' Signification." *Social Semiotics* 12, no. 3, 2002.

Craven, Peter. Review of *Readings/Writings* by Greg Dening." *Australian Review of Books* no. 209, April 1999.

Curthoys, Ann. "Revisiting Australian History: Including Aboriginal Resistance." *Arena* no. 62, 1983.

Damousi, Joy. *Depraved and Disorderly: Female Convicts, Sexuality and Gender in Colonial Australia*. Cambridge: Cambridge University Press, 1997.

Dasey, Patricia, ed. *An Australian Murder Almanac: 150 Years of Chilling Crime*. Adelaide: Nationwide News, 1993.

Davies, Susanne, and Sandy Cook. "Dying Outside: Women, Imprisonment and Post-Release Mortality." Paper given at "Women in Corrections: Staff and Clients" conference, Adelaide: Australian Institute of Criminology, 31 October–1 November 2000.

Davids, Cindy, and Linda Hancock. "Policing, Accountability and Citizenship in the Market State." *Australian and New Zealand Journal of Criminology* 31, no. 1, April 1998, pp. 38–68.

Davis, Angela, and Gina Dent. "Conversations: Prison as a Border: A Conversation on Gender, Globalization, and Punishment" (Panel Discussion). *Signs* 26, no. 4, Summer 2001.

Davison, Graeme. *The Use and Abuse of Australian History.* Crows Nest NSW: Allen and Unwin, 2000.

———. "Museums and National Identity." Paper to Museums Australia National Conference, Adelaide, 20 March 2002.

Denborough, David. "Inside/Outside." http://www.anu.edu.au/~a112465/XY/InOut.htm (accessed 10 September 2002).

Denton, Barbara. *Dealing: Women in the Drug Economy.* Sydney: University of New South Wales Press, 2001.

Dewan, Rikki. "In and Out of Prison." In *Women and Imprisonment* [discussion paper compilation]. Melbourne: Fitzroy Legal Service, 1995.

Dewar, Mickey. "If I was Writing my Own History I'd be a Hero...A Response to Professor David Carment on Making Museum History at the Museum and Art Gallery of the Northern Territory." *Australian Historical Studies* 33, no. 119, 2002.

———. "Forgotten fragments: the Story behind the Object." Paper to Museums Australia National Conference. Adelaide. 20 March 2002.

——— and Clayton Fredericksen. "Prison Heritage, Public History and Archaeology at Fannie Bay Gaol, Northern Australia." *International Journal of Heritage Studies* 9, no. 1, 2003.

Dovey, Kim. *Framing Places: Mediating Power in Built Form.* London: Routledge, 1999.

Dunbaugh, Frank. *Amicus curiae* brief to US Supreme Court in *Farmer v Brennan* (1993). "SPR—Stop Prisoner Rape." http://www.spr.org/en/farmer_argument.html.

Eastern State Penitentiary. Website. http://www.easternstate.org/ (accessed 10 March 2005).

———. "History of Eastern State Penitentiary, Philadelphia." http://www.easternstate.org/history/sixpage.html (accessed 10 Mar 2005).

Edwards, Amy, and Richard Hurley. "Prisons Over Two Centuries." United Kingdom Home Office. http://www.homeoffice.gov.uk/docs/prishist.html (accessed 10 March 2005).

Ellem, Barry. *Doing Time: The Prison Experience.* Sydney: Fontana Collins, 1984.

Fairall, Paul Ames. "Violent Offenders and Community Protection in Victoria—the Gary David Experience." *Criminal Law Journal* 17, no.1, February 1993.

Fremantle Prison. Website. http://www.fremantleprison.com.au/tours/tours8.cfn.

Friends of J Ward. "Frequently Asked Questions". http://www.jward.ararat.net.au/faqs.html.

Foucault, Michel. *Discipline and Punish: The Birth of the Prison.* Harmondsworth: Penguin, 1986.

Freidson, Eliot. "Celebrating Erving Goffman." *Contemporary Sociology* 12, no. 4, July 1983.

Frere, Marion. "Corporeal Punishment." PhD Thesis. University of Melbourne, 2000.

Gardiner, Dianne. "Show and Tell: Old Melbourne Gaol." *Open Museum Journal* 2: *Unsavoury Histories*, online. http://amol.org.au/craft/omjournal/abstract.asp?ID=16.

Garton-Smith, Jennifer. "The Prison Wall: Interpretation Problems for Prison Museums." *Open Museum Journal* 2: *Unsavoury Histories*, online. http://amol.org.au/craft/omjournal/ abstract.asp?ID=6.

Geason, S., and P. Wilson. *Preventing Graffiti and Vandalism*. Canberra: Institute of Criminology, 1990.

Geertz, Clifford. *The Interpretation of Cultures*. New York: Basic Books, 1973.

———. "Clifford Geertz on Ethnography and Social Construction." Interview by Gary Olson. *JAC* 11, no. 2, 1991. Archived. http://jac.gsu.edu/jac/11.2/Articles/Geertz.htm (accessed 29 July 2005).

George, Amanda. "Strip Searches: Sexual Assault by the State." In *Without Consent: Confronting Adult Sexual Violence, Proceedings of Conference 27–29 October 1992*, edited by Patricia Weiser Easteal. Canberra: Australian Institute of Criminology, Conference Proceedings no. 20, 1993.

——— and Sabra Lazarus. "Private Prison: The Punished, the Profiteers, and the Grand Prix of State Approval." *Australian Feminist Law Journal* 4, March 1995, pp. 153–73.

Goc, Nicola. "From Convict Prison to the Gothic Ruins of Tourist Attraction." *Historic Environment* 16, no. 3, 2002.

Goffman, Erving. *Asylums: Essays on the Social Situation of Mental Patients and Other Inmates*. Garden City NY: Anchor Books, 1961.

———. *The Presentation of Self in Everyday Life*. New York: Anchor Books, 1959.

Grabosky, Peter. *Wayward Governance: Illegality and its Control in the Public Sector*. Canberra: Australian Institute of Criminology, 1989.

Green, J. "The Writing on the Stall: Gender and Graffiti." *Journal of Language and Social Psychology* 22, no. 3, September 2003.

Greig, Deidre. *Neither Mad nor Bad: The Competing Discourses of Psychiatry, Law and Politics*. London: Jessica Kingsley Publishers, 2002.

———. "Shifting the Boundary Between Psychiatry and the Law: The Garry David Case Revisited." http://www.libertyvictoria.org.au/docs/psychiatry_and_the_law.pdf (accessed 29 Sept 2003).

———. "The Politics of Dangerousness." http://www.aic.gov.au/publications/proceedings/19/greig.pdf.

Grimwade, Cherry. "Diminishing Opportunities: Researching Women's Imprisonment." In *Harsh Punishment: International Experiences of Women's Imprisonment*, edited by Sandy Cook and Susanne Davies. Boston: Northeastern University Press, 1999.

Halsey, Mark, and Alison Young. "The Meanings of Graffiti and Municipal Administration." *Australian and New Zealand Journal of Criminology* 35, no. 2, 2002.

Hamilton, Paula. "The Knife Edge: Debates about Memory and History." In *Memory and History in Twentieth-Century Australia*, edited by Kate Darian-Smith and Paula Hamilton. Melbourne: Oxford University Press, 1994.

Hancock, W.K. *Australia*, Brisbane: Jacaranda Press, 1966 (1930).

Harding, Richard. *Private Prisons and Public Accountability*. Buckingham: Open University Press, 1997.

———. *Review of Suicide and Suicide Attempts in the Custody of the Office of Corrections, Victoria: Report*. Melbourne: Victorian Government, 1990.

Hebdige, Dick. *Subculture: The Meaning of Style*. London: Methuen, 1979.

Heilpern, David M. *Fear or Favour: Sexual assault of Young Prisoners*. Lismore NSW: Southern Cross University Press 1998.

Hibbert, Christopher. *The Roots of Evil: A Social History of Crime and Punishment.* Harmondsworth: Penguin, 1963.

Hinkson, Melinda. "Goliath Wins." *Arena Magazine* August–September 1993.

Hirst, J.B. *Convict Society and its Enemies: A History of Early New South Wales.* Sydney: George Allen and Unwin, 1983.

Howard league for Penal Reform. "A Short History of Prison." http://www.howardleague.org/studycentre/historyofprison.htm (accessed 25 February 2001).

Horne, Donald. *The Lucky Country* [revised edition]. Harmondsworth: Penguin, 1964.

Hume, L.J. "Bentham's Panopticon: An Administrative History" parts I and II. *Historical Studies* 15 and 16, nos. 61 and 62, October 1973, April 1974.

Hunt, Matthew. *Cunt: A Cultural History.* http://www.matthewhunt.com/cunt.html (accessed 20 February 2008).

———. "Cunt: Taboo, Patriarchy and Liberation." MA Thesis. Coventry University, 2000.

Ignatieff, Michael. *A Just Measure of Pain: The Penitentiary in the Industrial Revolution.* London: MacMillan, 1978.

Inglis, K.S. *Sacred Places: War Memorials in the Australian Landscape.* Melbourne: Melbourne University Press, 2001.

Jacobson-Hardy, Michael. "Behind the Razor Wire: A Photographic Essay." *Ethnography* 3, no. 4, pp. 398–415.

Jenkinson, Kenneth. *Report of the Board of Inquiry into Allegations of Brutality and Ill Treatment at H.M. Prison Pentridge.* Melbourne: State Government of Victoria, 1973.

———. *Report of the Board of Inquiry into Several Matters Concerning H.M. Prison Pentridge and the Maintenance of Discipline in Prisons.* Melbourne: Victorian Government, 1973.

Johnson, Grant. "Report to Director of Prisons, Office of Corrections, re Disturbance in 'B' Division on Saturday 7 January 1984." Melbourne: Office of Corrections, 1984.

Johnson, Holly. "Experiences of Crime in Two Selected Migrant Communities." Trends and Issues in Crime and Criminal Justice no. 302. Australian Institute of Criminology. http://www.aic.gov.au./publications/tandi2/tandi302.pdf (accessed 10 October 2005).

Johnston, Norman. *Forms of Constraint: A History of Prison Architecture.* Urbana Ill.: University of Illinois Press, 2000.

Jones, Ian. *Ned Kelly: A Short Life.* Port Melbourne: Lothian, 1995.

Kasakoff, Alice Bee. "Is There a Place for Anthropology in Social Science History?." *Social Science History* 23, no. 4, 1999.

Kelly, Paul. *The End of Certainty: Power, Politics and Business in Australia* (revised edition). St Leonards NSW: Allen and Unwin, 1994.

Kennedy, James. *Final Report of the Commission of Review into Corrective Services in Queensland.* Brisbane: Queensland Government, 1988.

Kent, D.A. "The Anzac Book and the Anzac Legend." *Historical Studies* 21, no. 84, April 1985.

Keon-Cohen, Bryan. "Dilemmas for the Law." http://libertyvictoria.org.au/docs/garry%20david.pdf.

Kerr, James Semple. *Design for Convicts: An Account of Design for Convict Establishments in the Australian Colonies During the Transportation Era.* Sydney: Library of Australian History, 1984.

———. *Out of Sight, Out of Mind: Australia's Places of Confinement, 1788–1988.* Sydney: S.H. Ervin Gallery, National Trust of Australia (NSW), 1988.

King, Jonathon. *Mary Bryant: Her Life and Escape from Botany Bay.* Pymble NSW: Simon and Schuster, 2004.

Kleinert, Sylvia. "Revisiting the Prison: Museums in a Penal Landscape." Round Table no. 15, "History and the Museum: New narratives?." 20th International Congress of Historical Sciences, Sydney 3–9 July 2005.

Klofas, J., and C. Cutshall. "Unobtrusive Research Methods in Criminal Justice: Using Graffiti in the Reconstruction of Institutional Cultures." *Journal of Research in Crime and Delinquency* 22 no 4, November 1985, pp. 355–73.

Koestler, Arthur. *The Invisible Writing: The Second Volume of an Autobiography: 1932–40.* London: Hutchinson, 1969.

Lake, Marilyn. *Getting Equal: The History of Australian Feminism.* St Leonards NSW: Allen and Unwin, 1999.

Lambert, Ronald D. "Reclaiming the Ancestral Past: Narrative, Rhetoric and the 'Convict Stain'." *Journal of Sociology* 38, no. 2, 2002, pp. 111–127.

Lawrence, Susan. "Approaches to Gender in the Archaeology of Mining." In *Redefining Archaeology: Feminist Perspectives*, edited by Mary Casey, Denise Donlon, Jeanette Hope and Sharon Wellfare. Canberra: Australian National University Publications, 1998.

Leach, Michael. "Hansonism, Political Discourse and Australian Identity." In *The Rise and Fall of One Nation*, edited by Michael Leach, Geoffrey Stokes and Ian Ward. St Lucia: University of Queensland Press, 2000.

Leibling, Alison. *Suicides in Prison.* London: Routledge 1992.

Lennon, John, and Malcolm Foley. *Dark Tourism.* London: Continuum, 2000.

Levin, Jack, and Arnold Arluke. *Gossip: The Inside Scoop.* New York: Plenum Press, 1987.

Loo, Tina, and Carolyn Strange. "'Rock Prison of Liberation': Alcatraz Island and the American Imagination." *Radical History Review* no. 78, 2000.

Ludowyk, Frederick. "Aussie Words: Larrikin." *Ozwords*, June 1998. http://www.anu .edu.au/andc/Ozwords/June_98/5._larrikin.htm (accessed 7 December 2004).

Lynn, Peter. *Inquiry into the Victorian Prison System: Instituted to Inquire into a Report on Allegations of Maladministration, Corruption and Drug Trafficking within the Victorian Prison System.* Melbourne: Victorian Government, 1993.

Manchester University, Dept of History of Science, Technology and Medicine. Course lecture notes. http://www.chstm.man.ac.uk/teaching/hs124_6htm (accessed 3 March 2003, no longer posted).

Magistrates Court of Victoria. Website ["History" search]. http://www.magis-tratescourt.vic .gov.au (accessed 17 May 2005).

Madman Entertainment. "Chopper's on DVD Again…!" http://www.madman.com.au/ations/ news.do?method=viewandnewsld=45 (accessed 6 October 2005).

MacCannell, Dean. *The Tourist: A New Theory of the Leisure Class.* Berkeley Ca.: University of California Press, 1999.

Macdonald, Nancy. *The Graffiti Subculture: Youth, Masculinity and Identity in London and New York*. Houndmills UK: Palgrave Macmillan, 2001.

MacIntyre, Alasdair. *After Virtue: A Study in Moral Theory*. Notre Dame: University of Notre Dame Press, 1981.

Macintyre, Stuart, and Anna Clark. *The History Wars*. Carlton, Vic: Melbourne University Press, 2004.

McCalman, Janet. *Sex and Suffering: Women's Health and a Women's Hospital: The Royal Women's Hospital, Melbourne 1856–1996*. Melbourne: Melbourne University Press, 1999.

McKercher, Bob, and Hilary du Cros. *Cultural Tourism: The Partnership Between Tourism and Cultural Heritage Management*. New York: Haworth Hospitality Press, 2002.

Maltin, Leonard, ed. *Movie and Video Guide* (1998 edition). New York: Signet, 1997.

Manne, Robert. "The Whitlam Revolution." In *The Australian Century: Political Struggle in the Building of a Nation*, edited by Robert Manne. Melbourne: Text, 1999.

———. *In Denial: The Stolen Generations and the Right*. Melbourne: Schwartz Publishing, 2001.

——— with David Corlett. *Sending them Home: Refugees and the New Politics*. Melbourne: Black Inc., 2004.

Marshall, Helen, Kathy Douglas and Desmond McDonnell. *Deviance and Social Control: Who Rules?* Melbourne: Oxford University Press, 2007.

Maxwell-Stewart, Hamish, and Susan Hood. *Pack of Thieves? 52 Port Arthur Lives*. Port Arthur, Tas.: Port Arthur Historic Site Management Authority, 2001.

Merlo, Pat. *Screw: Observations and Revelations of a Prison Officer*. Melbourne: Hudson 1996.

Merkel, Ron, QC. "'Dangerous Persons': To Be Gaoled for What They Are, or What They May Do, *Not* for What They Have Done." http://www.aic.gov.au/publications/proceedings/19/merkel.pdf (accessed September 2002).

Miller, Toby. *Visible Evidence Volume 2: Technologies of Truth: Cultural Citizenship and the Popular Media*. Minneapolis: University Of Minnesota Press, 1998.

Minogue, Craig W.J. "Human Rights and Life as an Attraction in a Correctional Theme Park." *Journal of Prisoners on Prisons* 12, 2002.

Ministry for Planning Panel. *Moreland Planning Scheme Heritage Interpretation Issue: Pentridge Prison Complex*, Report. Melbourne: Victorian Government, 2002.

Moreland City Council. Correspondence to Citizens Advocating Responsible Development (CARD), 27 August 2001.

Morrison, Richard. "The Management of Paradox: the Archaeology of the Port Arthur Landscape." *Historic Environment* 16, no. 3, 2002.

Mukherjee, Satyanshu. *Ethnicity and crime: A Report prepared for the Department of Immigration and Multicultural Affairs*. Canberra: Australian Institute of Criminology, 1999.

Nagle J, J.F. *Report of the Royal Commission into New South Wales Prisons*. Sydney: New South Wales Government, 1978.

National Archives of Australia. "Order-in-Council changing name to Tasmania 21 July 1855 (UK)." http://www.foundingdocs.gov.au/item.asp?sdID=35 (accessed 2 October 2005).

National Trust of Australia (Victoria). "Pentridge Under Threat." Media Release, 10 September 1998.

Neill, R. *White Out: How Politics is Killing Black Australia.* Sydney: Allen and Unwin, 2002.

Nicoll, Irena. "The Panopticon—Were Any Built and Where Are They?" http://www.ucl.ac.uk/ Bentham-Project/Faqs/fpanwher.htm (accessed 2 Mar 2005).

Nugent, Stephen, Meredith Wilkie and Robyn Iredale. *Violence Today: No. 8: Racist Violence.* Canberra: Australian Institute of Criminology, 1989.

O'Donnell, I., and K. Edgar. "Fear in prison." *The Prison Journal* 79, no. 1, March 1999.

Ombudsman WA. *Report on an Investigation into Deaths in Prisons.* Perth: Western Australian Government, 2000.

O'Meally, William John. *The Man They Couldn't Break.* Melbourne: Unicorn Books, 1980.

Orwell, George. "Good Bad Books." In *The Penguin Essays of George Orwell.* London: Penguin, 1984.

———. "Raffles and Miss Blandish." In *The Penguin Essays of George Orwell.* London: Penguin Books, 1984.

Palmer, Daniel. "In the Anonymity of a Murmur: Graffiti and the Construction of the Past at the Fremantle Prison." In *Historical Traces*, edited by Jenny Gregory. Perth: Centre for Western Australian History, 1997.

Port Arthur Historic Site. "Sunday 28 April 1996: A Brief Outline of Events." http://www.portarthur.org.au/pashow.php?ACTION=Publicandmenu_code=400.300 (accessed 12 August 2005).

Penney, Jan. "What is History in the Marketplace?" *La Trobe Forum* no. 17, Dec–Feb 2000–1, pp. 27–8.

Pentridge Piazza. Website. http://www.pentridge-piazza.com.au (accessed 13 May 2005).

———. "History" page. http://www.pentridge-piazza.com.au/pages/history.html (accessed 3 June 2005).

Perkin, Harold. *Origins of Modern English Society.* London: Ark, 1986.

Pringle, John. *Australian Accent.* London: Chatto and Windus, 1961.

Pubboy. Website ["Wild Colonial Psychos"]. http://www.pubboy.com.au/page/wild_colonial_phycos_tour.html [*sic*] (accessed 1 January 2005).

Quartly, Marian. "Convict History." In *The Oxford Companion to Australian History* (revised edition), edited by Graeme Davison, John Hirst and Stuart Macintyre. Melbourne: Oxford University Press, 2001.

Read, Mark Brandon. *Chopper: From the Inside: The Confessions of Mark Brandon Read.* [Kilmore, Vic.]: Floradale Productions 2001 (1991).

———. Personal website. Home page. http://www.chopperread.com (accessed 1 Sept 2006).

———. Personal website. Merchandising page. http://www.chopperread.com/Memor-abilia%20pages/Hab007.htm.

Read, Peter. *Returning to Nothing: The Meaning of Lost Places.* Cambridge UK: Cambridge University Press, 1996.

———. *Haunted Earth.* Sydney: University of New South Wales Press, 2003.

Reber, Arthur S. *The Penguin Dictionary of Psychology.* Harmondsworth: Penguin Books, 1985.

Rediker, Marcus. "How to Escape Bondage: The Atlantic Adventures of the 'Fugitive Traytor' Henry Pitman, 1687." Keynote address. "Escape" conference. Strahan, Tasmania, July 2003.

Reynolds, Henry. "'That Hated Stain': The Aftermath of Transportation in Tasmania." *Historical Studies* 14, no. 53, Oct 1969, pp. 19–31.

Rhodes, Lorna A. "Toward an Anthropology of Prisons." *Annual Review of Anthropology* 30, 2001, pp. 65–84.

Richards, Mike. *The Hanged Man: The Life and Death of Ronald Ryan*. Melbourne: Macmillan, 2003.

Richmond, Katy. "Fear of Homosexuality and Modes of Expressions of Sexuality in Prisons." *Australian and New Zealand Journal of Sociology: Symposium on Deviance, Crime and Legal Process* 14, no. 1, February 1978, pp. 51–7.

Rickard, John. "Lovable Larrikins and Awful Ockers." *Journal of Australian Studies* no. 56, March 1998.

Rosnow, Ralph, and Gary Fine. *Rumor and Gossip: The Social Psychology of Hearsay*. New York: Elsevier, 1976.

Round House [Perth]. http://www.freofocus.com/things2c/html/roundhouse.cfm (accessed 21 Dec. 2004).

Royal Commission into Aboriginal Deaths in Custody. *National Report*, 4. Canberra: Australian Government, 1991.

Russell, Emma. *Fairlea: The History of a Women's Prison in Australia 1956–96*. Kew, Vic.: The Public Correctional Enterprise, 1998.

Scott, Elizabeth. "Through the Lens of Gender: Archaeology, Inequality and Those 'of Little Note'." In *Those of Little Note: Gender, Race and Class in Historical Archaeology*, edited by Elizabeth Scott. Tucson: University of Arizona Press, 1994.

Scott, Margaret. *Port Arthur: A Story of Strength and Courage*. Milsons Point, NSW: Random House, 1997.

———. Speaker at the Tasman Institute for Conservation and Convict Studies. Port Arthur Heritage Site, July 2, 2003.

Senate Inquiry into Australian Children in Care. *Forgotten Australians: A Report on Australians Who Experienced Institutional or Out-of-Home Care as Children*. Canberra: Australian Government, 2004.

Smith, Babette. *Australia's Birthstain: The Startling Legacy of the Convict Era*. Crows Nest NSW: Allen and Unwin, 2008.

Strange, Carolyn. "From 'Place of Misery' to 'Lottery of Life': Interpreting Port Arthur's Past." *Online Museum Journal* 2, 2000. http://amol.org.au/omj/volume2/strange.pdf (accessed 12 March 2005).

——— and Michael Kempa. "Shades of Dark Tourism: Alcatraz and Robben Island." *Annals of Tourism Research* 30, no. 2, April 2003.

Summers, Anne. *Damned Whores and God's Police: The Colonization of Women in Australia*. Harmondsworth: Penguin, 1975.

Thompson, E.P. *The Making of the English Working Class*. London: Victor Gollancz, 1980.

———. "The Moral Economy of the English Crowd in the Eighteenth Century." *Past and Present* no. 50, 1971, pp. 76–136.

Tomsen, Stephen. "Hate Crimes and Masculinity: New Crimes, New Responses and Some Familiar Patterns." Paper to the 4th National Outlook Symposium on Crime in Australia: "New Crimes or New Responses." Canberra: Australian Institute of Criminology, 21–22 June 2001.

Tranter, Bruce, and Jed Donoghue. "Convict Ancestry: A Neglected Aspect of Australian Identity." *Nations and Nationalism* 9, no. 4.

Trollope, Anthony. *Australia and New Zealand*. London: Dawsons of Pall Mall, 1968 (1873).

Twomey, Christina. *Deserted and Destitute: Motherhood, Wife Desertion and Colonial Welfare*. Melbourne: Australian Scholarly Publishing, 2002.

Vadim, Roger. "'I Won't Let That Dago By': Rethinking Punk and Racism." In *Punk Rock, So What? The Cultural Legacy of Punk*, edited by Roger Vadim. London: Routledge, 1999.

Victoria. *Community Protection Act 1990*. Melbourne: Victorian Government.

———. *Mental Health Act 1986*. Melbourne: Victorian Government.

Victoria: Office of the Minister for Finance. "Government to Offer Coburg Prison Site for Redevelopment." News Release, 10 September 1998.

Vinson, Tony. "Reforming Prisons: A 1970s Experience." Paper to conference "History of Crime, Policing and Punishment." Canberra: Australian Institute of Criminology, 9-10 Dec. 1999.

———. *Wilful Obstruction*. Sydney: Methuen, 1982.

Walker, Graeme. "Aradale to Close as Work Proceeds on New Forensic Centre." Department of Human Services, Victorian Government. http://hnb.dhs.vic.gov.au/web/pubaff/medrel.nsf/0/e50f66f085869f4a2565a90022f07e?OpenDocument.

Wacquant, Loïc. "The Curious Eclipse of Prison Ethnography in the Age of Mass Incarceration." *Ethnography* 3, no. 4, December 2002, pp. 371–97.

Wales, E., and B. Brewer. "Graffiti in the 1970s." *Journal of Social Psychology* no. 99, 1976, pp. 115–23.

Walsh, Mike. "Black Hoods and Iron Gags: The Quaker Experiment at Eastern State Penitentiary in Philadelphia." http://www.missioncreep.com/mw/estate.html (accessed 10 Mar 2005).

Ward, Russel. *The Australian Legend*. Melbourne: Oxford University Press, 2003.

White, Rob, and Daphne Habibis. *Crime and Society*. Melbourne: Oxford University Press, 2005.

Wilson, David. "Millbank, the Panopticon and their Victorian Audiences." *The Howard Journal* 41, no. 4.

Wilson, Jacqueline Zara. "Dark Tourism and the Celebrity Prisoner: Front and Back Regions in Representations of an Australian Historical Prison." *Journal of Australian Studies* no. 82: *Colour*, 2004.

———. "Invisible Racism: The Language and Ontology of 'White Trash'." *Critique of Anthropology* 22, no. 4, December 2002.

———. "Relics of a Desperate Act: Escape and Containment in J Ward." *History Australia* 1, no. 1, December 2003.

———. Review: *Dumping Ground: A History of the Cherbourg Settlement* by Thom Blake. *History Australia* 1, no. 2, July 2004.

————. "Representing Pentridge: The Loss of Narrative Diversity in the Populist Interpretation of a Former Total Institution." *Australian Historical Studies* 37, no. 125, April 2004.

————. "The Incarcerated." In *Introducing Sociology: Place Time and Division*, edited by Peter Beilhartz and Trevor Hogan. Melbourne: Oxford University Press, 2006.

Wollen, Peter. "Introduction." In *Visual Display: Culture Beyond Appearances*, edited by Lynne Cooke and Peter Wollen. Seattle: Bay Press, 1995.

Woman and Imprisonment Group. *Women and Imprisonment.* Melbourne: Fitzroy Legal Service, 1995.

Wright, Russell. "Accounting for Our Souls." *Overland* no. 158, Autumn 2000, pp. 5–13.

Young, David. *Making Crime Pay: The Evolution of Convict Tourism in Tasmania.* Hobart: Tasmanian Historical Research Association, 1996.

INDEX